# DYING HARDER

## Action Movies
## of the 1980s

Colin M. Barron

## Other Books by
## Colin M. Barron

Running Your Own Private
Residential or Nursing Home

The Craft of Public Speaking

Planes on Film: Ten Favourite Aviation Films

# DYING HARDER

## Action Movies
## of the 1980s

Colin M. Barron

*Dying Harder: Action Movies of the 1980s* by Colin M. Barron.

First edition published in Great Britain in 2017 by Extremis Publishing Ltd., Suite 218, Castle House, 1 Baker Street, Stirling, FK8 1AL, United Kingdom. *www.extremispublishing.com*

Extremis Publishing is a Private Limited Company registered in Scotland (SC509983) whose Registered Office is Suite 218, Castle House, 1 Baker Street, Stirling, FK8 1AL, United Kingdom.

A CIP catalogue record for this book is available from the British Library.

ISBN: 978-0-9934932-7-0

Typeset in Goudy Bookletter 1911, designed by The League of Moveable Type. Printed and bound in Great Britain by IngramSpark, Chapter House, Pitfield, Kiln Farm, Milton Keynes, MK11 3LW, United Kingdom.

Front cover artwork is Copyright © Roka Pics at Shutterstock.
Back cover artwork and incidental stock images are Copyright © Pixabay.
Cover design and book design is Copyright © Thomas A. Christie.
Author images are Copyright © Raymond McFadyen.
Image credits and licences (if applicable) for illustrations have been stated alongside each photograph.

# CONTENTS

# DYING HARDER

## Action Movies
## of the 1980s

Colin M. Barron

# INTRODUCTION

## The Eighties:
## A Golden Era for Action Movies

ACTION movies of some kind have been with us since the early days of cinema, but it was in the eighties that they really came of age. For it was in that decade that some of the most exciting movies of all time were made, including *Raiders of the Lost Ark, Lethal Weapon, Die Hard, Commando, Predator, Aliens* and the first three *Rambo* movies, most of which spawned franchises which are still active. At the same time as this was happening, six James Bond films were released which are still regarded as some of the greatest offerings in the series. And many of the older action stars like Charles Bronson and Clint Eastwood made a few of their most interesting films during this decade.

In this opening chapter, I would like to discuss how the political events and trends in the eighties heavily influenced the motion picture industry in the UK and USA – particularly in the area of action movies – and how this has had an effect that persists to this day.

The decade opened with a weak, liberal President in charge in the USA. Jimmy Carter's Presidency was tarnished by his inept handling of the Iranian hostage crisis, culminating in a bungled rescue attempt by the US Armed Forces. This debacle directly inspired one Hollywood action picture, *The*

*Delta Force* (1986), which was originally scripted as a re-telling of the hostage rescue mission but showing what would have happened if it had succeeded.

Carter's standing was blighted by his perceived failure to resolve the crisis and it was no surprise when he lost the 1980 Presidential Election to the Republican candidate, former actor Ronald Reagan, who promised to make America great again, even putting four mothballed 'Iowa' class super-battleships back into service and stationing Tomahawk cruise missiles in Britain.

This more assertive projection of America's power, which forced the Soviet Union to compete in an arms race it could ill afford, was one factor which led to the eventual collapse of the USSR in 1991, following the dismantling of the Berlin Wall two years earlier. Another was the unsuccessful Russian invasion of Afghanistan in 1979, sometimes described as 'Russia's Vietnam', which ended with a humiliating withdrawal of Soviet forces about a decade later.

At the same time as this was happening, the USA was starting to heal from the trauma of its own unsuccessful war in Asia, namely the Vietnam conflict. President John F. Kennedy had first sent military advisors to the area in 1963, but by 1965 the US had become involved in a full-scale shooting war. From the start, the US military was forced to fight the war with one hand tied behind its back as – for most of the conflict – they were required to refrain from bombing most of North Vietnam, or carrying out a full-scale invasion of that country, either of which would probably have ended the war.

What worried the politicians back in the USA was that the Chinese or Russians might be provoked into sending military forces to help the North, which could even result in the conflict becoming a nuclear war. This had nearly happened in the Korean conflict. United Nations forces drove the North Koreans out the South and then invaded the North. They were on the point of complete victory when a vast force of Chinese troops intervened. Although an armistice was agreed in 1953, the war really ended in a draw rather than an outright victory. No peace agreement was ever signed – only a ceasefire – and this has had political and military ramifications which continue to this day.

Something similar happened in Vietnam, as a peace treaty was agreed in 1973. Unfortunately the North Vietnamese simply waited until the Americans had withdrawn and then invaded the South, achieving complete victory by 1975.

Thus the Americans were beaten and humiliated by a technically inferior (but more highly motivated) opponent, leading to a sense of national disgrace. In fact the US forces had fought bravely and did their best under difficult circumstances, but they had been let down by the politicians at home who had attempted to micro-manage every detail of the war from control rooms in the USA and thus had interfered with tactical decisions. The American media also contributed to the perceived failure in Vietnam with their biased reporting. The 1968 Tet Offensive (in which North Vietnamese forces invaded the South) was portrayed as a disaster for the US military, when in fact the North Vietnamese were driven back with huge losses.

All these factors lead to a large number of rather disenchanted veterans arriving back home. Many of them were suffering from Post Traumatic Stress Disorder (PTSD), a condition which was not well treated (or even properly recognised) at that time. Some were even addicted to heroin as a result of the efforts of the Vietcong to turn American soldiers into junkies. In addition, the proclamations of liberal activists had convinced many Americans that the failure of the US Forces in Vietnam could be blamed on the actions of individual soldiers. Thus returning war veterans were not always treated with the respect and compassion they deserved. This contrasts sharply to what happens nowadays as – in both the USA and UK – there is now a realisation that our servicemen and servicewomen must be supported and honoured even if we do not agree with the political motivations behind a particular war.

All these factors had an influence on action movies produced in the eighties. The ghost of Vietnam hangs over them. The first *Rambo* movie, *First Blood* (1982), dealt with the poor treatment of returning Vietnam veterans while the second, *Rambo: First Blood Part II* (1985), is really a wish-fulfilment fantasy depicting what might have happened if the US military had gained the upper hand in South East Asia. The Vietnamese soldiers in this film are – like the Germans in *Where Eagles Dare* (1968) – unable to shoot straight and are mown down in large numbers, while their Russian allies are portrayed as cruel sadists. It comes as no surprise to learn that this film was banned in the USSR, and the Russians even got their revenge by producing their own version in which the baddies were American capitalists!

Other films made during this decade reflect the Vietnam experience. Many of the heroes and villains in these films are revealed to be Vietnam veterans. *Lethal Weapon* (1987) is a good example as the hero, Martin Riggs, is revealed to be a former Special Forces sniper while the criminal gang he goes up against is made up of ex-servicemen.

The events in Afghanistan are also depicted in action movies of the eighties, notably *The Living Daylights* (1987) and *Rambo III* (1988) which both feature scenes of combat with Soviet forces, while *Red Dawn* (1984) reflects Cold War paranoia by depicting an actual invasion of the USA by Soviet paratroops.

The changing relationship between the Western Allies and the Soviet Union also informs the plots of these movies. *Who Dares Wins* (1982) – inspired by the real life Iranian Embassy siege in 1980 – has as its protagonist the 'People's Lobby', an anarchist group concerned at the American siting of nuclear missiles in Britain, particularly the Tomahawk Cruise missiles at Greenham Common and Polaris missiles at the US Navy Holy Loch base in Scotland.

But as the international situation changed, so too did the plots. The pragmatic General Leonid Pushkin in *The Living Daylights* – who agrees to work with Bond – is clearly inspired by Soviet leader Mikhail Gorbachev, who Mrs Margaret Thatcher once described as 'a man we can do business with' and was to be instrumental in achieving better relations with the West, laying the foundations for the eventual dissolution of the Soviet Union.

The eighties was also a decade in which traditional special effects technology reached a peak before CGI started to dominate the profession. *Die Hard*, for example, features some superb painted backdrops. The one used to depict the Los Angeles skyline, as seen out the windows of the office block, features animated lighting effects to depict moving traffic and different times of day. It is so realistic that is has been used in other movies and still exists in storage at the Fox lot. It is interesting to compare this with the crude painted skyscraper background with simple lighting effects used in

Hitchcock's *Rope* (1948), which is laughably unconvincing by comparison.

Techniques of miniature photography had also improved by the eighties, to the point where such shots were hard to tell from the real thing. Some shots of the Lockheed executive jet in *Goldfinger* (1964) are quite obviously of a model hanging on clearly visible wires against a painted backdrop, but equivalent miniature work of a radio-controlled C-130 Hercules transport miniature in *The Living Daylights* (1987) is totally convincing.

James Cameron's *The Abyss* (1989) was the first major feature to make extensive use of Computer Generated Imagery (CGI), but since then the technique has proliferated to the point where it has effectively replaced miniature work – even though, in my personal opinion, it produces results that can look very phoney.

Another entirely practical benefit for filmmakers of the changing international situation was that by the end of the decade onwards, it became possible to obtain genuine Soviet Bloc equipment for use in films. *The Living Daylights* (1987), for example, is set partly in Soviet-occupied Afghanistan but had to employ mainly Western vehicles and aircraft in the production as these were all that were available. Thus the transport aircraft which plays a key part in the plot was a Lockheed C-130 Hercules of the Moroccan Air Force, with Soviet decals applied, rather than a Russian Antonov. Similarly all the 'Soviet' armour in *Red Dawn* were mock-ups, based on American vehicles.

The availability of Eastern Bloc equipment also helped the makers of war films. Following the collapse of Communism, large numbers of Czech Tatra OT-810 halftracks were sold to Western collectors, and most have since been converted to resemble WW2 vintage German Sd. Kfz 251 armoured personnel carriers. If you see a German halftrack in a film or TV production these days, it is very likely to be a converted OT-810. Similarly, large numbers of Soviet tanks have been sold to Western collectors and the three replica Tiger I tanks which appear in *Saving Private Ryan* (1998) were constructed using Soviet T34/85 tanks.

The eighties also saw the continuing use of clichés in action films. I rather like them, and rather than groaning inwardly at their presence I greet them like old friends.

Here are some of my favourites: The hero is able to outrun any fireball or explosion. In *Raiders of the Lost Ark*, Indiana Jones outruns a huge boulder. In *Predator*, Schwarzenegger even outpaces a nuclear blast. The hero never runs out of ammunition and can fire hundreds of rounds without reloading. The hero is a super-marksman and always hits the target, even when using a pistol at very long range. If the hero is hit by a bullet, it will result in a 'flesh wound' which is easily treated, or else he has really been wearing a bulletproof vest under his clothing all this time and isn't harmed. Or he has been shot with blanks as a ruse to fool the bad guys. He knows how to defuse bombs, and always cuts the right wire. He survives car crashes without injury.

Any car can be 'hot-wired' in seconds by pulling any two wires from under the dash and twisting them together. Any car that is hit by bullets (or goes over a cliff) explodes in a huge fireball. The hero always has a magnificent toned physique, as does the heroine. Every woman fancies the hero. Sex scenes always go perfectly, and the hero never suffers from premature ejaculation or impotence. You never see fat people having sex. The woman always climaxes and there is no wet patch on the bed afterwards, or skid marks on discarded underwear.

Drugged drinks always work within seconds. The hero can fall off a moving vehicle (or fall down a lift shaft) without injury. No-one suffers from obesity, body odour, bad breath, acne, dandruff, varicose veins, or cellulite. Drunk, struck-off-the-medical-register doctors can be sobered up with black coffee in order to deliver babies. The only things they ask for are 'some blankets and lots of hot water'.

The hero can drive any car, truck, motorbike or armoured vehicle. He can drive a tank, load and fire all of its machine guns – plus its main gun – single-handed (even though tanks usually have a crew of 3-4 people), and fly a helicopter, jet fighter, airliner, bomber, submarine, transport plane, hovercraft or even spacecraft without any prior training.

The hero is an ex-Green Beret/CIA operative/policeman/detective who is approached to do one last mission. He refuses and then has to be coerced into doing it, either with the carrot or the stick.

All the problems are caused by a conspiracy involving the CIA, the FBI, the National Security Agency, a corrupt politician, or even the President. The hero has been wrongly accused of crimes, and no-one believes his story. He has a dark secret in his past, but in fact what happened wasn't his fault. There is a 'mole' leaking secrets to the bad guys. The hero is a maverick cop who only has 24 hours to solve the case. He has been let down by the legal system, so he has to take matters into his own hands. His boss is an incompetent bureaucrat who is obsessed with correct protocol. I could go on...

Lastly, another concept I would like to explore in this book is what I call the 'fantasy-reality axis'. If we take as an

8

example five films such as *The Dambusters, Star Wars, Goldfinger, Moonraker* and *From Russia with Love*, we can place them on a line representing the 'fantasy-reality axis', as follows:

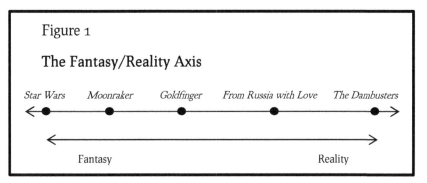

Figure 1

**The Fantasy/Reality Axis**

You will notice from this chart that *The Dambusters* would be considered the most realistic of the four films mentioned as it is effectively a dramatized documentary, while *Star Wars* would be the most fantastic. *From Russia with Love* is more realistic and less fantastic than *Goldfinger*, while *Moonraker* might be considered one of the most fantasy-orientated Bond films.

Applying this concept to some of the films in this book, it can be seen that the British film *Who Dares Wins* is the most realistic of those studied, while the most fantastic would probably be *Aliens. Predator* is also quite close to *Aliens* on the fantasy-reality axis, close enough to enable two 'crossover' movies to be made later, while *Lethal Weapon* is actually more fantastic and less realistic than most people imagine.

So in conclusion, then, the 1980s were a golden era for action films, reflecting what was happening in the world, and in the chapters that follow I will discuss some of them in greater depth.

# 1

# RAIDERS OF THE LOST ARK

## (1981)

*Lucasfilm Ltd.*

**Director**: Steven Spielberg
**Producer**: Frank Marshall
**Screenwriter**: Lawrence Kasdan,
from a story by George Lucas and Philip Kaufman

*R*AIDERS of the Lost Ark is one of the most remarkable films ever made, as it effectively created its own genre. It is certainly an action film (and a very good one at that), but it is most definitely not set in the real world of 1936 as it contains numerous anachronisms such as out-of-period aircraft and weapons, and its depiction of pre-WW2 Egypt is not accurate. Some of the stunts, fights and effects are even more over-the-top than in a James Bond movie, and the supernatural elements towards the end of the movie are like those in a horror film. Returning to my concept of the 'fantasy-reality axis' described in an earlier chapter, *Raiders of the Lost Ark* is much more fantastic and less realistic than most of the other action films described in this book.

*Raiders of the Lost Ark* can also be regarded as a milestone in film history, as it marked the first collaboration between two of the *wunderkinds* of modern cinema: Steven

Spielberg and George Lucas. The pair first met at UCLA on 19 January 1968 and have remained firm friends ever since. Following his direction of a series of amateur films, at the age of 22 Spielberg got a contract to direct TV episodes for Universal Studios which included two episodes of *Night Gallery* in 1969 and 1971 and one of *Columbo* in 1971. He also made *Duel* (1971), a cult TV movie about a motorist pursued by a truck whose driver is never seen. His first cinema feature was *Sugarland Express* (1974) starring Goldie Hawn, but his breakthrough movie was *Jaws* (1975) about a giant shark which terrorizes swimmers. Despite a troubled production, the film became the most successful movie of all time (although this gross has since been exceeded by other productions, with *Avatar*, 2009, currently holding the record).

Spielberg followed up *Jaws* with *Close Encounters of the Third Kind* (1977), which was also hugely successful. His next movie, the high-budget *1941* (1979), was a critical and commercial failure, but all the same Spielberg had a track record of successes with all his other films when he became involved with *Raiders*.

George Lucas was born in 1944 – two years before Spielberg – and first came to attention with the science fiction movie *THX 1138* (1971), starring Robert Duvall, which was based on a short film Lucas had made some years before when he was a student. His breakthrough movie though was *American Graffiti* (1973), starring Harrison Ford, which was highly successful. After this film had been completed, Lucas started thinking about his next project, which was to be a science fiction movie based on 1930s and 1940s serials such as *Flash Gordon* and *Buck Rogers*. The result (as everyone knows) was *Star Wars* (1977), which soon replaced *Jaws* as the most successful movie of all time.

In his brainstorming sessions for *Star Wars*, Lucas had come up with an alternative idea – a series of films about a playboy adventurer-cum-archaeologist who stole priceless artefacts from historic sites to finance his hedonistic lifestyle. At this stage, writer-director Phil Kaufman also contributed some story material, notably the concept of the Lost Ark of the Covenant as the 'McGuffin' of the story. (A 'McGuffin' is an object or device in a film which serves as a trigger for the plot. So, for example, the Lektor machine in *From Russia with Love*, 1963, would be the 'McGuffin' in that story.) Kaufman had to withdraw from the project in 1975 in order to direct *The Outlaw Josey Wales* (1976) for Clint Eastwood.

A few years later, in May 1977, Lucas was on holiday in Hawaii awaiting the critical and commericial reaction to the just-released *Star Wars* when he met up with Steven Spielberg, who told him that he had always wanted to direct a James Bond movie but one that was closer in style to the early entries in the series featuring Sean Connery. Lucas then explained that he had a project that might interest him.

The following year, at a brainstorming exercise held between 23 and 27 January 1978, Lucas, Spielberg and writer Lawrence Kasdan threw together their ideas to create what eventually became the first draft of the script of *Raiders of the Lost Ark*. The sessions were recorded and then transcribed, and these were used by Kasdan to write his script.

Originally the lead character was to be called Indiana Smith after Lucas's dog Indiana: a huge Alaskan Malamute who had a habit of sitting in the front passenger seat of Lucas's car when he was driving. This apparently was also the inspiration for Chewbacca in *Star Wars*.

Spielberg didn't like the name 'Indiana Smith' as he felt it was too much like Nevada Smith in the 1966 Steve McQueen movie of the same name, so the surname was changed to Jones. The appearance of the lead character was partly inspired by Fred C. Dobbs as portrayed by Humphrey Bogart in *The Treasure of the Sierra Madre* (1948) – directed by John Huston – who wore a felt hat, leather jacket, open-necked shirt, trousers and boots and carried a revolver as well as (in some scenes) a blazing torch. It was also suggested that Jones would be a poor pistol shot, but highly proficient with the bullwhip which became his trademark. As the original short Republic films which inspired the movie had included cliffhangers, Spielberg suggested that there should be several such dramatic highlights in the new feature.

As with *Star Wars,* a large number of paintings were commissioned depicting notable scenes in the production including Nazis digging in the desert, a Flying Wing aircraft, and the truck chase. A key inspiration for the latter shot was a monochrome photo from a *Zorro* film showing the hero transferring from a horse to a moving truck.

Harrison Ford was initially considered as the lead, but Lucas was reluctant to cast him as he had already used him in both *American Graffiti* and *Star Wars.* Various actors were screen-tested for the role, and eventually the part was given to Tom Selleck. However, all the publicity about him starring in the forthcoming blockbuster resulted in the producers of *Magnum P.I.* – a series which Selleck was contracted to, but which had not yet been given the go-ahead – deciding to greenlight the production, and consequently Selleck had to pull out of *Raiders.* As a result Harrison Ford was given the part. This whole affair was very similar to what happened to Pierce Brosnan in 1986 when he was chosen as the new James

Bond but had to withdraw when the producers of the cancelled TV series *Remington Steele* decided to make another season and held Brosnan to his contract, resulting in Timothy Dalton then being cast as Bond.

The other key piece of casting was Indy's old flame Marion Ravenwood. A large number of actresses were considered for the role, including Debra Winger and Jane Seymour, but in the end the part went to Karen Allen who had previously appeared in *Animal House* (1978) and *Cruising* (1980).

Some of Spielberg's previous movies had gone seriously over-budget with extended shooting schedules, but this time the American director was determined that he would bring in the movie under budget and under time. Just $17m was allocated to the production; quite a small amount for a movie which was to feature a lot of stunts and special effects.

The film was scheduled for production in the summer of 1980 with location work in France, Tunisia, Hawaii, England and the USA, with studio scenes shot at Elstree Studios in Borehamwood near London. Many of the Tunisian locations were the same as those used in *Star Wars* four years earlier.

The film opens with the Paramount logo which dissolves into a shot of a mountain peak in Hawaii that closely resembles the film company's motif. As the camera pulls back, we see Professor Indiana Jones (Harrison Ford) and his squad of helpers trekking through the jungle. One of their native porters uncovers a carving of a face and is terrified, while Satipo (Alfred Molina) discovers a pencil-sized poison-tipped dart stuck in a tree trunk.

At this point, a caption informs the viewer that this part of the film is set in 'South America 1936'. This scene –

which was filmed in Hawaii – was actually supposed to be in Peru, although this is not made clear in the final cut of the film. Jones stops to consult a rather worn map, and at this point his Peruvian guide Barranca (Vic Tablian) pulls a gun on him. Jones knocks the weapon out of his hand using his trusty bullwhip.

Shortly afterwards, Jones finds the entrance to the tunnel and prepares a cloth bag which is carefully weighted with soil. Meanwhile Satipo is dismayed to discover that his entire back is covered with spiders. The tarantulas were a real, though harmless, version of the spider, and Alfred Molina developed an allergic reaction to them which required treatment. As Jones makes his way down the tunnel he narrowly avoids falling into booby traps, some of which have previously claimed victims as evidenced by a number of rotting corpses which are impaled on spikes.

Satipo and Jones use a creeper to swing over a gaping chasm to reach the end of the tunnel but eventually they reach their prize – a gold idol which is sitting atop a cylindrical stone plinth. The reason for Jones preparing the weighted cloth bag now becomes clear – in order to remove the small statue he has to replace it instantly with the weighted bag of soil, otherwise he will trigger a booby trap.

With one deft movement Jones removes the idol and replaces it with the weighted bag. But it is clear that – despite Jones' precautions – things are starting to happen, as walls are coming down and there are alarming noises. Jones and Satipo have to get out of the temple fast!

As they run down the corridor Satipo jumps over the gaping chasm. As he turns round to face Jones, he asks the Professor to throw the golden idol to him. In return he will throw Jones his whip. But after receiving the idol, Satipo betrays the Professor and makes his escape. Eventually Jones manages to jump over the chasm and finds Satipo dead – he has been murdered with a knife. Jones retrieves the gold idol but is then pursued by a huge rolling boulder which he just manages to outrun. This is one of the most striking visual sequences in the movie and was filmed at Elstree Studios using a 22-foot fibreglass rock. Five cameras filmed this shot from different angles, and 10 takes were performed.

Eventually Jones finds himself at the tunnel entrance, but there is no respite for him as he is confronted by rival archaeologist Belloq (Paul Freeman) who is supported by a large band of hostile Hovito natives armed with spears, bows and arrows, and blowpipes firing poisonous darts. Jones is forced to surrender his revolver and the golden idol but then makes a break for it and races across the countryside pursued by a huge band of natives equipped with bows and arrows.

As he runs towards a river where his floatplane is moored, he screams at the pilot to start the engine so they can make a quick getaway. The aircraft used in this sequence was a 1933 Waco UBF-2 biplane owned by Hank Strauch, with the US civil registration N13075 and marked as OB-CPO. 'OB' indicates a Peruvian registration, while 'CPO' is thought to be a subtle reference to the droid C3PO in *Star Wars*.

The pilot, Jock (Fred Sorenson, who in real life was an airliner pilot and not an actor), is busy fishing in the river while standing on the aircraft's starboard float, and initially seems rather reluctant to terminate his angling in order to escape from the bloodthirsty natives intent on murdering him. Eventually he sees sense, climbs into the rear cockpit of the aircraft and starts the Continental R-670 radial engine. Jones jumps into the river, swims to the aircraft, climbs onto the starboard float and then into the front cockpit. As arrows fall around it, the plane accelerates and takes off. Jones is safe, but his problems aren't over yet as a snake – the pilot's pet, called 'Reggie' – is wriggling about the cockpit floor, and the Professor hates snakes!

This opening sequence sets the tone for the whole film (and its sequels), as it involves a mixture of action and tongue-in-cheek humour. It does raise a number of unanswered questions, though. How did Jones and his team get to the temple location in the first place, as the seaplane can only take one passenger? Or did Jones arrange for the seaplane to be waiting in the river just in case everything went wrong and there was only one survivor?

The next scene is set in Marshall College in the USA, where Jones lectures in archaeology. The exterior shots were of the University of the Pacific in Stockton, California, while the interiors were filmed at Ricksmansworth Masonic School for Girls in Hertfordshire, England. Most of Indy's class consist of young, attractive females who appear to be besotted with him. One girl student even has the word 'love' drawn on her right upper eyelid and 'you' marked on the eyelid on the other side, an idea which was suggested by assistant director David Tomblin.

Soon the bell rings, the lecture is over and Jones meets his old friend and colleague Dr Marcus Brody (Denholm Elliott), who informs him that two officers from U.S. Army Intelligence are waiting to see him.

The two military men, Colonel Musgrove (Don Fellows) and Major Eaton (William Hootkins), inform Jones that the Nazis are searching for his old mentor Abner Ravenwood, under whom Jones originally studied at the University of Chicago. The Nazis know that Ravenwood is an expert on the ancient city of Tanis in Egypt, and that he owns the headpiece of the Staff of Ra: a circular bronze medallion with a round crystal at its centre. Jones realises that the Nazis must be searching for the legendary lost Ark of the Covenant, the stone chest containing the broken remnants of the tablets on which the Ten Commandments were written and which allegedly possess amazing supernatural powers. Thus the Nazis believe that any Army which carries the Ark into battle will become invincible.

This part of the screenplay does have some basis in fact, as Hitler was indeed obsessed with the occult and one of the many reasons he lost the Second World War was that he had a tendency to consult astrologers rather than accepting the sage advice of his many able generals. General Erwin Rommel, for example, advised Hitler to abandon Africa after the Battle of El Alamein. Hitler refused and instead massively reinforced Tunisia, resulting in 250,000 Axis soldiers being taken prisoner when the campaign in North Africa ended in May 1943.

The two officers also inform Jones that the Nazis are currently carrying out an archaeological excavation of a site in the desert near Cairo which is believed to be the location of the lost, buried city of Tanis where the Lost Ark of the Covenant is thought to reside.

The Ark is understood to be located in the Well of Souls, and the only way of determining its location is to enter the so-called Map Room and allow light from the rising sun to stream through a porthole into the central crystal of the headpiece of the Staff of Ra. The resulting beam of light will then be projected as a tiny spot on a model of Tanis on the floor of the Map Room, giving the precise location of the Well of Souls. Thus the key to finding the Ark is to obtain the Staff or Ra, and this is the reason why the Nazis are currently searching for it.

The next scene is set in Jones' house, where the Professor is packing his suitcase as Brody arrives. As he throws his revolver into his suitcase, Marcus points out that man has been searching for the Ark for 3000 years.

The next day Jones sets off on his long journey to Nepal, boarding a Pan American Airways 'China Clipper' flying boat. The aircraft used in this sequence was a rare British Short Solent Mark III flying boat with a US civil registration N9946F, one of only two remaining in the world and located at Richmond Marina near San Francisco. The aircraft had been owned by Rick and Randy Grant since 1976 and hadn't flown since 1958. A background of docks was added using a matte painting by Alan Maley and the Pan American markings were applied by means of an optical effect, rather than the more common methods used in aviation films to apply temporary markings, namely self-adhesive vinyl decals or painted insignia applied with a washable, water-based paint. Process work was also used to make the flying boat appear as if it was floating in the water when in fact it was sitting on dry land.

The Solent was a civilian version of the Short Seaford Mk 1 flying boat, itself a more powerful and better-armed derivative of the RAF's famous Short Sunderland which played a key role in defeating U-boats in the Battle of the Atlantic.

At the time of filming the Solent – which was formerly owned by Howard Hughes – was under restoration, and the only one of its four Bristol Hercules engines which was in working order was the starboard outer. This was the one which is seen starting up in the film.

The next scene showing the Solent flying over the Golden Gate Bridge in San Francisco was achieved using a miniature, as was the following 'moving map' sequence depicting the flying boat travelling to Nepal. Jones's journey has not gone unnoticed, however, as a Nazi spy (played by effects supervisor Dennis Muren) is sitting a few seats behind him, his face partly hidden by a copy of *Life* magazine.

Sometime later, Abner Ravenwood's daughter Marion (Karen Allen) is engaged in a drinking competition with an Australian climber (Patrick Durkin) in her bar (the *Raven* bar) in Nepal. Money is changing hands as people are betting on the outcome. Marion's opponent seems to be gaining the upper hand as he consumes one more drink and then smiles. Then he collapses unconscious – Marion has won.

Suddenly Indy arrives. We don't see him at first, only his huge shadow on the wall to the right of Marion, as if director Steven Spielberg is suggesting visually that he is a 'larger than life' character. 'Hello Marion,' he says. But his old flame's joy at seeing him only last seconds as she promptly wallops him. 'I've come to hate you in the past ten years', she screams.

'I never meant to hurt you,' replies Jones.

'I was a child! It was wrong, and you knew it.'

It is clear that the pair had a passionate affair which ended acrimoniously a decade earlier, and the pain is still there. The past unfinished business over for the moment, Jones gets to the point. He is looking for a headpiece which Abner owned, but Marion tells him that her father is now dead. Jones then offers her 3000 dollars for the item with a further 2000 dollars once he gets back to the USA, but Marion simply asks him to come back the following day. 'See you tomorrow, Indiana Jones'. After Jones has departed,

Marion sits down and pulls out the headpiece from under her blouse. She has been wearing it around her neck like a medallion.

Suddenly diehard Nazi Arnold Toht (Ronald Lacey) arrives with a group of German and Nepalese heavies, and brusquely informs Marion that he has come to retrieve the headpiece. Marion claims she no longer has it but does know where it is, and tries to placate Toht with an offer of drinks for him and his men. Toht is far from happy at this offer and gets his men to restrain her while he retrieves a red-hot poker from the fire. He intends to torture Marion until she reveals the location of the headpiece.

Toht approaches Marion with the poker but, as it approaches her face, it is knocked out of his grasp by a bullwhip. 'Let her go,' says Indy as a fight breaks out. Soon bullets are flying and the displaced red-hot poker sets fire to a curtain, starting a blaze. Some of the barrels of liquor are punctured by stray bullets, and there is a nice comic moment as Marion glugs down some of the leaking jets of alcohol. She then hits a bad guy on the head with a bit of wood.

This whole scene is a homage to the bar-room fights in many Westerns in which a punch-up between just two people always escalates into a conflict which involves everyone in the room, even if they have been the best of friends a moment earlier, and must include at least one sequence in which someone is struck over the head with a bottle.

Amid the chaos, Toht tries to grab the headpiece but it has been heated up so much by the flames that it is scalding hot. He burns his right hand, forcing him to drop the medallion. Marion shoots a Nepalese bandit just as he is about to fire on Indy, and she then retrieves the headpiece by wrapping it in cloth. She and Indy escape from the bar unscathed. One of the heavies who dies in this scene is played by Pat Roach, who also appears as a Luftwaffe aircraft mechanic later in the film, while another is portrayed by Sonny Caldinez, a Trinidadian actor who was an 'Ice Warrior' in various *Doctor Who* stories between 1967 and 1974.

The next shot of a Douglas DC-3 airliner flying over the Himalayas is stock footage taken from the 1973 Peter Finch movie *Lost Horizon*, with a moving map display superimposed to depict the aircraft flying to Cairo.

All the Egyptian scenes in the movie were filmed in Tunisia, which was a popular location at that time as it had been used for shooting the first *Star Wars* picture in 1976. Around the same time Sir Lew Grade's miniseries *Jesus of Nazareth* (1977) was filmed there, as was *Monty Python's Life of Brian* (1979) which re-used many of the sets from the earlier production.

On a rooftop terrace in Cairo, Jones discusses the Germans' ongoing excavations in the desert and meets Sallah (John Rhys-Davies) – regarded as the finest digger in Egypt. Sallah reports that the German team had discovered the all-important map room three days earlier, so it is only a matter of days before they recover the Ark. He is scornful of the Germans' abilities though, as he feels there 'is only one brain among them': the archaeologist Belloq, whom Jones already knows.

Jones points out, though, that the Germans cannot find the Ark without the headpiece of the Staff of Ra, which he possesses. Sallah meanwhile is concerned about the Ark being excavated and opened, as it is 'not of this world' and 'death has always surrounded it'.

Soon after this meeting, Marion and Indy go for a stroll in Cairo and a friendly pet monkey accompanies them.

Suddenly they are attacked by several Arabs. Unlike most Bond pictures, all the fights in *Raiders of the Lost Ark* have a semi-comic quality which is typified by this sequence. Indy manages to make an Arab attacker stab one of his colleagues with a sword by getting out of the way at the last moment. Then he helps Marion to escape by putting her on the back of a haycart. Marion leaves the haycart but is followed by an Arab who chases her into a house – but she hits him over the head. Later she escapes her pursuers by hiding in a tall, empty wicker basket, but the pet monkey insists on sitting on top and crying, thus giving away her position.

Meanwhile a black-clad Arab warrior is threatening Indy with a scimitar. But instead of taking up the challenge Jones simply draws his revolver and shoots him. Originally this scene was scripted as a lengthy fight sequence, but as Harrison Ford was weakened by food poisoning he opted for a simpler solution which in the end provided for a very comic moment. Most of the cast and crew suffered from gastroenteritis during the lengthy shoot in Tunisia, but director Steven Spielberg remained in good health for most of the time by avoiding local produce and eating a large supply of Sainsburys canned food which he had brought from London.

After disposing of his attacker, Indy goes in search of Marion. He realises that she has been hiding in a laundry basket but can't find her. Suddenly he sees some Arabs putting a laundry basket in the back of a truck which is carrying ammunition and explosives. As the truck drives towards him, Indy shoots an Arab riding on the running board and then kills the driver. The truck promptly slews off course, travels up a ramp, turns over and explodes. Indy is despondent because he thinks he has just killed Marion.

This is another scene which illustrates that *Raiders of the Lost Ark* is a pure fantasy. Indiana Jones and his Nazi and Arab opponents kill anyone they like, but there is no comeback as the Egyptian police are nowhere to be seen. It is also highly unlikely that the pre-war Egyptian Government would have allowed an armed expedition by German forces on their soil. Though Egypt had been an independent country since 1922, the British still had a huge garrison in the country, particularly in Cairo and Alexandria, which was effectively an occupation force and it is hardly likely that they would have allowed Nazis to drive around Egypt killing anyone they wanted.

The next scene shows a rather traumatized Indy sitting outside the Marhala Bar, drinking from a bottle of whisky in an attempt to calm himself down after the death of Marion. The pet monkey is around his neck. Two Nazis arrive and ask him to go inside the bar, where he discovers his adversary Belloq smoking a Hookah 'water pipe'. Jones says that he would like to kill him, but Belloq points out that the two of them are actually very alike; an assertion which Jones refutes. Belloq then says that the Ark is like a transmitter, a radio for speaking to God, but Jones replies brusquely: 'If you want to talk to God let's see him together, I've nothing better to do'. Jones is perhaps suggesting rather obliquely that the two of them commit suicide as he is despondent at the death of Marion. This is the nearest that Jones ever comes to displaying a truly realistic emotional response to a situation in a film which is pure fantasy.

Belloq dismisses Jones' offer. Just then, Jones is rescued by Sallah's children who take him into the street. Later Sallah reveals that Belloq now has a copy of the headpiece. How he created it is never made clear in the movie, but production paperwork indicates that it was supposedly created from a cast of the scar on Toht's right palm which was effectively a branding caused by the scorching hot headpiece.

However in discussion with Sallah, Jones realises that the Germans don't have information about the exact length of the staff to which the headpiece should be attached. This data is contained in inscriptions on the reverse side of the headpiece, so Jones deduces that – as the Germans are using a staff which is not the correct length – they must be digging in the wrong place. As the two conclude their discussion, they discover that the monkey has died from eating poisoned dates – the Germans are still trying to kill them.

The next morning, as the sun is rising above the horizon Egyptian labourers are excavating what the Germans and Belloq believe to be the site of the Well of Souls. Close by, Indy and Sallah are preparing to enter the map room, an ancient building with a domed stone roof and an open porthole at one end. The plan is for Indy to enter the room, set up the staff and headpiece, and wait for the rising sun to shine through the porthole. At exactly 9.00 a.m. the sun has risen sufficiently for a stream of light to pass through the glass centre of the headpiece and cause a beam of light to be projected on a small area of a model of the city of Tanis, giving the exact location of the Well of Souls. The beam of light appears like a yellow laser beam, though it must be said that the science in this sequence is rather questionable as a focused beam of light would require both an aperture and an actual lens which weren't invented till the Middle Ages. Indy records the correct location in his notebook and then breaks the staff in two. He climbs out of the Map Room using a makeshift rope left by Sallah, which has been created from sheets and a Nazi swastika flag.

He then makes his way through the Nazi camp and is delighted to discover that Marion is alive and well, though bound and gagged in a tent. He takes off her gag but can't free her yet as it will let the Nazis know he is alive. Later he uses a surveyor's theodolite to determine the exact position of the Well of Souls.

Meanwhile the Nazi officers in charge of the excavation think it may be worthwhile interviewing Marion, but Belloq thinks she knows nothing. Though clearly devious, treacherous and on the wrong side, he is not a sadist like the Nazis. The Germans criticise him for his squeamishness but point out that they have 'the perfect man for this kind of work' – Toht, who has just arrived and gives a Nazi salute revealing that his right palm is scarred, branded with an impression of the headpiece, the only clue in the film that the Nazis have created their own replica of the crucial artefact.

Later, as the sun is setting, Indy and a gang of native labourers dig furiously to excavate the Well of Souls. The weather changes abruptly and a storm develops as they uncover first a stone surface, then an actual flagstone under the sand. They lever up the large slab, and Sallah wonders why the floor of the chamber they have uncovered is moving. He asks for a blazing torch to be thrown in, and discovers that the Well of Souls is filled with hundreds of snakes – something which Indy hates. Jones is appalled, but Sallah merely notices that they are 'Asps... very dangerous. You go first'. Meanwhile, Belloq visits Marion in her tent. He releases her bonds and offers her a meal on a tray. He also shows her a white dress in a box and says he would like to see her wearing it.

As the French archaeologist is entertaining Marion, Indy is descending a rope into the Well of Souls. As he reaches the floor he is confronted by a cobra. This scene was done using a real cobra but, as the creature was highly dangerous, a sheet of glass was placed between Harrison Ford and the reptile. Indy then calls on Sallah to join him, and he kills some of the snakes – creating a clear path to the Ark – by spraying them with petrol and then setting fire to them. This is another piece of 'Hollywood Science', as incinerating the snakes in this way would produce vast quantities of asphyxiating smoke which would have damaged Indy's lungs.

Initially 3,000 real snakes were obtained for this scene, but this was found to be insufficient and a further 4,000 had to be obtained including cobras and pythons. The numbers were then beefed up with fake snakes made from lengths of hosepipe.

Having dealt with the snakes, Indy and Sallah lift the lid of the stone chest containing the Ark. Jones is an expert on the occult and knows that he must not touch the Ark, so the two of them lift the golden artefact out of the stone chest using wooden poles. While this is happening, Marion has her own plan to escape from the Nazi camp. She will make Belloq take part in a drinking competition as it has been established earlier in the movie that she has an incredible tolerance for alcohol. Marion and Belloq have one drink after another. The French archaeologist soon becomes inebriated and Marion pretends to be as drunk as him, though she is really in command of the situation. She steals a knife and attempts to escape from the tent but backs into Toht.

A few moments later Belloq, Colonel Dietrich and Toht are strolling through their camp and spot Jones' digging party silhouetted against the setting sun. Realising that something is brewing, they rush to the site of the activity accompanied by a gang of native labourers and a large party of armed German soldiers. This is a continuity error in the film. During the initial entry into the Well the weather was dull, cloudy and stormy, and all of a sudden there isn't a cloud in the sky.

The Germans arrive just as the Ark is being brought to the surface. They take possession of the artefact, throw Marion into the Well of Souls where she joins Jones and Sallah, and replace the flagstone. Jones and his party are now sealed in the chamber, effectively buried alive.

But Indy is soon working on an escape plan. Seeing snakes emerging from holes in the wall, he realises there must be a further chamber beyond it which must lead somewhere. He climbs a statue of a Jackal, causing it to fall and break through the wall. Jones can now see sunlight streaming through a hole and realises this is their way out. Marion encounters the corpses of previous occupants of the Well who have died trying to escape but, despite this, Indy and his colleagues escape to the surface where they soon find that the Germans are planning to fly the Ark out using an aircraft.

The plane is an unusual 'flying wing' design which is actually wrong for the period. During WW2 the Horten Brothers produced designs for German 'Flying Wing' designs which were never actually built. After the war ended, these designs formed the basis of the American Northrop 'YB-35 Flying Wing' aircraft, which was developed into the jet-powered YB-49 bomber.

The flying wing aircraft which appears in *Raiders of the Lost Ark* is therefore an anachronism. A more accurate representation of a 1936 Luftwaffe transport aircraft would have been achieved by using a Junkers 52/3m trimotor, several examples of which were airworthy in 1980 including three with the Swiss Air Force, but it must be said that the Flying

Wing – inaccurate though it may be – does look very interesting visually, and makes for a very exciting sequence. Initial drawings for the replica aircraft showed a version with five engines and a model with four motors was produced. A full-sized version would have cost $750,000, but George Lucas saved about $250,000 just by opting for a twin-engined design. The non-flying replica, which had turning propellors and could taxi, was built by the Vickers Aircraft company (now part of British Aerospace) in England and shipped to Tunisia in sections.

The aircraft has a tricycle (nosewheel) undercarriage (which was very unusual for 1936), and is apparently armed with two 20mm cannon projecting from the wing leading edges plus two 7.9mm machine guns in a dorsal turret. It is supposedly powered by two liquid-cooled inline engines driving pusher propellors (though the exhaust stubs don't emit smoke or flames as they would on a real engine). Another inaccuracy is that the aircraft has large swastika markings on the upper wings, rather than the correct *Balkenkreuz* Luftwaffe markings.

A bald, muscular Luftwaffe aircraft mechanic (Pat Roach) hears the commotion and emerges from a tent. Stripping off his shirt, he starts to fight Indy. Roach also appeared as a Nepalese bandit earlier in the movie and later played Lippe in a lengthy fight sequence in *Never Say Never Again* (1983). As well as being an actor and stuntman, Roach was a professional wrestler and ran a gym.

The pilot of the aircraft then opens the canopy and tries to shoot Indy with his pistol, but he is knocked out by Marion who takes his place in the cockpit and manages to get into the dorsal turret where she opens fire on every target she can see. The pilot was played by producer Frank Marshall, who agreed to step in after the stuntman who was earmarked for the role fell ill.

By this time the flying wing is taxiing in a wide circle, and its starboard wingtip punctures a fuel bowser causing hundreds of gallons of petrol to leak onto the ground. As the fight with the aircraft mechanic continues, Indy drops his revolver on the ground while Marion continues to shoot up German vehicles. Over the rise, the main party of Germans see an orange fireball rising into the sky and realise things are going awry.

By this time the aircraft mechanic has given Indy a sound beating, but he makes the fatal mistake of walking backwards into one of the aeroplane's whirling propellors which cuts him to ribbons. As this was a family film, this was not directly depicted and is merely implied by a shot of fake blood splattering on one of the aircraft's fins. Quickly, Indy jumps on the Flying Wing to free Marion, but the canopy has jammed shut and Indy has to blast the catch with his revolver to get the Perspex hood open. The pair quickly flee the scene just as the leaking fuel catches fire and the aircraft explodes.

This sequence was one of the most trying to film, as the ambient temperature was as high as 130 degrees Fahrenheit and Harrison Ford suffered a leg injury when he was run over by the aircraft's undercarriage. Fortunately the aircraft's tyres had softened in the heat, and Ford only suffered ligament damage.

Now that the aircraft has been destroyed, Indy realises that the only option left to the Germans is to take the Ark in a truck to the nearest port and ship it out. He tells Marion and Sallah to make their way to Cairo and arrange transport out of the country by boat or plane. He is going after the truck and he doesn't have a plan. By his own admission, he is 'making it up as he goes along'.

Without further thought, Indy rides out of the German camp on a horse in pursuit of the German convoy which includes a heavy Mercedes LG3000 truck, a Mercedes G5 light truck, a Mercedes 320 staff car, and a motorcycle and sidecar combination. The Ark is being carried in a wooden crate in the largest vehicle in the convoy, a replica of a pre-war Mercedes LG3000 truck which was specially created for the film using an American GMC two-and-a-half ton truck of WW2 vintage. A new cab and front end were fabricated, and the ground clearance was raised to enable a number of stunts to be carried out which involved Indy holding onto the underside of the vehicle. Even with the increased height of the chassis above the ground a trench had to be dug in the road to enable the stunts to be carried out safely.

After catching up with the convoy, Indy jumps from his horse to the truck and fights off a German soldier to take control of the vehicle. At one point five Nazi troopers are clinging to the side and rear of the truck and attempting to enter the cab. Indy manages to force them off the vehicle by swerving into trees at the side of the road.

Indy then sets about eliminating his opponents by swerving from side to side and knocking them off the road. A German motorcycle/sidecar combo is knocked off the road and the light truck is forced off a cliff (in a sequence which resembles those seen in the classic war movies *The Guns of Navarone*, 1961, and *Where Eagles Dare*, 1968).

One of the highlights of this incredible stunt sequence is the 'gag' where Indy has been thrown through the windscreen onto the bonnet of the truck and then has to cling to the radiator. He holds onto the metal Mercedes badge at the top of the radiator, but it bends under his weight and he ends up under the chassis of the truck holding onto a rope. Eventually he finds himself dragged along the road behind the truck and manages to pull himself back and regain control of the vehicle. This whole sequence is an homage to a very similar stunt devised by veteran Hollywood stunt arranger Yakima Canutt, which appears in a number of classic movies including the John Wayne movie *Stagecoach* (1939). Often this stunt involved the hero finding himself under a stagecoach, being dragged behind it and then finally getting back on board. A variant on this stunt appears in the war movie *Tobruk* (1967), in which George Peppard's character gets under a moving German tank in order to affix a satchel charge.

Finally, having regained control of the truck, Indy eliminates the final German vehicle, a Mercedes 320 staff car which he forces off the road. Having beaten off the opposition, he heads into Cairo where he hides the truck in an empty shop front with the assistance of the local population who conceal the truck with a drape and a cart. Twelve period vehicles were acquired for the Tunisian scenes, but all the German trucks and cars were effectively replicas created by modifying British and American vehicles. Even the Mercedes staff car was a replica, made from Jaguar Mark 5 and Mark 9 components by Classic Cars of Coventry.

That evening at the dockside (supposedly Cairo but actually La Rochelle in France), Indy and Marion prepare to board a tramp steamer the *Bantu Wind* which is captained by a man called Simon Katanga (George Harris) who has agreed to take both them and the Ark home. They say farewell to Sallah and Marion kisses him.

The tramp steamer *Bantu Wind* was a real vessel – the *Abeer Delta* – which was found in a suitably rust-streaked state in Belfast. Just before filming began the owners had her repainted to pristine condition, requiring the film producers to dirty her down again to get the effect they required.

As the *Bantu Wind* sets sail, Marion and Indy relax in their cabin. Marion cleans Indy's wounds and discovers that the only part of Indy's body which doesn't hurt is his left elbow! Meanwhile, in the hold of the vessel strange noises and smoke are emanating from the wooden crate containing the Ark.

The next morning Indy and Marion wake up to discover that a German submarine has surfaced nearby. The vessel – an exact replica of a WW2 vintage 700-ton Type VII U-Boat specially constructed for the 1981 film and TV miniseries *Das Boot* – was loaned to the filmmakers by Bavaria Studios. As the boat could not be broken down and transported elsewhere, all scenes featuring the craft had to be shot at La Rochelle in France where the submarine was based.

A German boarding party quickly lands on the *Bantu Wind* and takes possession of the crate containing the Ark. Belloq insists on taking Marion with them, despite Katanga's protests. Katanga also claims to have killed Jones, but he is alive and well and hiding in one of the curved, cylindrical ventilation ducts on deck.

As the crew of the U-boat get back on board their vessel and get below, Indy swims to the German submarine, climbing onto the railed *Wintergarten* deck behind the conning tower. The crew of the *Bantu Wind* cheer loudly when they see what he has done. The captain of the U-boat is played by English actor Michael Sheard, who often played German soldiers and prominent Nazis in films and TV productions including Adolf Hitler in *Indiana Jones and the Last Crusade* (1989).

A moving map display then follows showing the submarine travelling to a small island North of Crete. The island (which looks a bit like Tracy Island in *Thunderbirds*) was a matte painting superimposed on footage of a large model submarine approaching an island off San Rafael in California. The U-boat in this sequence was a modified 25 foot miniature of a Japanese submarine which had been built for Steven Spielberg's previous film *1941* (1979).

Some behind-the-scenes photographs show that footage was shot showing Indy making the entire journey clinging to the submarine's periscope. In fact, U-boats of this era were really submersibles rather than true submarines, as they spent most of their time on the surface and only dived underwater for short periods to make an underwater attack or evade detection. They were also very slow underwater, so any lengthy journeys had to be made on the surface using their diesel engines.

The U-boat enters the anchorage in footage which was shot at a genuine wartime submarine pen in La Rochelle, France. Many of these facilities (and similar E-boat pens) were built on the French coast by the German Todt Organisation in WW2, and because they were constructed of thick reinforced concrete designed to withstand even a direct hit from the heaviest bomb they still survive to this day as they are almost impossible to demolish. This is the same reason that most of the coastal fortifications and flak towers built by the Nazis still exist.

As the U-boat docks, Indy emerges from cover, knocks out a German soldier and steals his uniform. However, he can't get the jacket to fasten as it is the wrong size. Another

German soldier of a higher rank stumbles across him and berates him about his appearance, so Indy knocks him out and steals his uniform which fits perfectly. This scene may be regarded as a satire on a cliché common in war movies in which Allied soldiers steal German uniforms which always fit perfectly (e.g. *The Guns of Navarone,* 1961, and two of Harrison Ford's previous movies *Force 10 from Navarone,* 1978, and *Hanover Street,* 1979, both feature such sequences).

As the crate containing the Ark sits on the deck of the U-boat awaiting transport, Colonel Dietrich confesses that he is uncomfortable about the necessity for 'Jewish Rituals' to activate the Ark, and Belloq agrees to perform this function. He also feels that the Ark should be opened now – and not when it gets to Berlin – to make sure that it performs its functions.

The next scene shows a column of Nazi troops marching across the island carrying a crate which contains the Ark. This scene was shot in what is now known as the '*Star Wars* canyon' in Tunisia. The troops are travelling to the location where they are going to open the artefact. Wearing a German uniform, Indy is accompanying them. As the group of soldiers pass some storage huts, he sneaks off to one side.

A few moments later the column is ambushed by Indy, who is standing on a rock above them carrying a shoulder-launched anti-tank rocket which he has presumably acquired from the huts. Articles about the film describe this weapon as a 'Panzerfaust', but this is incorrect. The Panzerfaust (literally 'tank-fist') was a simple, hand-held anti-armour weapon which used a small explosive charge to fire a powerful shaped-charge warhead at a tank. It was thus not a rocket but a type of recoilless gun and was held below (rather than above) the shoulder. It was not deployed by German forces until 1943.

The weapon shown in *Raiders of the Lost Ark* was a replica of a Chinese Type 56 weapon based on the Soviet RPG-2 (rocket propelled grenade), which didn't see service until 1962. In 1936 the only hand-held anti-tank weapons which existed would be rifle grenades (i.e. explosive grenades attached to the muzzle of a rifle and fired by the explosive force of a blank cartridge) and anti-tank rifles which were effectively large calibre rifles firing a bullet of about 0.50in calibre. The best-known anti-tank rifle was the British Boys rifle of 0.55in calibre which was obsolete by the start of WW2. The appearance of a rocket-propelled grenade launcher in *Raiders of the Lost Ark* is therefore a serious anachronism, as is the German troops' use of MP-40 submachine guns which did not enter service until 1940.

Indy threatens to blow up the Ark with his weapon unless the Nazis hand over Marion, but Belloq calls his bluff and Indy surrenders. Later Marion and Indy are tied to a stake while the Nazis prepare to open the Ark. A film camera, complete with swastika, is readied to record the event. This is another minor beef I have about *Raiders of the Lost Ark* – there is an excessive use of swastikas everywhere. Even the gantry crane in the submarine pen has one so you can't forget it is a Nazi installation. This is a common practice in many war movies. As one of my friends once said, talking about a famous war movie, 'If the movie featured a love scene the condom would have a swastika on it!'

Belloq dresses as a Jewish priest and utters incantantions in Hebrew as the Ark is opened. He is appalled when he discovers it is full of sand. Suddenly strange things start to happen – blue sparks like lightning surround the Ark, smoke wafts from it, and energy beams criss-cross the room.

Indy tells Marion to close her eyes, insisting that she mustn't look at the Ark.

Strange spirit forms appear from the Ark. Although looking initially like angels, they quickly change into malevolent skull-like forms intent on killing. Originally it was intended to create these spirit beings using traditional cel animation techniques, but this proved unconvincing and eventually these sequences were created using mannequins which were shot underwater using reverse filming techniques.

One by one, the Nazi soldiers are killed by energy bolts. Dietrich's skull shrivels up, Belloq's head explodes and Toht's face melts. This 'melting face' sequence was probably the most striking special effect in the movie, and involved taking an alginate cast of Ronald Lacey's head which was used to create an accurate gelatine mask over a fake skull which was then melted with heat guns. All the same, the footage had to be speeded up many times to create the stunning effect. As all the Nazis die, an energy bolt heads up to a cloud above the island and the lid of the Ark snaps shut, leaving Indy and Marion unscathed. They free themselves and hug.

Sometime later in Washington DC, Indy meets Dr Marcus Brody and the Army Intelligence chiefs. Marion is to be given a financial settlement which pleases Indy, but he is concerned about the fate of the Ark. He is reassured that it is somewhere safe while Brody asserts that it is a source of unspeakable power and has to be researched. They are told that top men are working on it.

As Indy and Marion leave the building, the archaelogist comments that they don't know what they've got, but Marion remarks that she knows what she's got – him. The final shot of the movie shows the Ark in a sealed, padlocked crate being taken by fork lift truck to the far end of a huge storage warehouse containing thousands of similar chests. One wonders what is in all these other boxes?

The film was released on 12 June 1981 and eventually made $384 million against a final budget of $18m. It was the most successful film of 1981, and spawned further Indiana Jones movies – namely *Indiana Jones and the Temple of Doom* (1984), *Indiana Jones and the Last Crusade* (1989) and *Indiana Jones and the Kingdom of the Crystal Skull* (2008). A fifth Indiana Jones film is planned for release in 2019. A spin-off TV series, *The Young Indiana Jones Chronicles*, was also aired between 1992 and 1996. The film was nominated for nine Oscars and won in five categories (Art Direction, Film Editing, Sound, Sound Effects Editing, and Visual Effects).

An amateur shot-by-shot remake of the original film called *Raiders of the Lost Ark: The Adaptation* was made by Chris Strompolos, Eric Zala and Jayson Lamb between 1982 and 1989. Although praised by Steven Spielberg, the amateur film has never been released on DVD or Blu-Ray, presumably for copyright reasons.

*Raiders* has also influenced many other films and TV productions. The 1999 version of *The Mummy* starring Brendan Fraser and Rachel Weisz owes more *to Raiders of the Lost Ark* than to the 1932 Boris Karloff movie on which it is supposedly based. A rebooted version of that movie starring Tom Cruise is planned for release in 2017, showing that the influence of Spielberg and Lucas's 1981 original continues to this day.

## *Raiders of the Lost Ark* (1981)
## Production Credits

Director: Steven Spielberg
Screenplay: Lawrence Kasdan
Based on a story by George
Lucas and Philip Kaufman

### Cast

Indiana Jones - Harrison Ford
Marion Ravenwood - Karen
Allen
Dr Rene Belloq - Paul Freeman
Major Arnold Toht - Ronald
Lacey
Sallah - John Rhys-Davies
Dr Marcus Brody - Denholm
Elliott
Satipo - Alfred Molina
Colonel Dietrich - Wolf Kahler
Gobler - Anthony Higgins
Barranca / Monkey Man - Vic
Tablian
Colonel Musgrove - Don
Fellows
Major Eaton - William Hootkins
Bureaucrat - Bill Reimbold
Jock - Fred Sorenson
Australian Climber - Patrick
Durkin
2nd Nazi - Matthew Scurfield
Ratty Nepalese - Malcolm
Weaver
Mean Mongolian - Sonny
Caldinez
Mohan - Anthony Chinn
Giant Sherpa / Aircraft
Mechanic - Pat Roach
Otto - Christopher Frederick

Imam - Tutte Lemkow
Omar - Ishaq Bux
Abu - Kiran Shuh
Fayah - Souad Messaoudi
Arab Swordsman - Terry
Richards
German Agent - Steve Hanson
Pilot - Frank Marshall
Young Soldier - Martin Kreidt
Katanga - George Harris
Messenger Pirate - Eddie Tagoe
Sergeant - John Rees
Tall Captain - Tony Vogel
Peruvian Porter - Ted Grossman
German Soldiers - Vic
Armstrong, Rocky Taylor, Alan
Austen, Nick Gillard, Romo
Gorrara, Chris Parsons, Rick
Lester, Peter Diamond, Harry
Fielder
Nazi Supporter - Darin
Chambers
German Lieutenant - Reg
Harding
Archivist - Barrie Holland
Gobler's Gunner - Billy Horrigan
The Boulder - Josh Ag
German Truck Drivers - Terry
Leonard, Sergio Mioni
Nazi Spy on Flying Boat -
Dennis Muren
Flying Wing Mechanic - Glenn
Randall Jr
U-Boat Captain - Michael
Sheard

Special Vocal Effects - Frank
Welker

**Producers**
Executive Producers: Howard J.
Kazanjian, George Lucas
Producer: Frank Marshall
Associate Producer: Robert
Watts

**Music**
Composer: John Williams

**Cinematography**
Director of Photography:
Douglas Slocombe

**Film Editing**
Film Editors: Michael Kahn,
George Lucas
Casting: Jane Feinberg, Mike
Fenton, Mary Selway
Production Design: Norman
Reynolds
Art Director: Leslie Dilley
Set Director: Michael Ford
Costume Design: Deborah
Nadollman

**Makeup Department**
Hairdresser: Mike Lockey
Chief Hairdresser: Patricia
McDermott
Makeup Artist: Dickie Mills
Key Makeup Artists: Tom
Smith, Jim Gillespie
Special Makeup Effects (ILM):
Christopher Walas

**Production Management**
Assistant Production Manager:
Patricia Carr
Production Supervisor
(Tunisia): Mohamed Ali Cherif
Production Manager (France):
Dorothy Marchini
Production Manager (Tunisia):
Hassine Soufi
Production Supervisor: Douglas
Twiddy
Production Manager: Robert
Watts

**Second Unit Director or
Assistant Director**
First Assistant Director: Carlos
Gill, David Tomblin
Second Assistant Directors: Roy
Button, Patrick Cadell
First Assistant Director
(France): Vincent Joliet
First Assistant Director
(Tunisia): Naceur Ktari
Second Assistant Director
(Hawaii): Louis G. Friedman
Second Assistant Director
(Second Unit): Michael Hook
Second Unit Director: Michael
Moore, Frank Marshall
Second Unit Assistant Director:
Julian Wall

**Art Department**
Property Master: Frank Bruton
Sketch Artist: Roy Carnon
Art Department Assistant:
Sharon Cartwright
Plasterer: Mick Chubbock

Supervising Plasterer: Kenneth Clark
Production Artist: Ron Cobb
Assistant Art Directors: Ken Court, John Fenner, Michael Lamont, Fred Hole
Draughtsman: George Djurkovic
Scenic Artist: Andrew Garnet-Lawson
Assistant Construction Manager: George Gunning
Production Artist: Michael Lloyd
Chief Buyer: David Lusby
Illustrator (ILM): Ralph McQuarrie
Construction Storeman: Dave Middleton
Head Plasterer: Bert Rodwell
Master Painter: Eric Shirtliffe
Modeller: Keith Short
Property Supervisor: Charles Torbett
Production Illustrator: Ed Verreaux
Décor & Lettering Artist: Bob Walker
Assistant Art Director (Tunisia): Hassen Soufi
Sketch Artist: David Negron
Property Master (Tunisia): Peter Hancock
Construction Manager: Bill Welch
Plasterers: Tony Vice, Andy Aitken
Plasterer Stand-by: Paul James
Poster Artists: John Alvin, Tom Jung

Art Department Design Work: Tony Boxall
Painter: Michael Finlay
Propery Buyer (Tunisia): Taieb Jallouli
Dressing Prop: Dave Midson
Sculptor: Brian Muir
Art Department: Kent State
Storyboard Artists: Dave Stevens, William Stout

**Sound Department**
Supervising Sound Effects Editor: Richard L Anderson
Sound Designer: Ben Burtt
Production Sound: Roy Charman
Foley Editor: John Dunn
Sound Effects Editor: Stephen Hunter Flick
Apprentice Sound Editor: Peter Grives
Recording Technician: Howie Hammerman
Re-recording: Steve Maslow, Gregg Landaker, Bill Varney
Sound Effects Editor: Mark Mangini
Sound Dubbing Technician: Kevin O'Connell
Dialogue Editor: Andy Patterson
Production Sound Maintenance: George Rice
Sound Boom Operator: John Salter
Supervising Dialogue Editor: Curt Schulkey

Sound Effects Recording: Gary Summers

Assistant Dialogue Editor: Eric Whitfield

Foley Artist: John Roesch, Vanessa Theme

Special Sound Effects: Alan Howarth

Foley Mixer: Greg Orloff

ADR Mixer: Lionel Strutt

Foley Recordist: Carolyn Tapp

Sound Effects: Randy Thom

**Special effects**

Special Effects Electrician: Chris Condon

Special Effects Carpenter: Roy Coombes

Senior Effects Technician: Peter Dawson

Special Effects Welder: Yves De Bono

Effects Tecnnician: Rodney Fuller

Effects Assistant: Ray Hanson, Ken Gittens

Effects Engineering: Terry Glass

Effects Technicians: Trevor Neighbour, Terry Schubert

Special Effects Equipment Supervisor: Bill Warrington

Mechanical Effects Supervisor: Kit West

Special Effects Assistant: Michael Dawson

**Visual Effects**

Assistant Effects Editor (ILM): Peter Amundson

Model Maker (ILM): Charlie Bailey

Matte Photography Assistant (ILM): Craig Barron

Stage Technician (ILM): William Beck

Optical Printer Operator (ILM): David Berry

Production Coordinator (ILM): Patricia Blau

Design Engineer (ILM): Mike Bolles

Electronics Engineer (ILM): Marty Brenneis

Computer Engineer (ILM): Kris Brown

Visual Effects Editorial Supervisor (ILM): Conrad Buff

Production Accountant (ILM): Laura Kaysen

Animator (ILM): Scott Caple

Electronics Technician (ILM): Melissa Cargill

Special Projects (ILM): Wade Childress

Still Photographer (ILM): Terry Chostner

Assistant Visual Effects Editor (ILM): Joe Class

Animation Supervisor (ILM): Samuel Comstock

Stage Technician (ILM): Dick Dova

Camera Operator (ILM): Don Dow

Animator (ILM): Loring Doyle

Visual Effects Supervisor: Richard Edlund

Animator (ILM): Judy Elkins

Optical Printer Operator
(ILM): John Ellis
Administration Assistant
(ILM): Chrissie England
Stage Technicians (ILM): Bobby
Finley III, Patrick Fitzsimmons
Optical Line-up (ILM): Warren
Franklin
Animation Supervisor (ILM):
Dietrich Friesen
Model Makers (ILM): Mike
Fulmer, Steve Gawley, Paul
Huston, Ease Owyeung, Samuel
Zolltheis, Bruce Richardson,
Wesley Seeds, March Thorpe
Laboratory Technician (ILM):
Tim Geldeman
Production Associate (ILM):
Miki Herman
Stage Technician (ILM)
Edward Hirsh
Electronic Systems Designer
(ILM): Jerry Jefress
Art Director Visual Effects
(ILM): Joe Johnston
Laboratory Technician (ILM):
Ed Jones
Production Accountant (ILM):
David Kakita, Shirley Lee
Animators (ILM): Sylvia
Keulen, Kim Knowlton, Scott
Marshall, John Van Vliet,
Garry Waller
Matte Photography (ILM): Neil
Krepela
Electronics Engineers (ILM):
Gary Leo, Mike MacKenzie
Matte Painting Supervisor
(ILM): Alan Maley

Electronics Technician (ILM):
Cristi McCarthy
Still Lab Technicians (ILM):
Roberto McGrath, Kerry
Nordoquist
Stage Technicians (ILM): John
McCleod, Peter Stolz
Supervising Stage Technician
(ILM): Ted Moehnke
Pyrotechnics (ILM): Thaine
Morris
Laboratory Technician (ILM):
Ducan Myers
Camera Operator (ILM): Bill
Neill
Optical Photography Supervisor
(ILM): Bruce Nicholson
Assistant Cameraman (ILM):
Clint Palmer
Machinist (ILM): Udo Pampel
Matte Artist (ILM): Michael
Pangrazio
Modelshop Foreman (ILM):
Lorne Peterson
Cloud Effects (ILM): Gary
Platek
Optical Printer Supervisor
(ILM): Kenneth Smith
Production Supervisor (ILM):
Thomas Smith
Assistant Effects Editor (ILM):
Howard Stein
Production Supervisor (IMAX):
Jason Pomerantz
Assistant Art Director (ILM):
Nilo Rodis-Janiero
Optical Line-up (ILM): Thomas
Rosseter, Mark Vargo

Effects Cameraman (ILM): Jim Veilleux
Production Coordinator (ILM): Laurie Vermont
Equipment Engineering Supervisor (ILM): Gene Whiteman
Electronics Technician (ILM): Bessie Wiley
Digital Compositor (Restoration): Chris Crowell
Digital Paint and Roto Lead (Restoration): Beth D'Amato
Damage Artist/Supervisor: Rejynna Douglass-Whitman

## Stunt Work
Stunt Performers: Vic Armstrong, Peter Brace, Gerry Crampton, Romano Garrara, Martin Grace, Reg Harding, Billy Horrigan, Wendy Leach, Terry Leonard, Sergio Mione, Rocky Taylor, Chuck Walkers, Bill Weston, Paul Weston, Peter Diamond, Richard Graydon, Rick Lester
Stunt Arranger: Peter Diamond
Stunt Coordinator: Glenn Randall
Stunt Doubles for Harrison Ford: Vic Armstrong, Martin Grace, Terry Leonard
Stunt Double for Karen Allen: Wendy Leach

## Camera and Electrical Department
Additional Photography:
Paul Beeson
Gaffer (Hawaii): Alan Brady
Cameramen (Second Unit): Wally Byatt, Gerry Dunkley
Still Photographer: Albert Clark
Gaffer: Martin Evans
Dolly Grip (Second Unit): Jim Kane
Head Rigger: Red Lawrence
Dolly Grip. Colin Manning
Second Assistant Cameraman (Second Unit): Eamonn O'Keefe
Second Assistant Cameraman: Danny Shelmerdine
Assistant Cameraman (Second Unit): Chris Tanner
Assistant Cameraman: Robin Vidgeon
Operating Cameraman: Chic Waterson
Operating Cameraman (Second Unit): David Worley
Electricians: Wick Finch, Ron Herschman
Ultra High-Speed Photography: Bruce Hill
Clapper Loader: Paul Kenward
Best Boy: Ray Meehan

## Costume and Wardrobe Department
Wardrobe Assistants: Ian Hickinbotham, Sue Wain
Wardrobe Supervisor: Rita Wakely

## Editorial Department
Assistant Film Editor (ILM): Duwayne Dunham

Assistant Film Editor: Bruce
Green
Colour Timer: Robert
McMillian
Negative Cutter: Brian Ralph
Assistant Film Editors: Phil
Sanderson, Colin Wilson
Apprentice Film Editor: Julie
Kahn Zunder

## Location Management
Location Managers (Tunisia):
Abdelkrim Baccar, Habid Chaari
Location Manager: Brian Coates
Location Manager (Hawaii):
Maile Semitokol

## Music Department
Orchestra Conductor: Carl
Fortina
Orchestra: London Symphony
Orchestra
Orchestrator: Herbert W.
Spencer
Music Recordist: Eric
Tomlinson
Supervising Music Editor:
Kenneth Wannberg
Musician (Xylophone): Don
Williams
Musician (Percussion): Jerry
Williams, Tom Raney, Steve
Schaeffer
Musician (Tuba): Tommy
Johnson
Music Supervisor: Lionel
Newman
Musician (French Horn): James
Thatcher

Additional Orchestrator: Albert
Woodbury

## Transportation Department
Transportation Captain
(Hawaii): Harry Ueshiro
Camera Car Driver: John Ott
Driver (Cast): Terry Pritchard

## Other Crew
Armourer: Simon Atherton
Assistant to George Lucas: Jane
Bay
Production Coordinator
(Tunisia): Arthur Carroll
Production Assistant: Gill Case
Assistant to Steven Spielberg:
Martin Casella
Production Assistant (France):
Junior Charles
Animal Handler: Michael
Culling
Stand-in for Harrison Ford: Jack
Dearlove
Animal Handlers: Jed Edge,
Steve Edge
Researcher: Deborah Fine
Assistant to Frank Marshall:
Barbara Harley and Patty
Rumph
Unit Doctor: Dr Felicity Hodder
Continuity (Second Unit):
Maggie Jones
Assistant to Howard J.
Kazanjian: Laura Kenmore
Associate to Steven Spielberg:
Kathleen Kennedy
Assistant Accountant: Michael
Larkins

Continuity: Pamela Mann
Doctor (Second Unit): Dr Hassam Moossun
Production Coordinator (Hawaii): Dan Nichols
Production Assistant: Daniel Parker
Location Accountant: Stefano Priori
Accountant (France): Stella Quef
Accountant (Hawaii): Bonne Radford

Unit Publicist: Derek Robbins
Fire Safety Coordinator: Alan Sutton
Accountant (Tunisia): Ridna Turki
Production Intern: Michael Bay
Office Production Assistant: Xavier Legris
Original Illustrations: Jim Steranko

# 2

# WHO DARES WINS

## (1982)

*Varius/Richmond Light Horse Productions*

**Director:** Ian Sharp
**Producer:** Euan Lloyd
**Screenwriter:** Reginald Rose

AS explained elsewhere in this book, the boom in action movies during the 1980s was largely an American phenomenon. But there was one British film made during this era – *Who Dares Wins* – which has been consistently underrated ever since. I would argue that, as well as being a hugely enjoyable action picture in its own right, it represented a milestone in the history of British cinema as it could have led to even greater things for its producer Euan Lloyd and star Lewis Collins if economic conditions in the UK in the early eighties had been better.

The genesis of the film lay in a highly publicised incident on 5 May 1980 when a troop of SAS operatives stormed the Iranian embassy in London, releasing the hostages and killing five terrorists. Up to that point the activities of the SAS had largely been shrouded in mystery. Formed in 1941 in North Africa by Colonel David Stirling, its initial role was to attack enemy airfields. Its first mission – which involved insertion of troops by parachute – was a disaster, so Stirling arranged for his men to be taken to the target and back in vehicles of the Long Range Desert Group (LRDG). Later still, the unit acquired is own transport (including the first American Willys Jeeps to arrive in North Africa) which were fitted with multiple machine guns for shooting up Axis aircraft parked on airfields. These tactics proved extremely successful, and by mid-1942 the SAS was destroying more enemy planes than the RAF's Desert Air Force.

In the 1970s, in response to a wave of aircraft hijackings and other terrorist attacks, the SAS developed tactics (and acquired special weapons and equipment) in order to counter these incidents, leading to the formation of a Counter Revolutionary Warfare Wing (22 SAS). Thus the regiment was perfectly trained and equipped to storm the Iranian embassy when it was taken over by militants in 1980. The SAS assault (known as 'Operation Nimrod') was broadcast live on television and was also witnessed first-hand by a number of Londoners who lived or worked nearby, including film producer Euan Lloyd.

Lloyd had worked in the British film industry since the early fifties. He was employed as a publicist for Warwick Films and his first big feature was *The Red Beret* aka *Paratrooper* (1953) which starred Alan Ladd, who became a lifelong friend. Warwick Films had been established by future James Bond producer Albert R. ('Cubby') Broccoli and Irving Allen. Later he worked on a number of Carl Foreman's films, including *The Guns of Navarone* (1961).

In the late sixties Lloyd became an independent producer. His films included three Westerns, *Shalako* (1968), *Catlow* (1971) and *A Man Called Noon* (1973), the David Niven film *Paper Tiger* (1975), and the hugely successful action picture *The Wild Geese* (1978) which starred Richard

Burton, Richard Harris, Roger Moore and Hardy Kruger. After seeing the successful SAS assault, Lloyd 'phoned his lawyer and registered five possible titles with the Motion Picture Association of America (MPAA) for a film about the SAS, including *Who Dares Wins* – the regiment's motto.

The first stage in making the film was the creation of a workable script, and this was a result of a collaboration between George Markstein, James Follett and Reginald Rose. A former journalist, Markstein had also worked in the British intelligence services and had written and edited many scripts for film and television including the highly acclaimed movie *Robbery* (1967), directed by Peter Yates, which featured a realistic car chase presaging the same director's work on the Steve McQueen film *Bullitt* a year later. Markstein is best known, though, for his role as the script editor of Patrick McGoohan's 1967 ITC series *The Prisoner*, and actually appears in the title sequence of each episode as the bespectacled, bald man sitting at a desk, with whom McGoohan's character has an argument as he hands in his resignation.

Over a period of a few months, Markstein produced his own ideas for a storyline, one chapter at a time. These were then turned into a novel – *The Tiptoe Boys* by James Follett – and a screenplay, *Who Dares Wins* by Reginald Rose, who had previously scripted *The Wild Geese*. For the American market the film was re-titled *The Final Option*, as the SAS and their motto 'Who Dares Wins' were not widely recognised in the USA.

Lloyd had only one person in mind for the leading role of SAS Captain Peter Skellen, and that was actor Lewis Collins who at that time was extremely well-known for his role of Bodie in LWT's highly successful series *The Professionals* (1977-83).

Born in Bidston, Birkenhead, near Liverpool in 1946, Collins trained as a hairdresser and had a number of celebrity clients including early sixties pop star Helen Shapiro. He was also a proficient musician and, by 1962, was friendly with Paul McCartney's younger brother Mike (who as Mike McGear later became a member of the Liverpool pop group The Scaffold, who had a number of hits including *Thank You Very Much* and *Lily the Pink*). At that time the Beatles' original drummer – Pete Best – had resigned, and auditions were being held for a replacement, so Mike McCartney suggested that Lewis should attend. However, Collins declined to participate on the grounds that he was making so much money as a hairdresser, and thus missed an opportunity to become a member of the greatest pop band of all time!

In 1964 Collins did become a member of a Liverpool pop band, The Mojos, but by 1966 the group had split up and Collins eked out a living in a variety of jobs including being a delivery van driver. In 1968 he decided to go into acting after hearing a play on the radio, and trained at the London Academy of Music and Dramatic Art. His first TV appearances were as a policeman in the BBC's *Z Cars* in 1973 and as a sailor in an episode of the BBC series *Warship* in 1974. His big break came in 1975 when he was chosen to play lodger Gavin Rumsey in the Granada comedy series *The Cuckoo Waltz*, with Diane Keen playing his landlady. The series, written by *Coronation Street* writer Geoffrey Lancashire (father of actress Sarah Lancashire), ran for two years and was hugely popular. It also lead to Collins being cast in an episode of *The New Avengers* in 1977, a decision which set in course a chain of events that would result in his starring role in *Who Dares Wins* five years later.

Ever since *The Avengers* had ended its eight-year run in 1969 there had been talk of bringing it back. Despite being off the air, the series had a strong fan following and the appearance of its two stars, Patrick MacNee and Linda Thorson, in a French TV commercial for champagne merely left devotees wanting more.

In 1975 a press conference was held in London at which it was announced that *The New Avengers* was to be made the following year at Pinewood Studios. Patrick MacNee was to return as John Steed but, due to his age, he was to have two much younger sidekicks in the form of Mike Gambit (Gareth Hunt) and Purdey (Joanna Lumley). The series was a success and led to a second run of episodes in 1977, many of which were filmed in France and Canada.

There were hopes that a third series of *The New Avengers* might be made, but this did not happen for various reasons and in early 1977 series creator Brian Clemens pitched the idea of an action series to be called *The A-Squad,* based around the activities of a fictional unit called CI5 which was dedicated to fighting criminals and terrorists. Filming commenced on what was now called *The Professionals* in the summer of 1977, with Gordon Jackson as CI5 chief George Cowley and Martin Shaw and Anthony Andrews as agents Ray Doyle and William Bodie.

Within a week of starting filming, Clemens realised that the chemistry between Shaw and Andrews just wasn't right. The two actors knew other well (they had appeared together in the 1975 film *Operation Daybreak*), and had similar personalities and acting styles. Clemens felt that a different actor, with a totally different personality, was required to play Bodie and remembered Lewis Collins, who had appeared with Martin Shaw in an episode of the second series of *The New Avengers* entitled *Obsession* which was broadcast by the ITV network on 7 October 1977.

Shaw and Collins had apparently not got on well during the filming of that episode, and that was exactly what Clemens was looking for: a bit of antagonism between them which led to a more interesting on-screen relationship. As Clemens put it very succinctly, Bodie and Doyle were to be like 'Nitro and Glycerine'.

Interestingly, Martin Shaw's character in *Obsession* isn't at all like Ray Doyle either in looks or personality. In particular, his hairstyle is different as he doesn't wear the curly perm he adopted for his role as Doyle. Lewis Collins, on the other hand, is virtually a prototype Bodie in this episode – especially as his haircut is identical to that which he would wear in his later role. Incidentally, using his past hairdressing skills Collins was at that time in the habit of cutting his own hair using mirrors, and the famous 'Bodie Cut' was his own creation. Throughout the episode, Collins's character – Kilner – wears a British Army battledress jacket, a garment he later wore in many publicity shots for *The Professionals*, and at one point says to Shaw's character Larry Doomer that: 'Maybe we should work together again. We make a good team'. This was probably just a coincidence, as at that point there was no indication he was being considered for a role in *The Professionals*.

57 episodes of *The Professionals* were made between summer 1977 and spring 1981, with the last of them not receiving their first broadcast till early 1983, and the series' two young stars became celebrities. Thus when pre-production started on *Who Dares Wins* in 1981, Lewis Collins

was really the only actor in Britain who could be considered for the role of SAS Captain Peter Skellen as he had the ideal credentials. Not only was he a fine actor who had a great experience of action roles, but he was in real life a part-time soldier – a member of the Territorial Army. At one point he had even applied to become a member of the Territorial SAS (21 SAS), but had been turned down because he was too well-known. Collins was also a parachutist, a skilled marksman with a keen interest in guns, held a private pilot's licence, and was an expert in various forms of unarmed combat.

It is unlikely that his co-star in *The Professionals*, Martin Shaw, would have been interested in the role of Captain Peter Skellen. Though a talented and versatile actor, he disliked the label that the media had given him of 'TV tough guy' and asked to leave the series after the first 13 episodes had been shot. The producers refused to allow him to depart as he had signed a four-year contract, and for the remaining three years Shaw repeatedly expressed his dissatisfaction with the role in a series of newspaper interviews.

The plot of *Who Dares Wins* was fairly simple, and involved the terrorist takeover of the American ambassador's residence by a group of anarchist, anti-capitalist terrorists known as 'The People's Lobby'. Leading them was a wealthy American woman called Frankie Leith, played by Australian actress Judy Davis. According to Euan Lloyd, Leith's character was based on two people – actress Vanessa Redgrave and American thespian Jane Fonda, who in the 1970s espoused a number of rather dubious left-wing causes. She had also travelled to North Vietnam during the height of the Vietnam War, and was photographed wearing a North Vietnamese Army helmet while sitting on a traversing Soviet-made anti-aircraft gun. This led to her being dubbed 'Hanoi Jane' by American servicemen.

Some reports on the making of the film have suggested that the role of Frankie Leith was actually offered to Fonda, who then declined. I have been unable to verify this rumour, but in the end the part was played by Davis – a highly acclaimed Australian actress who had received much critical praise for her role in *My Brilliant Career* (1979) and had just played the young Golda Meir in *A Woman Called Golda* (1979), a TV movie about the life of Israel's first woman Prime Minister.

A distinguished cast was assembled for the production which included veteran actor Richard Widmark as US Secretary of State Arthur Curry. The part was originally to have been played by William Holden, but his untimely death on 12 November 1981 put paid to this idea. Holden's death also caused a delay in shooting the film. Originally scheduled to start in November 1981, it didn't go before the cameras until 11 January 1982. Another notable cast member was Ingrid Pitt, who had appeared in *Where Eagles Dare* (1968) and subsequently starred in several Hammer horror films plus the British classic *The Wicker Man* (1974). Many of the crew who had worked on *The Professionals* were employed on *Who Dares Wins*, including director Ian Sharp and associate producer Raymond Menmuir.

The budget was set at $6m, and the film was nearly cancelled when one of the backers withdrew their funding a few weeks before shooting was due to start. In order to save the movie Euan Lloyd flew to New York by Concorde just before Christmas 1981 to obtain the missing $1m funding from two new backers.

The film opens with shots of Whitehall and Westminster on a dull winter's day. There is no pre-credits sequence, and instead the movie starts with simple white titles superimposed on the action accompanied by a short version of Roy Budd's exciting title theme.

Bearing in mind the simplicity of the titles, it is quite a surprise to learn that they were produced by Maurice Binder – best known for his highly elaborate credit sequences for numerous Bond films, plus the 'looking down a gun barrel' shot which has opened every 007 movie produced by Eon Productions.

An anti-nuclear protest march is in progress near the Ministry of Defence Buildings in Whitehall, consisting of CND members, Communists, Trade Unionists and members of the so-called 'People's Lobby'. Prominent amongst the protestors is Frankie Leith (Judy Davis), a highly intelligent yet deluded American.

As the march proceeds, a crossbow dart is fired from a nearby window and one of the protestors drops dead. In fact he is really Andrew Wilcox, an undercover agent working for British Intelligence.

This may have been a bit of 'plot recycling' by screenwriter Reginald Rose, as it is similar to the scene in *The Wild Geese* where Lt Pieter Coetzee (Hardy Kruger) kills some sentries with a crossbow. In James Follett's novel *The Tiptoe Boys*, Wilcox is shot with a 9mm handgun and is a lieutenant in the SAS. Later, at a meeting of security specialists, including members of Special Branch, MI5 and the SAS, Commander Powell (Edward Woodward) expresses his dismay at what has happened. His source of information has now been cut off, and all he knows is that the People's Lobby is planning an operation which will happen soon, be very destructive, and will involve a foreign power. Though he recognises that the majority of anti-nuclear protestors are committed to achieving their aims by peaceful means, he realises that the People's Lobby is comprised of deranged, anarchist hard-liners who will stop at nothing.

Colonel Hadley (Tony Doyle) says he has a suggestion. We don't get to hear what it is, because the action then shifts to an SAS training base on a sunny winter's day where a Range Rover driven by Trooper Baker (Ziggy Byfield) is approaching a checkpoint. The vehicle contains two officers, Captain Hagen (Bob Sherman) of the US Rangers and Captain Freund (Albert Fortell) of the West German GSG-9 anti-terrorist force, who are on temporary attachment to the SAS. In reality the SAS training camp would be at their HQ and barracks at Stirling Lines, Hereford, but these scenes were shot on the back lot at Pinewood Studios.

As the vehicle passes through the checkpoint, Freund and Hagen comment on the lack of formality in the SAS. There is no saluting, many people are wearing civvies, and everyone is on first name terms. The two officers are taken into a building where some SAS troopers are about to practice a hostage rescue mission, and they are introduced to Captain Peter Skellen who is wearing casual clothes, including a black body-warmer. Collins looks noticeably slimmer than he did in *The Professionals* and reportedly went on a diet for his role as Skellen, going from 14 stone to 12 stone 8lbs. He also has a different hairstyle, opting for a rather bouffant, blow-dried look. One also wonders if his character's name, Peter Skellen, was inspired by the similarly named Peter Skellern – a pop singer of the previous decade whose best-known hit was *You're a Lady* (1972).

After the introductions Skellen sits still in a chair, playing the part of a hostage, while four SAS troopers burst into the room shooting the targets representing terrorists and leaving him unscathed. After this dramatic event is over, Skellen gives the troopers feedback on their performance.

The next day Skellen, Freund and Hagen (plus three other SAS troopers) are taken to Wales to take part in a training exercise in Snowdonia. Carrying heavy British Army SLR rifles and backpacks, and dressed in camouflage battledress uniforms and green wool caps, the two foreign soldiers are to climb to a rendezvous point at the top of a hill some miles away. Captain Andy Steele (Maurice Roeves) tells Skellen to give them a full hour's start before setting off in pursuit with his men.

The two officers set off on their mission to the accompaniment of Roy Budd's highly evocative score, which at this point uses a synthesiser to convey the bleakness of the cold winter landscape. A talented jazz musician and composer, Budd provided the music for a number of British films of the 70s and 80s including *Zeppelin* (1970), *Get Carter* (1971), and Euan Lloyd's previous two blockbusters *The Wild Geese* (1978) and *The Sea Wolves* (1980).

Eventually the two officers reach the hilltop only to discover that Skellen and his men have somehow got there first. Almost immediately Skellen snaps and orders his men to truss up the two foreign soldiers with rope, tying their hands behind their backs and then securing them to their ankles, causing them great discomfort. The two men are then hooded (which also helps to disguise the fact that their parts are now played by two stuntmen wearing considerable padding beneath their uniforms). The principal stunt arranger for this film was Bob Simmons (who Euan Lloyd had known since his days with Warwick Films, as *The Red Beret* was Simmons' first picture), who worked on most of the James Bond pictures in the sixties and seventies and even appeared as Bond in the 'looking down a gun barrel' sequence in the first three movies in the franchise.

Skellen discards his rifle and kicks and punches the two officers as the other SAS soldiers look on. In the nick of time, a helicopter arrives containing Major Andy Steele and Colonel Hadley, who jumps out and orders Skellen to stop what he is doing. The small choppers which appear in the film are Westland Scouts, a light helicopter with a Rolls-Royce Nimbus gas turbine engine, derived from the Saunders-Roe P.531. Three Scouts were used in the filming, supplied by 656 Squadron of the Army Air Corps. Both the Scout and its naval derivative – the Wasp – saw considerable action in the Falklands War, which took place not long after shooting on *Who Dares Wins* concluded in the spring of 1982.

Originally the film was to use three civilian helicopters painted in Army markings but after the head of the SAS, Brigadier Peter De La Billiere, read the script he agreed to full cooperation and the Ministry of Defence supplied the three Westland Scout helicopters plus troops, vehicles, weapons and equipment, adding greatly to the authenticity of the movie.

A few days later Skellen faces a court martial at the SAS's Hereford barracks. The penalty for his abhorrent behaviour is either a return to his original (non-SAS) unit or expulsion from the Army. He chooses the latter option and resigns his commission.

The next scene is set at Portobello Market in London, where Skellen meets his contact Ryan (Norman Rodway) who is posing as a stallholder. In James Follett's novel, Ryan is revealed to be a sergeant in the SAS. Snow is falling as

Skellen and Ryan exchange information while they pretend to haggle, and it becomes clear that the incident in Wales and the subsequent court martial was a set-up to enable Skellen to be apparently kicked out the SAS. Snow which appears in film and TV productions is usually artificial, but in *Who Dares Wins* it was real as the production was filmed in the first quarter of 1982. Thirty stalls were originally booked for the filming of this scene, but only one was available on the day due to the poor weather and director Ian Sharp had to get round this problem by shooting with a long lens.

Skellen asks Ryan what he knows about the People's Lobby. He says that the two prime movers in the organisation are Frankie Leith and Rod Walker, and that they like to hang out at the Black Horse Club in Marlborough Road. Ryan also gives Skellen his codename for his undercover work, which is 'Destroy'.

Meanwhile, a hovercraft arrives at an unspecified English Channel port and one of the occupants – a Mr Malek (Aharon Ipale) – drives up to Customs in his burgundy Porsche 928S. He explains that he is visiting for both business and pleasure, and is given a 10 day visa. In the novel *The Tiptoe Boys*, Malek is Libyan and has been sent to the UK on the personal orders of Colonel Gaddafi. This scene is one of the biggest goofs in the film, because the type of hovercraft shown (an SR.N6) was a passenger-only craft which could not carry cars. The only British hovercraft which could carry vehicles at that time was the larger SR.N4. Furthermore, the actual hovercraft shown (operated by Hovertravel) was employed on services between the Isle of Wight and the mainland, and was never used for cross-channel trips.

Back in London, Skellen drives his 1980 Renault 5, 1300cc automatic car into the garage at his Mews flat. This scene was shot at 25 Kynance Mews, Kensington. The car, RLD 957W, was driven by Collins in the early eighties and was allegedly owned by his then-girlfriend Marion Sheffield. Skellen enters his flat and spends some time with his wife Jenny and baby daughter Samantha. Jenny is played by Rosalind Lloyd, daughter of producer Euan Lloyd, who also appeared in the *The Wild Geese* as the girlfriend of Roger Moore's character, Shawn Fynn. As Skellen plays with his daughter and enjoys his lunch, he tells Jenny that he is going to be overseas for a while and not to worry.

Around the same time, Malek arrives at the Banque Generale in London and asks for £600,000 to be given to various left-wing organisations, with £100,000 to go to the People's Lobby. The bank manager invites Malek to join him and his wife on a trip to the theatre, but Malek declines as he has to leave for Boston on Sunday. This scene was filmed in the Athenaeum Club in Pall Mall.

Some miles away in a barn at a secret location, terrorist Helga (Ingrid Pitt) is demonstrating the People's Lobby's latest acquisition – a cache of American-made MAC-10 Ingram submachine guns. A makeshift shooting range has been set up using CND logos as targets. Helga fires a quick burst with a MAC-10 and destroys the target. She describes the compact, boxy Ingram as 'one hell of a killing machine... a range of 100 metres with a 32 round magazine and a rate of fire of 1,000 rounds a minute'. In fact, the 9mm calibre version of the Ingram used in the film had a rate of fire of 1250 rounds a minute. Normally glamorous, Pitt managed to look unattractive during her scenes in *Who Dares Wins* by maintaining a sour expression.

The next scene is set in the aforementioned Black Horse Club in Marlborough Road where a group of left-wing

the US Strategic Air Command. Ford reports that members of the People's Lobby had staged a demonstration at the airport in protest at the visit, while Skellen remarks that the US delegation would make an ideal target.

That evening Skellen meets his contact (Ryan) under the arches of Waterloo Bridge and learns that Hagen had suffered a broken nose in the assault the previous night. Ryan explains that Colonel Hadley sends his apologies, as he had set up the incident to increase Skellen's credibility with Leith. Later Ryan rings Colonel Hadley from a nearby 'phone box, but as he leaves Helga's reflection can be seen in the window. The People's Lobby are closing in on him.

Skellen and Leith attend a rock concert and rally in a church (the Union Chapel in Islington again), where they are entertained by a rock band consisting of Jerry and Marc Donahue, Gerry Conway, and Dave Pegg singing *Right on Time*. Jerry and Marc Donahue had previously written and performed a track, *Dance of Death*, which featured in the party scene early in *The Wild Geese* (1978).

After this musical interlude the audience is addressed by Bishop Crick, who points out that 'if Jesus Christ was around today, he would be considered a militant radical'. His comments anger a crowd of racist skinheads in the audience, who start arguing with him. Eventually fights break out and everyone has to leave the rally, including a rather pleased Malek who is anticipating the following day's newspaper headlines about skinheads attacking a peace rally. 'Perfect', he says. It is implied that he has been involved in setting up this violent confrontation for political gain.

The next day, Skellen visits his mews flat and sets off on his red and black Harris Magnum Suzuki 100 motorcycle to meet Jenny and their baby Samantha at Holland Park. This particular bike was owned by Lewis Collins during the 80s. Skellen tells Jenny he loves her and the couple kiss passionately. Unfortunately, Skellen has failed to notice a blue Volvo 340 that has followed him from his flat. The vehicle contains Helga and a colleague Mac (Mark Ryan) from the People's Lobby, who photograph Skellen kissing his wife using a 35mm SLR camera with a telephoto lens. Later, Frankie Leith is shown the photos. Although she is angry that the surveillance operation has been carried out without her approval, she realises that Skellen must be working undercover and cannot be trusted.

Frankie returns to her flat at St Catherine's Dock and tells Skellen that he has to sleep on the couch that night. She explains that she doesn't sleep well when they share a bed, and she has a lot to do the next day. She also admits to being in a bad mood.

The next day Skellen boards a number 73 red double decker bus (a 1949 Leyland Terrier) at Trafalgar Square, but then jumps from the moving rear platform of the vehicle to escape a tail and immediately boards a second Number 24 bus for Highgate. Collins performed this stunt himself and was lucky not to suffer an injury. During his four-year stint on *The Professionals* he broke both ankles in two separate parachuting accidents on his days off. One of these incidents in the autumn of 1978 led to filming on series two having to be stopped for several months until his ankle had healed.

Skellen climbs to the top deck of the bus where he meets his contact, Ryan. He tells him that the People's Lobby is carrying out an operation that day, but he can't get any information out of Leith as she has clammed up. Ryan responds by giving him a 'phone number where he can be contacted at any time. Skellen gets off the bus and hails a taxi, but as he leaves Helga boards the bus unnoticed, sits in front of Ryan, and kills him with a squirt from a hydrogen cyanide spray which is disguised as a perfume bottle.

Later that day, Commander Powell discusses the situation with his colleagues. A terrorist attack is imminent, but they don't know where. As it looks as though Skellen may have been compromised, Colonel Hadley suggests putting a watch on his mews flat.

In a barn on the outskirts of London, the People's Lobby terrorists are preparing for action while Skellen visits Leith's flat and finds no-one there. He then goes to the People's Lobby HQ, where he is told that he will be taken to her.

Meanwhile, Leith and some of her colleagues hijack a bus containing a US Air Force Band from Lakenheath. They force the driver to go to the barn. En-route, one of the bandsmen tries to overpower the terrorists as the bus lurches on the winding country road, but Leith opens fire with her Beretta M12 sub machine gun and a female singer collapses dead. The bus reaches the barn, where they are interned and their places taken by People's Lobby terrorists dressed in US Air Force uniforms. Skellen, Mac and Helga arrive at the barn in her Volvo 340. Skellen is told to put on a bandsman's uniform but is not given a gun. Back in London, the Police Commissioner (Patrick Allen) is briefed on the situation but with no idea of the target there is little that the British police and security services can do.

In the barn used by the People's Lobby, Leith holds a briefing. Fifteen terrorists are going to take over the American ambassador's residence, where a formal dinner is being held that evening with many prominent guests including Arthur Curry (Richard Widmark), the American Secretary of State; Ira Potter (Robert Webber), head of the Strategic Air Command; Harrison Franklin (Don Fellows), the American Ambassador, and also Harold Staunton (John Woodnutt), the British Foreign Secretary. Skellen wonders why he has not been given a gun, only to be told by Frankie that his wife and child are being held hostage in order to ensure his cooperation.

As the terrorists prepare to leave the barn, Helga and a terrorist colleague overpower the uniformed policeman (Martyn Jacobs) outside Skellen's flat and force their way inside. Fortunately the altercation is witnessed by two plain clothed SAS men who are sitting outside in a yellow GPO Bedford HA van. They get on the radio and ask for a hostage rescue team to be sent as soon as possible.

In the meantime, the terrorists' coach arrives at the American Ambassador's residence, a large white stately home with extensive lawns and gardens in front of it. Some contemporary reviewers seemed to think the building was actually the 'American Embassy', and criticised the makers for not using the well-known building in Grosvenor Square. The same error appears on Wikipedia.

The building playing the part of the ambassador's residence is Heatherden Hall (aka Pinewood House), which forms part of the Pinewood Studios complex. It has itself appeared in many films and TV series which were shot at Pinewood. Two notable appearances were as the SPECTRE base where Rosa Klebb first meets 'Red' Grant near the beginning of *From Russia with Love* (1963), and as the British Intelligence HQ where Philip Calvert (Anthony Hopkins) arrives by helicopter at the start of *When Eight Bells Toll* (1971). Part of Heatherden Hall served as Pinewood's dining room, and a temporary tented meal room had to be provided during shooting of the film.

As the fake American band and Frankie Leith (who is wearing an evening gown so as to pass for a singer) makes their way to the front entrance, they are stopped by a security man who says they cannot go in. There is a moment of tension before he says that they must enter via the service entrance.

The terrorists make their way into the building and pull out weapons. All the terrorists carry MAC-10 machine pistols, except for Frankie Leith and Rod Walker who are armed with Beretta M-12 sub machine guns. Within a couple of minutes they have made their way to the dining room, where Frankie Leith makes her demands clear in a 'phone call to Commander Powell: they want the authorities to fire a nuclear missile at the US Navy Polaris submarine base in the Holy Loch in Scotland, and if this demand is not met then all of the hostages will die. Furthermore, the resulting nuclear explosion is to be televised so that everyone in the world can witness the devastation caused by an atomic blast.

Powell asks Frankie what is going to happen to the population of South West Scotland, and she says they have 18 hours to evacuate them (actually this is a script error, as the Holy Loch is in North West Scotland). Frankie then moves all the wives to the room next door, while Arthur Curry, Ira Potter and Harold Staunton debate the ethics and moralities of nuclear war, and the policy of deterrence, with her.

Meanwhile, a Range Rover leaves Hereford. Inside is an SAS hostage rescue team tasked with resolving the situation at Skellen's mews flat. As the SAS men drive to London, a small team of plain-clothed policemen and SAS men make their way to the property next door, taking care to make as little noise as possible. After having been let in, they clear furniture and start to make preparations to blow their way into Skellen's flat using an explosive charge attached to the party wall. While this is going on, the police have arrived in strength outside the American ambassador's residence, accompanied by TV crews. The lawns and gardens in front of Heatherden House have featured as a location in a number of films and TV series. The pre-credits sequence of *From Russia with Love* (1963) was shot there, as were scenes for the classic *UFO* episode *Mindbender* (1970).

Leith asks Skellen for advice on whether the hostages should be dispersed throughout the building, and he advises her to keep them together as it will avoid spreading her men to different locations. In fact, he is giving her misleading advice to make the forthcoming SAS assault easier.

Commander Powell uses a loudhailer to contact Frankie, and she asks for press and TV coverage. Powell agrees to this, and in return suggests that she releases the servants. Frankie says she is willing to let the servants go, but not the wives of the delegates as Powell wants. Powell then asks for permission to tap the 'phones, as it will make it easier for her to contact him because she will only have to lift a receiver. After conferring with Skellen, she agrees to this as well.

Meanwhile, the police and SAS team continues its preparations to assault Skellen's flat and asks his neighbour to put on some loud music to cover the sound of drilling. Back at the American ambassador's residence, Commander Powell asks Frankie for more time and she says that they have till 3.00 p.m. the next day. Powell begs her for a few hours more.

Frankie asks one of her terrorists to accompany Skellen to the library and to keep any eye on him. Once there, Skellen asks to use the bathroom. As soon as he is inside with the door locked, he uses a shaving mirror to signal to the police outside using reflected light from police spotlamps. Skellen starts off by signalling 'S...A...S' by Morse Code, followed by his codename 'Destroy'. Colonel Hadley realises it is Skellen signalling and replies. Skellen asks for the SAS assault to be carried out at 10.00 a.m., and Hadley replies that he will have to get the Home Secretary's consent. He will let him know that this has been agreed by cutting the power to the house for three seconds. Skellen agrees to create distractions just before the assault. Outside the bathroom the terrorist guarding Skellen is becoming suspicious, but the SAS captain finishes his signalling, flushes the toilet, and comes out.

As this is happening, the team at the mews are drilling through the plasterboard on Skellen's side of the party wall, using a hand drill to make as little noise as possible. They insert a tiny CCTV camera into the hole so they can see what is going on next door. Two SAS troopers arrive at the flat.

Back at the American ambassador's residence, Ira Potter has coffee with the other male hostages and decides to make an attempt to overpower the single terrorist who has been left guarding them. Potter assaults the man and tries to grab his gun, but is shot dead. Leith runs into the dining room to find out what has happened. She slaps the terrorist responsible across the face, calling him an 'idiot'. The 'phone rings. It is Commander Powell, wanting to know what has happened. Leith assures them it was nothing more than an accidental discharge, but Powell is suspicious and subsequently 'phones the Home Secretary, recommending that the SAS be given permission to assault the building.

A few hours later, as dawn breaks, three Westland Scout helicopters take off from the SAS's Hereford base, each carrying SAS troopers wearing black combat uniforms and balaclavas. Each trooper carries a Heckler and Koch MP5 submachine gun with several spare magazines, a 9mm pistol, a gas mask, and stun grenades. The assault force includes Captains Hagen and Freund, who have come to witness the action.

The large, light grey building resembling an aircraft hangar seen in the background as the Scouts depart is the 007 Stage at Pinewood. This structure, which was officially opened by former PM Harold Wilson in December 1976, was originally constructed to house the *Liparus* supertanker set for *The Spy Who Loved Me* (1977). It has since been used in many other films and has been rebuilt twice, having burned down during the making of *Legend* (1985) and again towards the end of shooting on *Casino Royale* (2006).

Back at Skellen's flat, the SAS are about to blow through the wall. Helga tries to take Samantha away from Jenny, resulting in a fight breaking out between the two women. A hoop of explosive has been attached to the party wall and two SAS troopers, wearing full black combat gear and respirators and carrying Tokagypt 58 pistols, stand on either side of the proposed entry point, their backs to the wall as they cock their weapons. Just as Helga is about to shoot Jenny, the power to Skellen's flat is cut, plunging it into darkness as the SAS trigger the explosive charge which blows a hole in the wall. Immediately the two soldiers burst through the wall, illuminate the two terrorists with their torches, and shoot them dead.

As the siege at Skellen's flat ends, the three Scout helicopters – each with four SAS troopers clinging to their sides, with their feet on the choppers' skids – arrive over the American ambassador's residence. Quickly, the SAS soldiers abseil down ropes and take up positions on the roof. The terrorists inside the building start to panic, as they can hear the helicopters arriving but don't know what is going on. They look out the windows and see the three Scouts landing. Skellen spreads some disinformation, claiming that it is just top brass arriving. In fact twelve heavily-armed SAS troopers are on the roof, and the terrorists have only minutes left to live. These scenes were enacted by serving members of the SAS.

As the terrorists continue to panic, a fourth Westland Scout arrives. Two SAS troopers (actually dummies) hang underneath the skids of the aircraft from cables, each carrying a M201-Z 37mm grenade launcher. As the helicopter approaches the building the troopers fire their weapons, blowing out the windows and allowing them to enter the property. One of the windows subjected to an explosive entry was located in the office of producer Elliott Kastner, who later complained that his office stank of smoke for years afterwards!

As the assault starts, Skellen makes his move, grabbing one of the terrorists' MAC-10s and shooting him dead. He then rapidly changes his position in an acrobatic move to shoot two other terrorists in the dining room. By now, the SAS assault is in full swing. Troopers abseil down the sides of the building and burst in through windows, while others blow off door hinges using Remington 870 shotguns.

Soon the SAS work through the building, methodically throwing stun grenades into each room before spraying the bad guys inside with bullets. The hostages are released and are taken outside the building to safety. Skellen shoots another terrorist (Tony Osoba) before killing Rod, who is preparing to fire at the released hostages through a window.

One piece of realism in the film is that Skellen is seen to reload his MAC-10 with fresh magazines taken from dead terrorists.

Eventually Skellen meets the SAS rescue force and they join up to hunt down the last remaining terrorist, none other than Frankie Leith herself. Suddenly Frankie comes out of a room where she has been hiding, clutching a submachine gun. She confronts Skellen, but neither of them seems able to shoot the other. Suddenly Major Andy Steele arrives and kills Leith with a burst of fire from his MP5.

'Slowing up, Peter,' he says.

With the crisis over, Skellen goes outside where he meets Hagen and Freund again. This time they know he was working undercover and the encounter is more friendly.

The final scene of the film is set in Whitehall the following day, where a Government Minister (Paul Freeman) meets Malek. They are dismayed at the outcome of the terrorist attack, but realise there may be other opportunities in the future. It is clear that there is some kind of collusion going on between these two individuals.

The film ends with a superimposed caption giving statistics on the number of attacks by terrorists on embassies throughout the world. *The Red Flag* plays in the background. This is the unofficial anthem of the Communist Party and is often played at Labour Party conferences. The end credits play to the accompaniment of the full version of Roy Budd's exciting main title theme.

*Who Dares Wins* was released on 26 August 1982 and was one of the most successful British films of the year. The critics, though, were mixed in their views. *The Guardian*, unsurprisingly, described the film as 'terrible', while the short-lived *Cinema* magazine slated the movie for its 'political intolerance'. Demonstrations were held outside cinemas showing the film by left-wingers, who claimed it was attacking the CND. Euan Lloyd's earlier film *The Wild Geese* (1978) had also been criticized by left-wingers, as it was made in South Africa before the end of apartheid and its London premiere was picketed by anti-apartheid protestors.

It should be noted, however, that critics' views are often not shared by the general public, and *Who Dares Wins* became one of these films which was loved by audiences but hated by critics – rather like *The Professionals* TV series, which attracted huge ratings and a fan following but was reviled by reviewers at the time of its original broadcast. Though *The Professionals* is now regarded as one of the finest TV action series ever made and continues to sell well to this day in DVD and Blu-Ray formats, it was not highly regarded by most critics at the time of its original broadcast.

Appreciation of the film came from an unlikely source – film director Stanley Kubrick, who 'phoned Euan Lloyd to tell him how much he enjoyed the movie and how he thought the casting of Judy Davis was a brilliant idea. US President Ronald Reagan also loved the film, and viewed it at a private screening at Camp David after Euan Lloyd took a copy to the USA by Concorde following a request from one of the President's staff. Reagan was ecstatic at the film, and gave Euan Lloyd many positive comments about the production which were used (with his full permission) in subsequent publicity. However, this worked against the film as when word got out that Reagan liked it, the liberal establishment in Hollywood blacklisted the movie, resulting in it not being shown in most American cinemas as no distributor was willing to screen it.

Following the completion of *Who Dares Wins,* Lewis Collins was considered as a replacement for Roger Moore as

James Bond and had an interview with Cubby Broccoli. Unfortunately Broccoli took a dislike to Collins, who he considered arrogant and aggressive, and opted to continue with Roger Moore. Collins later considered this to be the greatest setback of his career.

However, the future still looked bright for Collins in the summer of 1982 because Euan Lloyd planned to follow up the success of *Who Dares Wins* with three further films featuring his new star. *Wild Geese 2*, costing £5.5m, was also to star Richard Burton, reprising his role of Colonel Faulkner from the earlier *Wild Geese* picture; *Macau* was to be filmed in the Far East with a budget of £9.5m, while *Battle of the Falklands* (aka *Task Force South*) was to be budgeted at £10m and deal with SAS and SBS operations during the 1982 South Atlantic conflict.

As things turned out, only one of these three films was ever made – *Wild Geese 2* (1985), which starred Scott Glenn instead of Lewis Collins. The other two proposed films were scrapped because of the likely high cost, and instead Collins made three forgettable foreign action pictures and appeared as policeman George Gently, a sidekick to Michael Caine's character, in a 1988 TV miniseries about Jack the Ripper.

In 1997, Collins was approached about reprising his role of Bodie who would now be the head of CI5 in a new TV series *CI5: The New Professionals*. However, Collins declined the offer as he had by then moved to the USA, and the CI5 boss (now called Harry Malone) was subsequently played by his old *Who Dares Wins* co-star Edward Woodward. Five years later, Collins made his final appearance on TV as a dodgy doctor facing criminal charges in an episode of ITV's *The Bill*.

Following this, Collins retired from acting to set up a computer company. In 2008 he was diagnosed with cancer, and in 2013 he died. Commenting on his death, *The Professionals* creator Brian Clemens confirmed that he would have made an excellent James Bond. Collins was an actor, a musician, a part-time soldier, a weapons expert, and had a private pilot's licence. Had things turned out differently, he could have been a member of The Beatles or indeed played James Bond. He might even have achieved both goals. Euan Lloyd, who died in 2016, was often described as 'The Last of the Gentlemen Producers', and made several excellent films. He nearly managed to make the only film about the Falklands War. So *Who Dares Wins* represents a milestone in the history of the British cinema, as it could have led to even greater things for both its star and its producer if economic conditions in the UK in the early eighties had been different.

The film was also a likely inspiration for ITV's series *Ultimate Force* (2002-06). Although starting off as an attempt to put Chris Ryan's successful novels on screen, some of the series' episodes appear to be have been inspired by *Who Dares Wins*. The first episode, *The Killing House*, deals with a bank siege while another – *Just a Target* – deals with an SAS trooper infiltrating an anti-capitalist group. That particular story features an anti-globalist activist called Marisal, played by New Zealand-born actress Anne-Marie Plowman who also turns up in the very last episode, *Slow Bomb*, as an American terrorist (Braun) intent on exploding a nuclear bomb in London.

In 2016 it was revealed that Collins' co-star in *The Professionals*, actor Martin Shaw, was to star in *6 Days*, a film about the 1980 Iranian embassy siege which inspired

*Who Dares Wins*. Thus the legacy of that event continues to this day.

# *Who Dares Wins* (1982)
## Production Credits

Director: Ian Sharp
Screenplay: Reginald Rose
Book: James Follett
Story Outline: George
Markstein

### Cast

Captain Peter Skellen - Lewis
Collins
Frankie Leith - Judy Davis
Arthur Curry - Richard
Widmark
Commander Powell - Edward
Woodward
General Ira Potter - Robert
Webber
Colonel Hadley - Tony Doyle
Rod Walker - John Duttine
Bishop Crick - Kenneth Griffiths
Jenny Skellen - Rosalind Lloyd
Helga - Ingrid PittRyan -
Norman Rodway
Major Andy Steele - Maurice
Roeves
Hagen - Bob Sherman
Freund - Albert Fortell
Mac - Mark Ryan
Police Commissioner - Patrick
Allen
Malek - Aharon Ipale
Sir Richard - Paul Freeman
Baby Samantha - Briony Elliott
Pop Group - Jerry Donahue,
Marc Donahue, Gerry Conway,
Dave Pegg
Harkness - Alan Mitchell

Mr Martin - Richard Coleman
Sergeant Pope - Nigel
Humphreys
Neil - Stephen Bent
Policeman at Mews - Martin
Jacobs
Bank Manager - Raymond Brody
Immigration Officer - Andrew
McLachlan
Special Branch Man - Oz Clarke
Butler - Peter Geddis
Baker - Ziggy Byfield
Pickley - Michael Forrest
Ambassador Franklin - Don
Fellows
Senator Kohoskie - Alan Gifford
Harold Staunton - John
Woodnutt
Williamson - Nick Brimble
MP - Michael Godley
Mary Tinker - Meg Davis
Melissa - Lynne Miller
US Security Man - Christopher
Muncke
Newscaster - Anna Ford
Newscaster - Bill Hamilton
US Marine Guards - Alan
Polonsky, Martin Grace
Terrorists - Tariq Yunus, Bruce
White, Patrick Gordon, Niall
Padden, Tony Osoba, Glyn
Baker, Ben Howard, Alan
Renwick, Peter Turner, Simon
Heywood, Ralph Arliss, Ewan
Stewart, Billy McBain

SAS Technician - Martin
Denning
Policeman - Harry Fielder
Girl on Bus - Jillian Gibbs

## Producers
Executive Producer: Chris
Chrisafis
Producer: Euan Lloyd
Associate Producer: Raymond
Menmuir

## Music
Composer: Ray Budd

## Film Editing
Film Editor: John Grover
Casting: Esta Charkham
Production Design: Syd Cain
Art Direction: Maurice Cain

## Makeup Department
Hair Stylist: Jeannette Freeman
Make-up Artist: Neville
Smallwood
Assistant Make-up Artists:
Eddie Knight, Tommie
Manderson
Production Manager: Ron
Purdie

## Second Unit
Third Assistant Director: Chris
Brock
Second Assistant Director:
Michael Murray
Assistant Director: Bill Westley

## Art Department
Graphic Artist: Maurice Binder
Carpenter: Paul Duff
Assistant Art Director: Jim
Morahan
Carpenter: Trevor Nichol
Buyer: Sid Palmer
Construction Manager: Michael
Redding
Dressing Prop: Bob Sherwood
Set Dresser: Robin Tarsnane
Property Master: Arthur Wicks

## Sound Department
Sound Recordist: David Crozier
Boom Operator: Colin
Dandridge
Dubbing Mixers: John Hayward,
Richard Langford
Dubbing Editor: Derek Holding
Assistant Dubbing Editors:
Chris Lloyd, Bob Mullen
Chief Dubbing Mixer: Gordon
K. McCallum
Sound Assistant: Guido Reidy
Re-recording Mixer: Graham V.
Hartstone

## Special Effects
SFX Supervisor and Visual
Effects: Nick Allder
Assistant SFX Supervisor: John
McGoldrick
Stunts: Roy Alon, Del Baker,
Andy Bradford, Terry Cade,
Dorothy Ford, Terry Forrestal,
Martin Grace, Lucien Morgan,
Greg Powell, Joe Powell, Denise
Ryan, Stuart St Paul, Tip

Tipping, Malcolm Weaver,
Steve Whyment
Action and Stunt Arranger: Bob
Simmons

## Camera and Electrical Department

Still Photographers: Graham
Attwood, Peter Kernot
Video Assist: Kevin Brookner
Clapper Loader: John Ignatius
Grip: John Payne
Camera Operator: Bob Smith
Gaffer: John Tythe
Focus Puller: Derek Worley

## Costume and Wardrobe Departments

Wardrobe Assistants: Gloria
Barnes, John Hilling, David
Murphy

Assembly Editors: Peter Davies,
Matthew Glen
Location Manager: Peter Carter
Transportation: Howard Pugh
Armourer: Simon Atherton
Technical Research Advisor: Ian
Black
Assistant to Producer: Mo
Coppiters
Production Accountant:
Carolyn Hall
Assistant Production
Accountants: Penny Forrester,
Pauline Granby
Publicist: Derek Robbins
Assistant to Producer: Helene
Thejll
Continuity: Alison Thorne
Choreographer: Anthony Von
Last
Floor Runner: Kevin Westley

# 3

# THE TERMINATOR

## (1984)

*Orion Pictures*

**Director**: James Cameron
**Producer**: Gale Anne Hurd
**Screenwriters**: James Cameron and
Gale Anne Hurd

*T*HE *Terminator* fits into a number of pigeonholes, as it can be considered a science fiction/horror/action/ slasher film. My own view is that it constitutes a sub-genre of the action picture known as the 'science fiction action movie', and two other productions which are also part of this genre would be *Aliens* (1986) and *Predator* (1987) – both of which are discussed elsewhere in this book.

The film was the brainchild of James Cameron, who was then unknown but is now arguably the world's greatest moviemaker, having directed the two biggest-grossing movies of all time, *Titanic* (1997) and *Avatar* (2009). Born in 1954 in Kapuskasing, Ontario, Canada, he originally studied physics at Fullerton College in 1973 and then switched to English before dropping out of college in the autumn of 1974 to earn a living as a truck driver. However, Cameron was fascinated by film making and after seeing *Star Wars* in 1977 vowed to become a director. He soon learned a great deal about every aspect of the craft and became a special effects designer, model-maker, artist, and production designer on several films including John Carpenter's *Escape from New York* (1981).

Later that same year, Cameron was in Rome working as a special effects designer on a low-budget movie called *Piranha II: The Spawning* when he fell ill with food poisoning. During his brief illness, he had a bad dream involving a skeletal metal robot emerging from flames clutching two knives. This gave him the inspiration for one of the final scenes in what eventually became *The Terminator*, and was the starting point for his screenplay. Since the robot existed in the future and an entire film set in this period would be very expensive, the answer was to bring the robot to the present, hence the time-travel element which forms a key part of the plot.

There was nothing new about the idea of killer robots. A 1965 monochrome episode of the British TV series *The Avengers* called *The Cybernauts* involved humanoid metal androids (the 'Cybernauts' of the title) which home in on their victims and kill them with powerful karate chops. The robots – which were created by deranged wheelchair-bound scientist Dr Armstrong (Michael Gough) – zeroed in on a small radio transmitter concealed inside a pen, gifted by Armstrong, which the victim carried in their jacket. Invulnerable to bullets, the Cybernauts smashed their way through doors to get to their targets. Utterly convincing on screen, the principal robot was portrayed by a stuntman wearing a simple blank silver mask with fake rivets, a heavy woollen coat, black leather gloves, black hat and trousers, and dark glasses to conceal the eyeholes in the mask.

The Cybernauts proved so popular that they returned in 1967 in the first colour series of *The Avengers* in an episode entitled *Return of the Cybernauts*. This time the metal monsters homed in on the heartbeat of their victims using an illicitly obtained ECG recording, and in one exciting sequence a Cybernaut bashes through a wooden fence, stops a moving car and then hauls its victim out through a hole it has smashed in the roof.

The third and final appearance of the Cybernauts to date came in a 1976 episode of *The New Avengers* – *The Last of the Cybernauts?* – in which the robots are controlled by a joystick and TV link. Eventually the villain – Kane (Robert Lang), who has overcome paralysis by turning himself into a 'half Cybernaut, half human' – is defeated after being sprayed with quick-setting plastic, an idea possibly borrowed from Episode 3 of the *Doctor Who* Cyberman story *The Wheel in Space* (1968) in which a Cybermat (a small metallic rodent-like creature) is immobilised in a similar fashion.

As I have indicated above, the Cybernauts only appeared three times on British television, but in 2014 footage was posted on YouTube taken from a 'Mexican Cybernauts movie' (sic). This came from the 1968 Mexican film *Luchadoras vs el Robot Asesino,* directed by Rene Cardona, which apparently was one of a series of Mexican films involving female wrestlers! Many of the scenes in this movie appear to have been lifted wholesale from *Return of the Cybernauts,* and the appearance of the robot is identical. One wonders why it did not trigger a lawsuit from the makers of *The Avengers?*

The idea of a person travelling back in time to kill someone, and thus altering history in the process, is also not new. In the 1972 *Doctor Who* story *The Day of the Daleks* (written by Louis Marks), a number of guerrillas from a future Earth ruled by the Daleks travel back to the present in order to assassinate British diplomat Sir Reginald Styles, who they (wrongly) believe set off a bomb to destroy a peace conference, thus triggering a nuclear war which gave the Daleks an opportunity to invade the Earth for a second time.

Harlan Ellison's teleplay for a 1964 episode of American sci-fi series *The Outer Limits*, entitled *Soldier*, also features a trooper travelling back in time from a post-nuclear war apocalypse to the present moment, and the similarity between this screenplay and *The Terminator* led to a legal action after Cameron's film was released as I shall describe in more detail later in the chapter.

Science fiction films often have high budgets, but *The Terminator* was originally to cost just $4m (though this was later increased to $6.5m), not a large sum when you consider the vast amount of special effects, miniature work and stunts in the picture. By comparison, the British action thriller *Who Dares Wins* (1982) cost $6m to make and had relatively few special effects when compared with the American picture.

For the role of the Terminator, Cameron cast former bodybuilding champion turned actor Arnold Schwarzenegger, whose career was on the up. Although Cameron had originally intended the Terminator to be an averagely-proportioned man who possessed incredible physical strength, he changed his mind after meeting the Austrian-born actor. With his background in bodybuilding, Schwarzenegger brought an intense physicality to the role and even his Austrian accent worked to his advantage. As Cameron later said, 'his voice had a synthesised quality... as if they hadn't quite got it to work correctly'.

Accounts vary on whether Lance Henriksen was seriously considered for the role. What is beyond dispute is that he did dress up as the Terminator for a meeting with studio executives, with his make-up consisting of fake cuts and gold foil over his teeth. Some concept art for the Terminator with Lance Henriksen's likeness was also prepared by James Cameron, but eventually the director opted to have a super-muscular Terminator – a decision which probably contributed greatly to the movie's popularity.

A large number of prominent Hollywood actresses auditioned for the role of Sarah Connor, and – if reports on the Internet are to believed – these included Sharon Stone, Geena Davis, Debra Winger, Kelly McGillis, Kathleen Turner, and even Glenn Close. In the end, though, the role was given to the relatively unknown Linda Hamilton.

27 year old Michael Biehn was cast as Sgt Kyle Reece, the soldier from the future who comes to rescue Sarah and becomes her lover. Biehn became one of Cameron's 'repertory company', playing similar military roles in *Aliens* (1986) and *The Abyss* (1987).

The film was produced by Cameron's then-wife Gale Anne Hurd, who bought the screenplay from her husband for the token sum of one dollar. Hurd, who worked for Orion Pictures, was the producer, with John Daly of Hemdale Pictures as executive producer.

Cameron's screenplay called for extensive creature effects, and these were provided by Stan Winston who had provided the amazing transformations in John Carpenter's 1982 remake of *The Thing* and who later went on to work on Cameron's next film *Aliens* (1986). Other effects, such as the future war sequences, were created by a large team from Fantasy II Film Effects.

The film was originally scheduled for shooting in 1983, but was delayed by nine months to allow Arnold

Schwarzenegger to meet his commitments on *Conan the Barbarian*. During this recess, Cameron wrote the screenplay for his next film – *Aliens* (1986) – and also wrote a first draft of *Rambo: First Blood Part II* (1985).

The film opens with a caption which reads 'Los Angeles 2029 AD.' Strange, alien-looking hovering aircraft float over a desolate smoke-filled landscape as they shoot at everything that moves with laser cannon. Later in the film, we learn that these craft (plus their tracked, land-based equivalents) are known as Hunter-Killers (HKs), and apparently their appearance and weaponry was inspired by the Martian war machines in *War of the Worlds* (1953). Soldiers in futuristic battledress, armed with hand-held laser weapons, run for cover as a lengthy caption appears on screen:

'The Machines Rose from the Ashes of a Nuclear Fire. Their war to exterminate mankind has raged for decades. But their final battle would not be fought in the future. It would be fought here. In the present. Tonight.'

Then the titles appear, accompanied by Brad Fiedel's synthesised score with its pounding five-note 'Terminator Theme', supposedly representing a mechanical heartbeat.

After the titles, a caption informs us that it is now 'Los Angeles 1984'. Amidst smoke and what looks like a miniature electrical storm, the Terminator arrives, played by the incredibly muscular Arnold Schwarzenegger. He is naked and immediately confronts three nearby punks (who are clowning around next to a 'pay as you view' telescope) and demands their garments.

'Give me clothes,' he says.

Two of them refuse to comply and are swiftly killed by the Terminator. The third, played by Bill Paxton, is so terrified he strips off all his clothing and runs away.

Meanwhile, in a nearby alley another naked man with a more average muscular build materializes from the future. To achieve this effect a stuntman dropped about four feet from a lying position on a wooden plank mounted between two stepladders, fortunately not injuring himself in the process. The second time traveller is Sgt Kyle Reese (Michael Biehn), a soldier from the year 2029.

Reese immediately confronts a tramp in the alley and robs him of his trousers. He steals a revolver from a policeman and holds him at gunpoint while he asks him the date, which is Thursday 12 May. Before he can find out the year he is chased by other cops and breaks into a department store where he steals a raincoat and other clothing items. As he makes his way out of the shop he also manages to purloin a pump-action shotgun from a police car. Reece saws off most of the wooden stock and fits a makeshift sling made from rope to allow the weapon to be easily concealed. Now suitably armed, he finds a 'phone box and rips out a page from the telephone directory containing the names, addresses and 'phone numbers of the three people in LA called Sarah Connor.

The next morning (in one of the few daytime shots in the movie, as it was mainly filmed at night), 19 year old Sarah Connor rides to work on a Honda motor scooter. She arrives (slightly late) at the diner and stamps her card.

In the meantime, the Terminator steals a station wagon by smashing the driver's window with his fist and then hot-wiring the ignition and starter motor using the usual Hollywood method of ripping out a few wires and twisting them together.

As the Terminator drives off, Sarah is having a bad day at work. The diner is busy, she is overworked, and then she spills food on a customer. As she leans forward to clean the customer's trousers a young child puts a scoop of ice cream in the pocket of her uniform. One of her fellow waitresses sees her predicament and makes the profound philosophical observation: '100 years from now, who is going to care?'

On the way to his next victim, the Terminator stops at a gun store where he asks for several weapons including a '0.45 Longside laser sighting pistol, a 12 gauge auto loader shotgun, a phased plasma rifle in the forty watt range and an Uzi 9mm submachine gun'. The 'phased plasma rifle' is obviously a weapon from the future and thus is not in stock, but the proprietor is able to supply the other items plus copious amounts of ammunition.

The shop owner says he will have to wait a couple of weeks before he can uplift the handgun (due to the paperwork and legalities involved), though he can have the rifles straight away. But the Terminator shoots him with the shotgun and leaves with all the guns. Soon afterwards, he turns up at a phonebox, pulls out the occupant, and steals a page of the phonebook containing the names and addresses of the three Sarah Connors who live in Los Angeles (though the Terminator clearly hasn't considered the possibility that Sarah has an ex-directory number!).

Later, the Terminator arrives at the address of the first Sarah Connor listed in the 'phone book. As his station wagon comes to a halt, its left front wheel crushes a toy truck underfoot, hinting at the devastation that is to come later in the movie. The truck is an exact replica of the cab unit of the articulated tanker which appears towards the end of the film. As Sarah answers the door, the Terminator grunts just two words of dialogue:

'Sarah Connor?'
'Yes?'

Having confirmed her identity, the Terminator kills her with a single round from his laser sighted .45 pistol, then fires a few more rounds into her body for good measure.

A few hours later, Sarah is still working at the diner when she hears a news item on the television. A lady called Sarah Connor, 35 – a mother of two – has been killed at her home.

'You're dead,' notes one of her fellow waitresses.

But Sarah remains unperturbed.

Meanwhile, Reese has stolen a car of his own. As he rests in the driver's seat, parked near a building site, a tracked excavator rolls past and he has a flashback about fighting tank-like HK vehicles in the future. As one them trundles past, he flings a grenade under one of its caterpillar tracks and blows it up. This was part of the highly realistic miniature filming. Two-dimensional cut-outs were used to represent devastated buildings and smoke helped to create a sense of perspective. Actors were added to the foreground of these scenes using both back and front projection.

Now Reese and a soldier colleague jump into an old car, which has been converted into a makeshift anti-aircraft vehicle by cutting off the roof and fitting a laser cannon in the rear (which was apparently a modified Browning M2 0.50in cal water-cooled machine gun). As the car speeds off it exchanges fire with a pursuing Hunter Killer aircraft. Suddenly the car is hit, crashing as Reese is jolted back to reality.

Later, Sarah Connor and her flatmate Ginger (Bess Motta) are in their flat preparing for their dates. The 'phone rings and Sarah picks it up. A man starts talking dirty to her, telling her what he would like to do to her. Sarah realises it is

Matt (Rick Rossovich), Ginger's boyfriend, and passes the 'phone to her.

In a nearby police station Detective Hal Vukovick (Lance Henriksen) and Lieutenant Ed Traxler (Paul Winfield) have discovered that a second person called Sarah Connor has been killed, and reflect that they may be facing a 'pattern killer' who is out to murder everyone with that name.

Around the same time, Sarah is checking her ansaphone for messages and discovers that her date for that evening (Dan) has cancelled, so she decides to go out on her own using her Honda scooter. The ansaphone message was voiced by James Cameron himself. As she is leaving her flat, Reese follows her in his car.

Just after she has left, the 'phone rings – it is the police, desperately trying to contact Sarah – but the call is picked up by her ansaphone. Ginger is too busy to hear it, having sex with her boyfriend while listening to her cassette Walkman with a pair of headphones.

As Ginger and Matt continue with their copulation – unaware of the danger they are in – Sarah is enjoying a meal and a drink in a bar. A TV news item mentions that two people, both called Sarah Connor, have been murdered and that police are hunting the killer. Suddenly, realising her life may be in danger, Sarah grabs a phonebook from a nearby payphone and deduces that someone is intent on assassinating all the Sarah Connors in the directory and that she will be next.

Feeling anxious, she leaves the bar. As she walks along the street she realises she is being followed by a man (Kyle Reese), so she manages to lose him and ducks into a nightclub, the *Tech Noir*. This nightclub was created especially for the film, and was so realistic that many LA citizens wanted to come inside and use its facilities – not realising it was merely a film set. Sarah makes a bee-line for the payphone inside the nightclub. Although it is working, all the lines are busy.

As Sarah continues with her attempts to contact the police, the Terminator has arrived at Sarah's flat. Ginger has finished her lovemaking with Matt and, Walkman headphones still in place, she is dancing as she makes her way to the kitchen to prepare a post-coital snack. As she takes items out the fridge and food cupboard, the Terminator enters Ginger's bedroom where he starts to fight with Matt. Though an obviously fit and well-muscled man, Matt is no match for the powerful cyborg. He is quickly killed after both he and the Terminator burst through the bedroom door. Ginger screams in terror, but is executed as she tries to flee.

As the Terminator is about to leave the scene, he hears an incoming message on the ansaphone. It is Sarah, saying she is at the *Tech Noir* nightclub. She gives the address. The Terminator knows he has to go there to complete his mission. Before he departs, he rummages through Sarah's drawers and finds her address book and university ID card. He now knows exactly what she looks like. Back at the nightclub, Sarah has finally managed to get through to the police and speaks on the 'phone to Lieutenant Traxler, who tells her to stay where she is as help is on its way.

By now Reese has arrived at the nightclub and is stalking Sarah, though at this point she does not know he is trying to protect her. Then the Terminator arrives and quickly identifies Sarah. He aims his .45 Longside pistol at her, projecting a small dot of red laser light on her forehead. Just as he is about to pull the trigger, Reese breaks cover and pulls out his pump action shotgun from beneath his coat. He fires several rounds at the Terminator, knocking him to the ground with the sheer kinetic energy of the projectiles and temporarily stunning him. But the Terminator is not killed, and within seconds he gets up again and opens fire with his Uzi 9mm submachine gun at the fleeing crowds. Sarah is not hit, but is trapped under the body of one of the Terminator's victims. As she lies on the ground, pinned down by the dead body, the Terminator cocks his Uzi and takes careful aim. Just as he is about to pull the trigger, Reese fires again – this time knocking the Terminator through a large plate glass window.

Before the Terminator recovers, Reese grabs Sarah by the hand, uttering the immortal line of dialogue: 'Come with me if you want to live'. They run out of the nightclub and down an alley, pursued by the Terminator. At this point, we see a 'Terminator's Eye View' of the proceedings which resembles the HUD (Head Up Display) of a fighter aircraft.

Reese and Sarah get into his car. As they drive off at speed, the Terminator climbs onto the windscreen and tries to smash his way in. Reese reverses at high speed and hits a police car, the impact throwing off the Terminator, allowing the pair to escape. However, the Terminator steals a police car and sets off in hot pursuit, leading to a furious car chase. The Terminator uses the police car radio to find out what is going on, and one of its many capabilities is revealed: it can exactly mimic any human voice it has heard.

As Reese drives like a maniac through the streets of LA, he tries to explain to Sarah what is going on. He is Sergeant Kyle Reese, who has been sent back in time from the year 2029 to try and prevent her assassination by a Terminator – effectively metal robots looking a bit like skeletons. These 'endo-skeletons' are covered with real living flesh to enable them to pass for humans. Though earlier 600-

series Terminator models had rubber flesh and could be easily identified, the new T-800 Model 101s have real human skin and muscles, and even have bad breath and sweat meaning they are hard to spot.

Terminators don't feel pain. They have no remorse. They can't be bargained with. Once they have been programmed to carry out a mission they will execute it.

Sarah asks Reese if he can stop the Terminator and he says that he is not sure, bearing in mind the limitations of the contemporary weaponry he is forced to use. Reese drives into a car park and steals another car to try and fox the Terminator. As he breaks the steering lock and hot wires the car, he explains a bit more about what is happening.

The Terminators have been produced by Cyberdyne Systems. In the near future, the machines produced by Cyberdyne – in particular the Skynet defence satellite system – have become self-aware and decide to eliminate mankind by starting a nuclear war. However, some humans survive and set up a resistance army to fight the machines. Others are used as slave labour, and Reese shows Sarah a tattoo rather like a bar code on his forearm.

One of the key resistance leaders is John Connor, Sarah's as-yet-unborn son, and Skynet wants to damage the future resistance movement by killing Sarah in 1984, thus preventing the birth of John Connor.

Suddenly the Terminator arrives in a police car, and another car chase on a freeway follows. But this time several police cars appear and, after an exchange of gunfire, the Terminator eventually crashes his vehicle. Reese and Sarah are surrounded by several police vehicles and are forced to surrender. There is no sign of the Terminator though, as he has apparently fled the scene. Reese and Sarah are taken to the police station where Reese is interrogated by Dr Silberman (Earl Boen), a criminal psychologist.

Meanwhile, the Terminator breaks into a building where he carries out some much-needed 'surgery' on his flesh outer body following his car crash. He cuts open the flesh of his right forearm so he can repair some damaged control rods. The surgery over, he folds back the skin and applies a bandage.

The Terminator also has to do some work on the area around his left eye which has been damaged. Many of these shots were achieved using a life-sized animatronic puppet of Schwarzenegger's head which took weeks to build. Totally convincing, the only thing that indicates that it is not the actor's real head is that its movements are slightly jerkier than a real human one. A larger-than-life-size model of the Terminator's left eye was also created, incorporating a real camera aperture. With the left eye now working properly, the Terminator covers the damage with a large pair of Gargoyles sunglasses.

Back at the police station, Dr Silverman continues to question Kyle Reese but is sceptical about his story. He asks why, if Reese had really come from the future, he didn't bring a ray gun with him and has to rely on contemporary weapons? Reese explains that the Time Displacement Equipment only works with living organisms, so inanimate objects (such as weapons) can't be transported through time.

A little later, Sarah watches a monochrome video recording of Silberman's interview with Reece, who comes across as a deranged lunatic. Drexler suggests that the Terminator's invulnerability to bullets and shotgun shells could be explained by the fact that he probably wore body armour and shows Sarah a Kevlar vest that policemen wear on operations. She is beginning to doubt Reece's story, but is not sure. She asks how the Terminator could punch his hand through a car windscreen, and Vokavich speculates that he may have been taking PCP – a drug which would prevent him feeling any pain. PCP (also known as Phencyclidine or 'angel dust') is an anaesthetic agent which was popular as a recreational drug in the eighties. Vokavich tells Sarah that she must need some sleep, and suggests she has a rest on the couch. He reassures her that there are 30 cops in the building and she is quite safe.

As Sarah is dropping off, the Terminator arrives at the front desk of the police station claiming to be a friend of hers, but the on-duty cop says he can't see her.

'I'll be back,' says the Terminator.

This has become one of the most famous lines in movie history, but was nearly 'I will be back' as Schwarzenegger thought it was more appropriate dialogue for a machine. He was overruled by James Cameron, who wanted the line delivered as scripted. 'I don't tell you how to act, you don't tell me how to write,' he is reported as saying.

A moment later the Terminator drives his car through the front of the police station and jumps out armed with his Uzi machine pistol and an Armalite AR-18 automatic rifle. Quickly the Terminator rips out the main electricity supply cable with his bare hands, plunging the building into darkness. The police arm themselves with M-16A1 rifles from the armoury but their guns prove useless against the metal killing machine. In the confusion Reece breaks free and finds Sarah. They escape in a stolen car and head for the country.

Unfortunately their car soon runs out of petrol and they have to push it off the road. As they take shelter, shivering, in a nearby culvert, Sarah applies a makeshift field dressing to Reece's right forearm as she asks him about her son John.

Reece reveals that he volunteered for the mission as he wanted to meet the legendary Sarah Connor. Sarah is perplexed, because the Sarah Connor that Reece talks about is obviously tough and organised whereas she 'can't even balance her cheque book'. Reece is unchanged in his views though, and recites a personal message from her son John telling her she must survive so he can exist in the future.

Sarah asks Reece to tell him more about the future war, and he explains how the Hunter Killers (HKs) use infrared vision to find resistance fighters in the dark. He remembers an incident when a Terminator infiltrated their camp and caused carnage. The Terminator in this sequence was played by Franco Columbu, one of Arnold Schwarzenegger's workout buddies. The alarm was raised by two Alsatian dogs, who were able to detect the difference between humans and Terminators and barked a warning. In the resulting firefight the only photo he had of Sarah (a small Polaroid print) got burned. Sarah falls asleep and dreams about this future war, and when she awakens remembers that the resistance uses dogs to sniff out Terminators.

In the interim, the unshaven and rather dishevelled-looking landlord of a cheap guest house knocks on the door of a bedroom as he puffs on a cigar. 'Hey, buddy! You got a dead cat in there or something?'

Inside the bedroom, the Terminator considers possible linguistic responses in a 'menu' display inside his head and selects the best option:

'Fuck you, asshole.'

Unperturbed, the proprietor sets off down the corridor, pushing his cleaning trolley before him as the Terminator continues to study Sarah's address book.

Meanwhile, Sarah and Reece have arrived at the Tiki Motel and ask for a room with a kitchen. Sarah says she is dying for a shower. Reece has to go out for supplies so he gives Sarah a handgun for her protection. A deleted scene reveals that this weapon was given to him by Lieutenant Traxler during the police station massacre.

Later, having had her shower, Sarah is sitting on the bed wrapped in a towel on the 'phone to her mother who implores her to give her a contact number. Though she knows she shouldn't really do this, she gives her the Tiki Motel's 'phone number. Unbeknown to Sarah, her mother is dead – killed in her cabin – and she is speaking to the Terminator, who can impersonate anyone's voice with pitch-perfect accuracy. After Sarah has hung up, the Terminator rings the number he has been given and finds out the address of the motel. He immediately leaves on a motorcycle.

Back at the Tiki Motel, Reece arrives with two paper bags of groceries. Sarah wonders if he has bought food for dinner but his provisions include mothballs, corn syrup and ammonia, the ingredients required to make home-made explosives.

Reece gets to work with Sarah's assistance and prepares six pipe bombs. As they construct the munitions, Sarah asks Reece if he has a special person in the future. To her surprise, he reveals he fell in love with Sarah after seeing her Polaroid photo. The couple then kiss and make love. Soon after they have finished having sex, the Terminator arrives at the motel and they are forced to flee the building.

Reece steals a pick-up truck, and a high-speed car chase ensues in which they are followed by the Terminator who is firing bursts from an automatic weapon. While travelling fast, Reece swaps places with Sarah so that he can attack the pursuing Terminator with his stock of pipe bombs. Reece lights the bomb fuses with a cigarette lighter and flings them out the passenger window one at a time, resulting in near misses which do not damage the Terminator. As he is about to throw a fourth bomb he is hit by a burst of gunfire causing him to drop the ordnance next to his truck. The device explodes, injuring him further. By now the Terminator has run out of ammunition for his Uzi and is relying on his pistol.

As his bike comes alongside the pick-up truck, Sarah pulls on the wheel, causing the vehicle to swerve and knock down the Terminator's bike. Unfortunately, Sarah's sudden manoeuvre also makes the pick-up overturn and the couple (by now both injured) have to climb out of the vehicle.

A large articulated fuel tanker of the J G Oil Company (the J and G stood for James Cameron and Gale Anne Hurd) drives past at speed and runs over the Terminator, who grabs onto the underside of the vehicle, showering sparks everywhere. The truck driver brings his vehicle to a halt and jumps out of the cab to find out what has happened. He is immediately killed by The Terminator, who jumps into the truck and tells the other occupant to get out. Quickly, the Terminator starts the vehicle, turns it round and chases after Sarah, mounting the kerb as he does so.

Reece races after the vehicle and shoves a lit pipe bomb into an open tube at the rear of the tanker, then dives into a large metal bin to take cover. Within seconds the tanker explodes in a massive conflagration. This was one of the most impressive pieces of miniature filming in the entire production, and is totally convincing. A one-sixth model of the fuel tanker was built and destroyed using 42 separate charges. The first take was a failure because a wire pulling the model accidentally ripped the front axle from its mounting, and a new miniature vehicle had to be built in just a few days.

The Terminator staggers through the inferno as its outer flesh body is consumed by the flames. Then, apparently killed, it collapses on its funeral pyre. The distributors wanted to end the film at this point, but Cameron put his foot down and insisted that the closing scenes he had scripted be shot and included in the final cut. He was right, because the last few minutes include some classic moments of cinema.

Sarah wanders amongst the wreckage and discovers the wounded Reece. Then, as the couple embrace, the Terminator comes back to life like a malevolent phoenix rising from the ashes. For the first time we see the Terminator endoskeleton in its full technological glory: a glistening metal robot with glowing red eyes and skull-like head. Some scenes featuring the endoskeleton were achieved using a full-sized animatronic puppet, which only existed from the waist up and was worked from below by an operator. For shots showing the robotic Terminator in its entirety, a complete stop-motion puppet was used and in these scenes the movement is a little more jerky.

Despite their injuries, Sarah and Reece make their way into a nearby factory which employs robot machine tools (rather like the Fiat Strada factory which appeared in TV commercials in the early eighties). Reece switches on the machinery in order to impede the Terminator's tracking devices and bolts the door behind them. This does not deter the robot, who starts breaking down the door. Eventually he makes a hole large enough to put a hand through, lets himself in, and then chases the couple through the factory.

Reese tries to fight the skeletal Terminator with a metal bar, but is unable to damage it. He then lights his last pipe bomb and sticks it into the waist of the Terminator. A few seconds later it explodes, effectively amputating the robot's body below the waist. Reece is killed and Sarah receives a large shard of metal in her left thigh. But the Terminator is still alive, and crawls towards Sarah determined to kill her with his metal hands. With the last of her energy, Sarah crawls under a large hydraulic press. As she escapes out the far side the Terminator follows her, and Sarah presses a large rubber button which brings the press down on the machine creature.

'You're terminated, fucker,' she says as the press squeezes the last bit of life out of the robot and its glowing red eyes fade to black. For this scene, a simple mock-up of the Terminator was made using foam-core and metal foil. The smoke is actually from a cigarette. Sarah collapses in exhaustion as the sound of police car sirens is heard in the background.

In the next, penultimate scene Sarah is lifted into an ambulance as Reece's corpse is taken away in a body bag (which was actually a suit bag obtained from the trunk of James Cameron's car). Scenes deleted from the final cut of the picture revealed that the factory was owned by Cyberdyne Systems, and that the Terminator's CPU chip had been found in the wreckage and was sent to Cyberdyne's research and development division, thus leading to the eventual creation of the Terminator in a future time. Therefore this chip was itself in a time loop, rather like the pocket watch in *Somewhere in Time* (1980).

The final scene of the movie is set in Mexico, several months later, where a heavily-pregnant Sarah has stopped at a gas station in her CJ-7 Jeep. She has an Alsatian dog on the passenger seat (obviously to detect Terminators), a revolver in her lap, and is dictating a series of audiocassettes to advise her unborn son.

A Mexican boy approaches her and takes a Polaroid picture of her for five dollars. The resulting print is the very same photo which John Connor gives to Kyle Reece in 2029. Sarah drives off along the highway as dark clouds gather on the horizon, and the end title credits roll.

*The Terminator* premiered on 26 October 1984, and proved to be one of the most successful films of the year. It also proved very popular in VHS, DVD and Blu-Ray formats.

Author Harlan Ellison loved the film but felt it was too similar to *Soldier*, a 1964 episode of *The Outer Limits* which he had written. As a result he took out a legal action, which meant that all future releases of *The Terminator* credited his works as a source of inspiration.

In 1991 a sequel – *Terminator 2: Judgment Day* – followed, with a vastly increased budget. In this new story, set 10 years after the original, Skynet tries to interfere with the past for a second time by sending another Terminator back in time. But this is a T-1000 'liquid metal' shape-shifting Terminator which is even harder to stop than the original. Arnold Scharzenegger returned in this sequel, playing a T-800 Terminator sent back in time by the resistance to protect John Connor.

James Cameron had originally planned to include a T-1000 Terminator in the 1984 original, but discounted the idea as special effects technology wasn't up to the job in the eighties. By 1991, though, the newly developed Computer

Generated Imagery (CGI) technology could be employed for this task.

*Terminator 2* also featured a number of ideas which were filmed for the 1984 original but were subsequently deleted, such as a technician discovering a microchip in the wreckage of the Terminator at the factory and Sarah's suggestion that they blow up the HQ of Cyberdyne Systems.

Further sequels followed: *Terminator 3: Rise of The Machines* in 2003, *Terminator: Salvation* in 2009 and *Terminator: Genisys* in 2015, plus a TV series *Terminator: The Sarah Connor Chronicles* (2008-09) with English actress Lena Headey replacing Linda Hamilton. However, most critics would agree that none of these matched the 1984 original for sheer thrills and originality. It is without a doubt one of the greatest films ever made.

# *The Terminator* (1984)
# Production Credits

Director: James Cameron
Screenwriters: James Cameron
and Gale Anne Hurd

## Cast
The Terminator ⁄ Arnold
Schwarzenegger
Kyle Reese ⁄ Michael Biehn
Sarah Connor ⁄ Linda Hamilton
Lt Ed Traxler ⁄ Paul Winfield
Detective Hal Vukovich ⁄ Lance
Henriksen
Matt Buchanan ⁄ Rick Rossovich
Ginger Ventura ⁄ Bess Motta
Dr Peter Silberman ⁄ Earl Boen
Pawn Shop Clerk ⁄ Dick Miller
Nancy ⁄ Shawn Schepps
Desk Sergeant ⁄ Bruce M.
Kerner
Future Terminator ⁄ Franco
Columbu
Punk Leader ⁄ Bill Paxton
Punks ⁄ Brad Rearden, Brian
Thompson
Policemen ⁄ William Wisher Jr,
Ken Fritz, Tim Oberhaus
Cop in Alley ⁄ Ed Dogans
TV Anchorman ⁄ Joe Farago
TV Anchorwoman ⁄ Hetty
Lynne Hurtes
Station Attendant ⁄ Tony
Mirelez
Mexican Boys ⁄ Philip Gordon,
Anthony Trujillo
Derelict ⁄ Stan Yale

Customers ⁄ Al Kahn, Leslie
Morris, Hugh Farrington,
Harriet Medin, Loreee Frazier,
James Ralston
Cleaning Man ⁄ Norman
Friedman
Ticket Taker ⁄ Barbara Powers
Tanker Driver ⁄ Wayne Stone
Tanker Partner ⁄ David Pierce
Phone Booth Man ⁄ John E.
Bristol
Reporter ⁄ Webster Williams
Bar Customer ⁄ Patrick Pinney
Bartender ⁄ Bill W. Richmond
Truck Driver ⁄ Chino 'Fats'
Williams
Motel Customer ⁄ Greg Robbins
Wrong Sarah ⁄ Marianne
Muellerleile
Sentry ⁄ John Durban
Dancer ⁄ Marian Green
Policeman ⁄ J. Randolph
Harrison
Punk ⁄ David Kristin
Bar Patron ⁄ Darrell Mapson
MacDougal ⁄ John Stuart West

## Producers
Executive Producers: John Daly,
Derek Gibson
Producer: Gale Anne Hurd

## Music
Composer: Brad Fiedel

## Cinematography

Director of Photography: Adam Greenberg

## Film Editing

Film Editing: Mark Goldblatt
Casting: Stanzi Stokes
Art Direction: George Costello
Set Decoration: Maria Caso
Costume Design: Hilary Wright

## Make-up Department

Make-up Department Head: Jeff Dawn
Hair Stylists: Kyle Sweet, Peter Tothpal
Assistant Makeup Artist: Melissa Street
Special Make-up Effects: Brian Wade

## Production Management

Executive in Charge of Production: Bruce M. Kerner
Post-Production Supervisor: Donna Smith

## Second Unit Director or Assistant Director

Additional First Assistant Director: Thomas A. Irvine
First Assistant Director: Betsy Magruder
Second Unit Director (Action): Jean-Paul Quellette
Second Assistant Director: Robert Roda

## Art Department

Assistant Art Director: Shay Austin
Construction Supervisor: John S. Curran
Property Master: Tommy Estridge
Carpenter: Mark Freedman
Assistant Property Master: Kerry Jennings
Scenic Artists: Amy McGarry, Kristen McGary
Art Assistants: Kurt Meisenbach, Jewel Myrow, Steven Rinehart, Jennie Ryan, Linda Shoeneck
Assistant to Art Director: Joe Rainey
Set Dresser: Cynthia B. Rebman
Carpenters: David Reece, Stephen Reece
Lead Man: Gary Shoeneck
Set Dresser: Greg Wolf
Property Maker: Christopher Gilman
Painter: Joe Koiwai

## Sound Department

Re-Recordist: Jennifer Barin
Assistant Sound Editor: Elizabeth Barnard
Supervising Editor: Tom Belfort
Boom Operator: Ken Brocious
Supervising Sound Editor: Davie Campling
Foley Artist: Gordon Daniel
Sound Effects Editors: Greg Dillon, Karola Storr, Jim Fritch, Gary Shepherd, Horace

Manzanares, Gil Marchant,
Mike Le-Mare, Rob Miller, Jim
Klinger
Synthesized Sound Effects:
Robert Garrett
Machine Room Operator:
Gabriel Guy
Re-Recording Mixers: David J.
Hudson, Mel Metcalfe, Gary
Rizzo, Terry Porter
Sound Editor: Stephen Kearney
Production Sound Mixer:
Richard Lightstone
Sound Design Consultant: Gary
Rydstrom
Foley Artist: Tom Post
Digital Mix Technician: Tony
Sereno
Sound Utility: Gabriel Cubos

## Special Effects

Terminator Special Effects: Jack
Bricker, Richard Landon, Shane
Mahan, David B. Miller, John
Rosengrant, Brian Wade
Terminator Mechanical Effects:
Ellis Burman Jr, Bob Williams,
Ron MacInnes
Special Effects: Frank De Marco,
Robert George
Special Effects Coordinator:
Ernest De Farino
Terminator Effects Creator:
Stan Winston
Special Effects Technician:
Roger Kelton, R. Bruce
Steinheimer

## Visual Effects

Stop Motion Effects: Doug
Beswick
Production Assistant: Don
Bland
Technical Assistant: Steven
Fagerquist
Graphic Animation Effects:
Ernest D. Farino
Optical Effects (Image 3): Phil
Huff
Camera Operator: John Huneck
Production Supervisor: Leslie
Huntley
Model Shop Supervisor:
Michael Joyce
Model Makers: Paul Kassler,
Gary Rhodeback
Terminator Stop Motion: Pete
Kleinow
Optical Effects: Laurel Click
Matte Artist: Ken Marschall
Rear Screen Projectionist:
Gerald McClain
Process Photography
Cinematographer: Austin
McKinney
Production Assistant: Jane A
Pahlman
Camera Assistant (Process
Work): Eric Peterson
Special Optical Consultant:
Mark Sawicki
Pyrotechnics and Fire Effects:
Joe Viskocil
Special Effects Supervisor: Gene
Warren Jr
Visual Effects Engineer: Kris
Brown

Stop-Motion Electronics: Sam
Longoria
Animation Assistant: Bret
Mixon
Stop Motion Model: Ted Rae
Stunts: Anthony Cecere, Jeff
Dashnow, Hill Farnsworth, J.
Suzanne Fish, Ken Fritz, Marian
Green, Tom Hart, Gene
Hartline, Jean Malahni, Gary
McLarty, Frank Orsatti, Jim
Stern, Pete Turner, Cynthia
Brannon, Eddy Donno, Jeff
Habberstad, Glenn R. Wilder,
Rob King, Lee Waddell, Monty
Jornan
Stunt Double (Arnold
Schwarzenegger): Peter Kent
Stunt Double (Linda Hamilton):
Jean Malahni

## Camera and Electrical
## Department
Focus Puller: Bernard Auroux
Gaffer: Dennis Bishop
Grip: Bruce Byall
Camera Operator (Inserts):
Anne S. Coffey
Second Unit Director of
Photography: Chuck Colwell
Grip and Equipment (Second
Unit): Mario Davis
Best Boy: Mark Ellensohn
Additional Camera Operator:
Alec Hirschfeld
Camera Operator (Second
Unit): Sean McLin
Dolly Grip: David Michels
Electrician: Mark Morton

Best Boy (Electric): Tim Morton
Grip: Elliott Nachbar
Electrician: Mark Petersen
Camera Assistant: Vance Piper
Still Photographer: Joyce
Rudolph
Video Playback Operator:
Roger Schweltzer
Key Grip: Dylan Shepherd
Camera Assistant (Insert
Photography): Gary Wagner
Electrician: Rick West
Grip: Tim Collins, Travy
Neftzger, John Janusek, Pascal
Franchot
Additional Cinematographer:
Donald D. Jackson
Electricians: Kyle T. McDowell,
Barry Seybert, Mark A. Shelton
Best Boy Grip: Philip Sloan

## Casting Department
Extras Casting Coordinator:
Greg Robbins

## Costume and Wardrobe
## Department
Costume Supervisor: Deborah
Everton
Costumer (Second Unit): Julie
Gombert
Costume Production Assistant:
Virginia Hartman

## Editorial Department
First Assistant Editor: Lorna
Anderson
Associate Editor: Michael
Bloecher

Assistant Editor: Spike Allison
Hooper
Negative Cutter: Mary Nelson
Colour Consultant: Peter
Silverman

**Other Crew**
Location Manager: Joseph A.
Luuzzi
Music Consultant: Budd Carr
Music Post Production
Coordinator: Robert Randles
Music Editor: Emilie Robertson
Transportation Captain: Wayne
Nelson
Transportation Coordinator:
Wayne Stone
Transportation Captain: Ike
Mizen
Assistant to Producer: Polly
Apostolof
Assistant Production
Accountant: Jo Barnett
Production Assistant (Second
Unit): Terry Benedict
Production Coordinator: Kathy
Breen
Title Designer: Ernest D. Farino
Assistant to Producer: Randy
Harrison

Set Production Assistant:
Deborah Herbert
Production Assistant: Scott
Javine
Script Supervisor (Second Unit):
Sharon Kirkpatrick
Publicist: Andrew Marx
First Aid: Pattison Newberry
Set Production Assistant:
George Parra
Utility Man: Kevin E.
Papperson
Craft Service: Eric Rasmussen
Talent Coodinator: Michael
Thomas Slifkin
Assistant to Producer: Lisa
Sonne
Assistant Production
Coordinator: Anne St Johns
Production Accountant:
Marilyn Tasso
Script Supervisor: Brenda
Weisman
Financial Services: Frans J.
Afman
Extras Wrangler: Lisa G.
Girolami

Acknowledgement given to the
works of Harlan Ellison.

# 4

# RAMBO: FIRST BLOOD PART II

(1985)

*Carolco Pictures*

**Director**: George P. Cosmatos
**Producer**: Buzz Feitshans
**Screenwriters**: Sylvester Stallone
and James Cameron

CONVENTIONAL wisdom decrees that sequels are usually inferior to the films which spawned them, and I would generally agree with this assertion. However, there are some movies which buck this trend, and examples might include *Aliens* (1986) which is discussed elsewhere in this book. The long-running series of James Bond films also illustrate this phenomenon, as *Goldfinger* (1964) is generally considered to be superior to *From Russia with Love* (1963), which in turn is thought by most critics to be better than *Dr No* (1962).

Although Sylvester Stallone himself feels that *First Blood* (1982) is the best of the quartet of *Rambo* films that have been made to date, I have a great liking for the second movie in the series as it established many of Rambo's trademarks – the beefy guy shooting an M60 from the hip, the bow firing explosive-tipped arrows, expertise with knives, and minimal dialogue. It also resulted in 'Rambo' becoming a word in the dictionary; something which did not happen after the first film in the series.

*Rambo: First Blood Part II* was of course a sequel to *First Blood* (1982), a successful action picture which had a very troubled history. Ten years earlier in 1972, while the Vietnam War was still raging, author David Morrell published his book *First Blood* about a war veteran called Rambo (no first name was ever given) who returns to the USA and is harassed by the police in the town of Madison, Kentucky. He is picked up by the local Police Chief, Teasle, who drives Rambo to the city limits and drops him off, but when the ex-soldier simply walks back to the town he is arrested and charged with vagrancy.

The cops throw him in a cell and try to cut off his long hair and shave him against his will. The experience causes Rambo to snap as it reminds him of being a POW in Vietnam (it is implied that he is suffering from PTSD as he has flashbacks). He assaults the policemen and escapes to the countryside on a stolen motorbike. Eventually he is hunted down by a mixed force of policemen and National Guardsman who are joined by Rambo's old commanding officer, Colonel Sam Trautman. The book ends with Rambo considering suicide by exploding a stick of dynamite against his chest. Eventually he dies after being shot in the head by Colonel Trautman.

The book was a hit, and the film rights were bought by Columbia Pictures who then sold them on to Warner Brothers. Over the next decade the story passed through three companies and eighteen screenplays. Finally the rights were acquired by Andrew G. Vajna and Mario Kassar, two film distributors who wanted to become producers.

Various actors were considered for the role of Rambo including Michael Douglas, John Travolta, Nick Nolte, Steve McQueen and Al Pacino. Curiously, Nick Nolte was also a candidate to play the Rambo-like character of Colonel John Matrix in *Commando* three years later, while Steve McQueen (who died in 1980, aged 50) was eventually considered too old to play a Vietnam vet.

Eventually the role went to Sylvester Stallone, whose career was already at its peak following a series of successful films including the *Rocky* franchise. As was to be the case with all the *Rambo* movies, Stallone co-wrote the screenplay, on this occasion with Michael Kozoll and William Sackheim.

Veteran actor Kirk Douglas was lined up to play the crucial role of Rambo's mentor, Colonel Sam Trautman, but pulled out at the last moment – reportedly because he disagreed with Stallone's decision to change the ending so that Rambo survived. His place was taken by Richard Crenna, who had to start work on the movie at short notice with little time for preparation.

The film was a success, making $125m internationally against a budget of $14m. Although it originally received varied reviews from critics, it is now regarded as a cult classic. All this must have come as a pleasant surprise for Sylvester Stallone, because the first cut of the movie reportedly ran for three and a half hours and the actor briefly considered buying the movie and then destroying it as he felt it might sink his career.

In view of the success of *First Blood*, a sequel was planned for 1985. Thus Stallone's decision to keep Rambo alive at the end of the first movie was a very wise move.

After all, studio executives reportedly considered a sequel to *Thelma and Louise* (1991) until someone pointed out that the titular characters had both died at the end of the first movie as they had driven their car off a cliff!

*First Blood* had been filmed in Hope, British Columbia (which was standing in for Hope, Washington State) in early 1982, in freezing conditions. The sequel was shot entirely near Acapulco, Mexico in hot weather in the summer of 1985, with some studio scenes lensed at Churubusco Studios. Acapulco was a popular holiday resort, and the area stood in for both Thailand and Vietnam.

The director was George P. Cosmatos, a Greek-American who had helmed the rather quirky war movie *Escape to Athena* (1979) and was later to direct Stallone for a second time in *Cobra* (1986). The screenplay was written by James Cameron and Sylvester Stallone. Cameron was waiting for Arnold Schwarzenegger to become available for the filming on *The Terminator* (1984), and during this nine-month recess he wrote both *Rambo: First Blood Part II* and *Aliens* (1986). Cameron reportedly wrote all the action sequences for the *Rambo* film while Stallone provided all the political content. It is possible that Cameron's work on *Rambo: First Blood Part II* influenced his screenplay for *Aliens*, as the latter can be considered a parable on the Vietnam War.

The film begins with a shot of a sun-baked quarry. Originally this scene was to be filmed in a prison, but no suitable location could be found in Mexico. A group of convicts are engaged in hard labour, breaking up stones, watched by armed warders. Amongst them, clad in a denim shirt and trousers, is John Rambo who is serving his sentence for criminal acts committed during the events depicted in *First*

*Blood* (1982) – a film which, since the release of the second *Rambo* movie, has been referred to as *Rambo: First Blood* on the cover of VHS, DVD and Blu-Ray releases though the actual titles on the film remain unchanged.

As Rambo continues with his monotonous and exhausting work, an old friend observes him through the heavy wire fence. It is his old colleague and mentor Colonel Trautman (Richard Crenna), who also featured in *First Blood*.

He calls Rambo over to talk to him. 'How are you doing?' asks the Colonel.

'Good', replies Rambo.

'Sorry to see you in such a hellhole. You know I said I'd help you.'

Rambo has been sentenced to five years hard labour. But then the Colonel makes an astonishing offer. There is the possibility of a Presidential pardon, if Rambo will agree to be temporarily reinstated in the US Army. This will be in order to carry out one more covert mission which involves the reconnaissance of a prison camp in Vietnam – the same one he had escaped from in 1971. Rambo is to find out if there are any American POWs in the camp.

This part of the plot was based on fact, and was very topical because around this time (1985) there was a widespread belief in the USA that a number of American prisoners – perhaps as many as 2,500 – were still being held captive by the Vietnamese. These people were known as MIAs (Missing in Action), and were a political hot potato at the time.

Rambo agrees to the mission, and Trautman says that the next time they meet they will both be in Thailand. I like this scene because it is a reversal of the usual cliché in action movies where a disgraced ex-Special Forces soldier, pilot, policeman, mercenary, detective etc. – who has a lot of skeletons in his cupboard – is asked to do one more mission. What usually happens is that the hero refuses and has to be persuaded to carry out the task either with a positive incentive to comply or else some kind of punishment if they do not cooperate. Presumably this is usually done for dramatic reasons, even though in real life most people would just say, 'Fine, I'll do it'.

As Trautman leaves, Rambo makes the poignant comment: 'Do we get to win this time?' Although seemingly a throwaway remark, this line is a metaphor for the whole Vietnam conflict as one of the reasons America lost the war was because politicians kept interfering with military decisions.

A brief title sequence then runs, played out over footage of a Buddha statue (actually carved from Styrofoam) and a Bell 206B Jet Ranger helicopter flying over paddy fields on its way to a forward air base in Thailand. Although the entire production was filmed in Mexico, great efforts were expended to make the countryside look like the Far East, and a large paddy field of rice was sown to complete the illusion.

The helicopter lands at a Thai airfield (actually a Mexican air force base), and Rambo jumps out and meets his colleagues including Trautman and Ericson (Martin Cove). He is also introduced to the mission controller, a rather shifty character called Murdock (Charles Napier) who looks at one of his computers and confirms that Rambo was born on 6$^{th}$ July 1947 (exactly a month after Sylvester Stallone's birthday) and joined the US Army on 6$^{th}$ August 1964. During his military career, Rambo had 59 kills and won numerous decorations including the Congressional Medal of Honour.

As Murdock sips a soft drink, he outlines the details of Rambo's mission. He is to carry out a reconnaissance of a Vietnamese prison camp in order to confirm the presence (or absence) of American POWs and take photographs. Although he will be provided with advanced weapons, these are for self-defence only and he is under orders *not* to engage the enemy. If any POWs are found they will be extracted by a Delta Force assault team, led by Colonel Trautman.

Rambo studies aerial photos of the POW camp. He is to be dropped by parachute at low altitude from an executive jet, modified for its clandestine role by the application of a coat of matt black paint. The aircraft used for this sequence was a North American Rockwell 1121 Aero-Commander supplied by the Mexican Air Force, a small twin-jet airliner which looks similar to the famous Lear Jet, although why it was painted matt black for this sequence is unclear since this would only be helpful at night and Rambo intends to parachute by day.

Trautman and Rambo walk outside the hangar to discuss the forthcoming mission and, as they do so, they pass a line of three Pilatus PC-7 Turbo Trainer aircraft of the Mexican Air Force with their national insignia covered with self-adhesive vinyl Thai Air Force roundels. They return to the control room. Rambo looks at the banks of computers that have been set up in the room and Trautman explains that all this hardware has been obtained to ensure the success of his mission. In addition he will be supplied with all the equipment he needs for his personal safety. Trautman proclaims that he will have the best weapons in the world, but Rambo points out that the mind is the best weapon – another reference to the Vietnam War, where the technologically superior USA was outsmarted by a more determined enemy.

As Rambo leaves to prepare for his mission, Murdock asks Trautman if the ex-soldier is mentally unbalanced. However Trautman replies that Rambo is nothing more than a killing machine and what others consider 'hell' is his home.

The next scene shows close-ups of parts of Rambo's muscular body as he readies his equipment for the mission and loads his camera with 35mm film. These shots are similar to those in *Commando* (1985) with Arnold Schwarzenegger, and are one of the reasons the two films are often compared.

As the Aero-Commander is prepared for the mission, the warrior packs a stash of conical, high-explosive warheads for his bow: an aluminium and fibreglass Hoyt Spectra Custom Bow which was specially made for the film. This weapon only weighed six pounds, and was able to be quickly dismantled to fit in a tube which could be easily carried on the body. This was to be his signature weapon in this film and the following one, *Rambo III* (1988).

As he boards the jet, Trautman reminds him that he has only 36 hours to get in and out. If there is any trouble he is to proceed to a hilltop extraction site which is marked on the map. The aircraft taxies out and takes off, heading for Vietnam and – as it flies away – Murdock expresses doubts about the viability of the mission. 'We're here to clean up a mess,' he says.

Sometime later, over Vietnam, Rambo dons a helmet and goggles and prepares to jump from the open passenger door on the port side of the aircraft. Most of his weapons and equipment are contained in a separate bag which is designed to dangle beneath his parachuting body on a nylon strap and hit the ground first (something that has been standard practice for parachute troops for decades). Unfortunately something goes wrong with his jump, and he finds himself trapped against the port side of the fuselage just in front of the engine intake. The only way to free himself is to saw through the nylon strap attaching his harness to the kit bag. Rambo takes out his combat knife, cuts through the webbing, and parachutes to safety. He has lost most of his weapons and equipment, except for his combat knives and special bow and arrows which he had fortunately attached to his body. The scene of Rambo struggling to free himself was achieved using a mock-up of the Aero-Commander with Stallone's body suspended from black-painted wires. The interior shots of the aeroplane's cabin were also done using the replica in the studio, while the actual parachute jump was done for real.

As the aircraft turns round and returns to base, Murdock is convinced Rambo must be dead but Trautman persuades him that he should give him the benefit of the doubt as he still has 36 hours to complete his mission.

Meanwhile, Rambo has survived his low-level parachute drop without injury and is running through the jungle when he bumps into his female contact Co Bao (Julia Nickson). Co asks him why he is late, and he replies that he got 'hung up': the nearest that Rambo gets to a Bond-style quip in the film. Co tells him she has arranged for a boat to take him down the river to the camp, and wonders why he has come all this way to see what will in all probability be an empty building.

Co and Rambo make their way to a jetty, where they board a vessel owned by local pirates. She has promised them a lot of money to take them to their destination and back. As there were no suitable rivers near the filming location, all these scenes were shot on a lake.

Rambo is concerned that they may encounter Vietnamese patrol craft, but the pirate leader opens a chest and shows him a cache of weapons which includes a Soviet RPG-7 rocket launcher; a shoulder-launched anti-tank weapon powerful enough to destroy a small vessel.

Back at the Thai military base, Colonel Trautman is studying a 35mm slide of the Vietnamese POW camp with interest, holding it up to the light.

In the meantime, as the boat makes its way downriver, Co asks Rambo if he wants to eat and then enquires how he got involved in all this. He explains that after he left the US Special Forces he 'moved around a bit' and then returned to the USA, where he discovered there was a 'war against soldiers returning from the war': a reference to the events of *First Blood.*

Co then asks him why he was picked for the mission, and he speculates that it was because he was regarded as 'expendable'. He then notices that Co is wearing a green onyx pendant round her neck and she explains that it brings her good luck.

Back at the Thai airfield, Trautman is itching for a piece of the action and insists that he be allowed to be part of the extraction team who will be going in by helicopter to rescue Rambo and the others. Reluctantly, Murdock agrees.

As Rambo's boat approaches the nearest point on the river to the Vietnamese POW camp the soldier prepares his weapons, screwing explosive warheads onto some of his arrows. Co wonders why he is doing this, as he is under orders not to engage the enemy.

As Rambo prepares to disembark from the boat, an attractive young woman drives up to the front gate of the

POW camp on a moped and talks to the guard. She is a local prostitute who has come to offer her services to the soldiers.

A little later, Rambo cuts through the wire fence with his combat knife and sneaks into the camp. By this time one of the Vietnamese officers, Lt Tay (George Cheung), is having sex with the prostitute as the Special Forces soldier crawls into the gap under the hut and observes the scene.

The camp is largely built from bamboo and has a watchtower with a spotlight but, as yet, no-one has spotted the intruder. Moving stealthily, Rambo makes his way through the camp and finds several POWs with beards and ragged clothes imprisoned in rat-infested bamboo cages. After wading into the river, he frees one POW who is tied to a tree next to the water.

Suddenly a Vietnamese guard comes out of the bushes and is swiftly killed by Rambo with a throwing knife. Another soldier positioned at the top of a bamboo watchtower points a searchlight at him but he too is rapidly executed by a well-aimed arrow fired from Rambo's bow. Hearing the commotion, Lt Tay emerges naked from the hut to see what is going on. Another Vietnamese soldier spots Co but is killed by an arrow.

The next morning the prison camp guards discover that one of the POWs is missing and a soldier raises the alarm by blowing a whistle. Back at the Thai airbase, an armed Bell UH-1 Huey helicopter is readied for action. Its windows are being cleaned and its door-mounted M6o machine gun is being loaded with ammunition. The crew (including Trautman) board the helicopter, and it takes off just as Rambo, Co and the POW cross a river and then trek through the jungle, pursued by a large force of Vietnamese soldiers.

Rambo's party makes it to the jetty, and they board the vessel which sets off down the river. Soon afterwards the Vietnamese force arrives but – as they lack the means to pursue their quarry – an officer calls for assistance on the radio. As it was hard to find Asian extras in Mexico, most of the Vietnamese soldiers were played by workers in local Chinese restaurants in Acapulco.

Sometime later, as Rambo's boat heads downriver to safety, another vessel appears and heads towards them. It is a Vietnamese Navy patrol boat armed with heavy machine guns. Suddenly the crew of Rambo's boat pick up weapons and turn them on their passengers. Rambo realises he has been betrayed and, to emphasise the point, the boat's captain slaps him on the face.

But he has picked a fight with the wrong guy. Quickly, Rambo pulls out two small, concealed knives from his belt, stabs one of the crew, and grabs his pump-action shotgun. Within a matter of seconds he has killed most of his opponents. One surviving crew member climbs onto the roof of the cabin and is immediately killed by Co, who fires up through the ceiling with an AKM (an improved version of the famous AK-47 Kalashnikov assault rifle).

By now the Vietnamese patrol boat is closing on its quarry, and one of its crew opens fire with twin M3 Browning 0.50in cal machine guns. The M3 was an improved version of the famous M2 gun used in WW2, but with various modifications to increase its rate of fire from 600 to 1200 rounds per minute. It arrived too late to see service in the Second World War, but it was used in various post-war aircraft – particularly the North American F-86 Sabre fighter, which saw action in the Korean War, and was also used as an anti-aircraft weapon.

Rambo tells the POW and Co to jump for safety while he engages the enemy vessel. Opening the wooden chest, he takes out an RPG-7 rocket launcher, puts it on his shoulder and fires a single round. The patrol boat explodes in a huge, orange fireball, but Rambo's troubles aren't over as one of the crew of his boat – who has been wounded but not killed – grabs him round the throat. After a brief struggle, Rambo kills him with a knife.

Rambo jumps from the vessel – just as the burning hulk of the Vietnamese patrol vessel collides with it – and swims ashore, where he joins Co and the POW.

Rambo is now armed with an AKM, and the three fugitives race through the jungle heading towards the hill which is the extraction point. Vietnamese mortar bombs fall around them as they advance to their objective. On board the Huey, Trautman learns they are just three minutes out.

As the trio heads towards the top of the hill, pursued by a large force of soldiers, the crew of the Huey see what is happening. The door gunner on the helicopter open fires on the Vietnamese troops with his M60 as the chopper comes in for a landing.

Back at the Thai operations room, the men are excited by the report that Rambo has found an American POW and they are going to be extracted. But Murdock is aghast at the news, and orders the mission to be aborted with the helicopter to return to base immediately without picking up Rambo and his two colleagues. On board the chopper, Trautman tries to persuade the crew to disregard the order but finds himself held at gunpoint.

This part of the plot is very similar to a crucial scene in the British movie *The Wild Geese* (1978), in which a force of mercenaries lead by Colonel Alan Faulkner (Richard Burton), having successfully carried out their mission, is about to be extracted from an African airfield by a Lockheed Hercules transport aircraft. Unfortunately at the last moment the instigator of the mission, businessman Sir Edward Matherson (Stewart Granger), does a deal with the bad guys and the 'Herc' is ordered to take off immediately without picking up the soldiers.

The helicopter extraction having been abandoned, Rambo is forced to surrender. Back at the Thai air base, Trautman angrily confronts Murdock. 'It was a lie, a whole damn lie, just like the war. You're just a stinking bureaucrat trying to cover his ass!'

Murdock points out that Rambo was just supposed to take pictures, not rescue anyone, while Trautman retorts that if the photos had shown anything they would no doubt have been mysteriously lost!

Murdock counters with the revelation that in 1972 the USA had agreed to pay North Vietnam $4.5 billon war reparations as part of the eventual peace settlement. The USA had reneged on the deal and, as a consequence of this, the North Vietnamese had held onto some of their POWs. It wasn't feasible for the USA to restart the war as it would cost billions of dollars, so the issue of MIAs was being swept under the carpet. He ends his rant by warning Trautman not to bring up the subject again. This part of the plot is pure fiction, as the USA never agreed to pay reparations.

As the two men argue, Rambo is being held captive in the Vietnamese prison camp. Wearing only a loincloth with his arms tied to a branch above his head, the soldier is forced to remain in a large cesspit filled with sewage and leeches. The authentic brown colour of the fake cesspit was achieved using a large quantity of instant coffee!

A helicopter arrives, another Bell UH-1 Huey – this time armed with twin rocket pods, a pair of General Electric GE134 7.62 mm miniguns, and door mounted M60 machine guns. It carries the orangey-red star of the Vietnamese armed forces. This is a technical error in the film, as the Vietnamese forces used exclusively Soviet equipment. But as no Russian-made helicopters were readily available to film-makers in the days before the fall of the Berlin Wall and the collapse of Communism, US equipment was often employed instead.

The helicopter lands, and a squad of Soviet troops arrives including several Spetsnaz Special Forces troops and three officers including Lt Col Podovsky (Steven Berkoff). Berkoff was a distinguished actor, author, playwright and theatre director who was also a well-known face in film and TV productions. One of his earliest TV appearances was as a Moonbase Interceptor pilot in Gerry Anderson's series *UFO* (1969-70). He also played Adolf Hitler in the TV miniseries *War and Remembrance* (1988).

Podovsky salutes the Vietnamese commander and then asks for Rambo to be removed from the cesspit for interrogation. 'These people are so vulgar; they lack compassion', he says as he removes a leech from Rambo's body with his combat knife. He then asks for the American soldier to be cleaned up and taken into the hut for interrogation.

Later, in the bamboo shack, a somewhat cleaner Rambo is brought in for questioning. Podovsky asks for one guard to remain along with his assistant, Sergeant Yushin (Vojo Goric), and for the others to go. Podovsky starts off by being reasonable but it is obvious that the taciturn American soldier is not going to cooperate as he is unwilling to even give his name.

Podovsky puts his combat knife on some hot coals to heat it up and drinks tea as he explains what he has in mind. He wants Rambo to speak on the radio to his HQ and make a statement condemning the USA as well as apologising for his espionage and his aggression towards the Vietnamese people (both the WW2 Japanese and the North Vietnamese put pressure on POWs to condemn their own countries in return for better treatment, a flagrant breach of the Geneva Convention).

Podovsky switches on the radio and puts the microphone in front of Rambo but the Special Forces soldier just says 'Fuck you' and refuses to comply with his request. As Podovsky continues with his attempts to coerce the America into denigrating his country, Co arrives at the front gates of the camp on a moped (the same one we saw earlier), posing as a prostitute.

Meanwhile, Podovsky has resorted to tougher methods to break his captive. He tortures him with electric shocks and then reads out a transcript of a conversation over the radio between the crew of the American Huey helicopter and their base which confirms that the chopper was ordered to abort the mission and return to Thailand, leaving Rambo to his fate. Interestingly, the transcript doesn't tally exactly with the dialogue we heard earlier in the film.

'These are the people you protect', says Podovsky.

Rambo is given more electric shocks and is threatened with a red-hot knife. Podovsky then takes the weapon and sears Rambo's left cheek. He then tells his colleague to put the hot knife in the POW's left eye. The man is then thrown to the ground and kicked.

Eventually Rambo agrees to talk on the radio and grabs the stem of the desk mike. By this time Podovsky's patience is running out. 'Do it now!' he says.

Rambo tunes the radio dial to the correct frequency and gives his call sign '22056, Lone Wolf receive'. The operations room answers his call and Murdock asks Rambo for his position: 'Give us your position and we'll come and pick you up'.

But Rambo says just a few words, 'Murdock, I'm coming to get you!' This was a Stallone trademark, as the actor liked to play people who said as few words as possible.

Without any further warning, Rambo attacks his captors. He is helped by Co, who has just arrived. Soon the American is armed with an AKM assault rifle and several grenades, and the pair flee from the building pursued by Vietnamese soldiers. Within a moment they have reached the perimeter of the camp. Rambo throws grenades to delay his former captors, and then lifts up the barbed wire with his bare hands allowing Co to crawl under it. They race into the jungle as a Vietnamese helicopter follows them, desperately trying to locate the pair with its spotlight.

The next morning the sun rises over the Thai base as Murdock and Trautman await further developments. In Vietnam, Rambo is resting by a river as Co washes his wounds. She asks him if he has any plans once all this is over, and he says that he intends to return to the USA and take Co with him. The two kiss. Suddenly a Vietnamese soldier appears out of the jungle and shoots Co with an AKM. Rambo returns fire but he is too late to save Co who dies in his arms.

Back at the Thai airbase, Trautman announces that he wants to lead a mission to rescue Rambo with departure in just one hour, but Murdock is furious and orders the Colonel to be placed under house arrest – he is not allowed to leave the base.

In Vietnam, Rambo is preparing for a major battle. As a way of honouring the deceased Co he wears her onyx pendant around his neck and puts on a headband.

He is being hunted by a mixed force of Spetsnaz Soviet Special Forces and regular Vietnamese soldiers. Rambo kills several Russian troops with arrows and his knife as he is chased into a village. More Vietnamese soldiers arrive in a truck and disembark. As they head off in pursuit of the American soldier, a Vietnamese officer discovers a spilled petrol can on the ground. But it is a booby trap set by Rambo and – as the officer examines it – the American soldier lights a trail of petrol, exploding the can and killing the officer in the resulting conflagration.

As the Vietnamese are still recovering from this assault, Rambo fits conical explosive warheads to two arrows and fires them at the enemy troops. He then destroys some Vietnamese army vehicles parked on a bridge next to the village with the same weapon. Next, he runs across rocks at the foot of a waterfall. Lieutenant Tay tries to shoot him with an AKM but then, out of ammunition, switches to a pistol instead but simply can't hit the soldier (this is actually quite authentic, as the AK-47 and AKM are quite inaccurate at long range – particularly on sustained automatic fire – as the barrel tends to kick up with the recoil, and pistols are useless at medium and long range). Rambo simply waits until the officer has used up all his ammo and then kills him with a single explosive arrow.

At this point, the Vietnamese Huey arrives carrying a bomb under its belly. The weapon looks like a beer keg. It drops its ordnance, resulting in a huge orange fireball. It is never explained whether the 'bomb' is supposed to contain napalm or even a fuel/air explosive.

Rambo easily outruns the expanding fireball (a favourite action movie cliché), and then dives under the surface of the water as the chopper drops to extremely low altitude in order to chase him. The helicopter hovers low over the water as the door gunner tries to spot him. Suddenly Rambo emerges from the water and pulls out the door gunner, who falls to his death. He climbs aboard the chopper, fights Sergeant Yushin, and throws him out. He then approaches the cockpit, causing the pilot to jump out. Rambo has now taken command of the helicopter and flies towards the POW camp, approaching with the rising sun behind him so he can't be seen.

Rambo systematically devastates the camp with the chopper's rockets and two forward-firing mini-guns which each have a rate of fire of 3,000 rounds per minute. After working over the camp for a few minutes and killing most of the defending troops, Rambo lands and – armed with the M60 machine-gun which he has dismounted from the door gunner's position – races to free all the POWs.

After releasing the prisoners, he shepherds them to the waiting helicopter. But one Russian soldier is still alive, though wounded. He reaches for his AKM and fires at the chopper, wounding one POW. Rambo kills him with a burst from his AKM.

With all the POWs aboard, Rambo takes off. Suddenly a Soviet Hind helicopter gunship appears, piloted by Podovsky. The Mil-24 Hind was one of the most feared weapon systems deployed by Soviet Bloc forces during the

Cold War as it carried a heavy weapons load on stub wings and a nose turret, including cannon, machine guns and rockets.

At the time of filming no real Hinds were available in the West, so an airworthy replica was created by modifying an Aerospatiale SA.330J Puma transport helicopter, an aircraft which had a similar-shaped fuselage to a real Hind although it lacked the narrow tandem cockpit of the genuine article.

The Hind proceeds to chase the Huey round the sky, peppering it with machine-gun fire. As the two aircraft fly low over the POW camp, part of the Hind's weapons load on the starboard stub-wing falls off. This was an accident during filming, but looked so good it was kept in.

Eventually the Huey is hit and, trailing smoke, descends towards the river bed. Podovsky grins in satisfaction and looses off another rocket from the Hind's pods, but can't see the effect because of all the smoke. As his view clears he sees the Huey lying on the river bed, apparently disabled, and closes in for a better look. As he hovers in front of the smaller helicopter, Podovsky sees Rambo slumped in the left hand pilot's seat. Suddenly the American soldier jumps into action. He is not dead at all. Grabbing an M72 66mm Light Anti-Armour Weapon (an American one-shot 'throwaway' bazooka, sometimes referred to as the LAAW, the LAW or the LAWS rocket) and placing it on his shoulder, the US soldier fires a missile through the shattered windscreen of the Huey, destroying the Hind.

'Playing dead to get a better shot at the enemy' is a common cliché in movies. Malcolm McDowell's character Gresham uses a similar ploy at the beginning of *Aces High* (1976), when he lands his supposedly stricken SE5.A fighter in a field and apparently collapses unconscious at the controls in order to escape being shot down by a German two-seat biplane. As the Germans land nearby and walk to the British fighter to investigate, he opens the throttle, takes off, and then strafes the Germans and their plane from the air. Charles Bronson's character Jay Killian adopts a similar ploy in *Assassination* (1987), when he pretends to be dead in order to shoot a bad guy at close range.

The M72 LAW has featured in many action films, but its use in this particular scene seems odd because logically a Soviet or Vietnamese helicopter would carry a Russian anti-tank weapon such as the RPG-7 seen earlier in the movie. Also, firing a LAW or RPG-7 in the confined space of a helicopter cabin would result in considerable backblast which would incinerate everyone sitting behind Rambo! Close examination of this scene using freeze-frame suggests that this sequence was shot with footage of both American M72 LAW and Soviet RPG-7 weapons and then edited together, as the close-up of Rambo pulling the trigger was achieved using an RPG-7.

The opposition now eradicated, Rambo lifts off in the Huey and heads for the airbase in Thailand. He gives his call sign 'Lone Wolf' and explains that he is making an emergency landing with American POWs aboard. The jubilant crew of the operations room rush out to greet Rambo as the still-smoking helicopter arrives.

As soon as the chopper lands, Rambo jumps out, takes the M60 from its door mounting and rushes into the hangar where he enters the control room and riddles the computers with bullets, finally ending his assault with a primal scream.

Murdock is quaking with fear after Rambo's assault and is clearly nervous about what he intends to do next. He tries to justify his actions without much success:

'I don't make the orders. I take them just like you... it was just supposed to be another assignment.'

But the soldier is unimpressed and pushes Murdock onto the desk, holding his combat knife high in the air above him. With one dramatic movement he slams the knife into the desk beside Murdock's head.

'You know there are more men out there. Find them, or I'll find you!'

In the final scene of the picture, Rambo walks outside the hangar. In the background, fire crews are dowsing the now-blazing Huey with foam. He is met by Trautman, who speculates that he may get a second 'Medal of Honour' (presumably a Congressional Medal of Honour) for his actions. But the soldier is unimpressed.

'Give it to them', he says, pointing at the POWs. 'They deserve it more.'

Trautman then suggests that Rambo might like to rejoin the US Armed Forces on a permanent basis: 'Stop running, come back to us'. But the warrior is unrepentant and turns down the offer. This is another similarity with the Arnold Schwarzenegger film *Commando* (1985), as it also ends with General Kirby asking Matrix to reform his unit – an offer which the Colonel refuses.

'The war may be wrong; don't hate our country for it,' says Trautman, but it is clear that all Rambo wants is for his country to love war veterans and take care of them, a re-stating of one of the main themes of the first Rambo picture, *First Blood.*

*Rambo: First Blood Part II* was released on 22 May 1985 and was a great success both critically and commercially, making $150m at the box-office against a budget of $40m. Following the film, the word 'Rambo' became common parlance. Indeed, some critics described Sigourney Weaver's character, Ellen Ripley in *Aliens,* as being 'Rambolina'.

One fan of the film was the current President of the USA, Ronald Reagan. After viewing the movie he said that it had given him a lot of ideas on how things should be done! As the reader may recall from reading an earlier chapter of this book, Reagan was also a fan of the hawkish British movie *Who Dares Wins* (1982).

In view of the success of the second *Rambo* movie, a further sequel – *Rambo III* – was made in 1987 and released the following year. This movie opened with Rambo living and working in a monastery in Thailand, having received a Presidential pardon for crimes committed during the events depicted in *First Blood* (1982). He is visited by his old mentor Colonel Trautman, who wants him to take part in a covert mission to Soviet-occupied Afghanistan. Rambo refuses but when the mission goes wrong and Trautman is captured, Rambo is forced to travel to Afghanistan to rescue his old friend, a course of action which involves several battles with the occupying Soviet forces.

This film was partly filmed in the Negev desert near Eilat in Israel, resulting in some spectacular landscapes being captured on film. The Israeli Defence Forces (IDF) supplied many military vehicles for this section of the film, including some rather anachronistic WW2 vintage American-made White M3 halftracks, portraying Soviet vehicles. The final battle scenes in the movie were shot in Arizona using a large number of mock Soviet vehicles originally created for *Red Dawn* (1984). A British Alvis Saracen six-wheeled APC and Ferret Scout car can also be glimpsed in this scene.

The fourth and (to date) final film featuring the character, simply entitled *Rambo,* premiered in 2008. This time the action took place in Burma (also known as Myanmar), and involved Rambo rescuing some missionaries from the clutches of the evil military regime in the country. The film received a lot of praise for its authentic battle scenes, which have been compared to those in *Saving Private Ryan* (1998), and for drawing attention to the horrific problems in Burma.

A fifth and final Rambo film has been under consideration since 2008 and has undergone numerous drafts. One early version of the screenplay, written by Stallone himself, involved the character's daughter being kidnapped and him going after the gang responsible for the crime, a plot which appears to have similarities with the successful films *Taken* (2008) and its sequel *Taken 2* (2012), both starring Liam Neeson. The film was reportedly to be shot in Bulgaria.

Another, later version of the screenplay retained the abduction but had the film set in Mexico City. Later still, Stallone himself claimed that the new *Rambo* film was to be called *Rambo: The Savage Hunt* and was to be based on the James Byron Huggins sci-fi novel *Hunter*. The plot involved Rambo and a team of special forces soldiers hunting a half-human beast created by genetic research. The plot of this version of the proposed sequel sounded a bit like that of the Arnold Schwarzenegger film *Predator* (1987), and it should be noted that the original title of *Predator* was to be *Hunter*!

However, by 2010 Stallone was instead considering a prequel to *First Blood* to be called *Rambo: Last Stand*, with a script by Sean Hood. Then the idea was dropped and Stallone went back to the notion of a further sequel. A press release around this time suggested the film would be called *Rambo: Last Blood*. On 5 January 2016 Stallone announced that his involvement with *Rambo V* was now over, but by May he was again talking publicly about another sequel. At the time of writing (March 2017), a Fox TV series involving Rambo's son is under development and a reboot *Rambo* film without Stallone and directed by Ariel Vromen has also been announced, so it is likely that we have not seen the last of the character.

### *Rambo: First Blood Part II* (1985)
### Production Credits

Director: George P. Cosmatos
Screenplay: Sylvester Stallone
and James Cameron
Story: Kevin Jarre
Based on Characters Created by
David Morrell

### Cast

John Rambo - Sylvester Stallone
Col Samuel Trautman - Richard
Crenna
Marshall Murdock - Charles
Napier
Lt Col Podovsky - Steven
Berkoff
Co - Julia Nickson
Erickson - Martin Kove
Tay - George Cheung
Banks - Andy Wood
Captain Vinh - William Ghent
Sergeant Yushin - Vojo Goric
Captain Kinh - Dana Lee
Gunboat Captain - Baoan
Coleman
Lifer - Steve Williams
POWs - Don Collins,
Christopher Grant, John
Sterlini, Alain Hocquenghem,
William Rothlein
Prison Guards - Tony Munafo,
John Pankow
Russian Pilot - Tom Gehrke
Russian Soldier - Mason Cardiff
Chief Radio Operator - Roger
Cudney
Tay's Soldier - Jeff Imada

Radio Operator - John Sabol

### Producers

Associate Producer: Mel Dellar
Producer: Buzz Feitshans
Executive Producers: Mario
Kassar, Andrew Vajna

### Music

Composer: Jerry Goldsmith

### Cinematography

Director of Photography: Jack
Cardiff

### Film Editing

Film Editors: Larry Bock, Mark
Goldblatt, Mark Helfrich, Gib
Jaffe, Frank E. Jimenez
Casting Director: Rhonda
Young
Production Designer: Bill
Kenney
Set Decoration: William Skinner
Costume Designer: Tom
Bronson

### Makeup Department

Hair Stylists: Bertha Chiu, Kay
Cole
Make-up Creator: Leonard
Engelman
Make-up Artists: Elvira
Oropeza, Pamela Westmore

## Production Management
Production Manager (Mexico):
Anuar Badin
Production Manager: Fred
Rollin

## Second Unit Director or
## Assistant Director
First Assistant Directors: Mario
Cisneros, Fred Rollin
Second Assistant Director:
Patrick Kinney
Second Unit Director: Peter
MacDonald

## Art Department
Assistant Art Director: Roy
Barnes
Greensman: Donald Butterworth
Prop Master (Mexico): Martin
Cardenas Moreno
Set Decorator (Mexico):
Enrique Estevez
Construction Coordinator:
Howard Hester
Art Director (Mexico): Agustin
Ituarte
Illustrator: Fred Lucky
Prop Master: Dennis Parrish
Set Painter: Ward Welton
Production Buyer: Moises
Pineda

## Sound Department
Supervising Sound Editor: Fred
J. Brown
ADR Editor: Juno J. Ellis
Stereo Sound Consultant: David
W. Gray

Sound Editor: Denise Horta
Re-Recording Mixers: Rick
Kline, Donald O. Mitchell,
Kevin O'Connell
Foley Artist: Margie Denecke
Assistant Sound Editor:
Michelle Pleis
Sound Editor: Michele Sharp
Sound Mixer: Rob Young

## Special Effects
Special Effects (Mexico):
Federico Farfan
Special Effects Coordinator:
Thomas Fisher
Special Effects: Jay King,
William Purcell, Cliff Wenger Jr.

## Stuntwork
Stunt Performers: Simone
Boisseree, Brad Bovee, Phil
Chong, Yukio Collins, Danny
Costa, Mark De Alessandro,
George Fisher, Joseph Hieu,
Jeffrey Imada, Robert Jauregui,
John Michael Johnson, Steve
Kelso, Eric Lee, Harry Mok,
Danny Munson, Vernon Paul
Rieta, Bill Ryusaki, Benjamin
Raymond Scott, John Wendall,
Clay Scott, Daniel Thomas
Wong, Anthony Cecere, Jay
King
Stunt Coordinator: Richard
'Diamond' Farnsworth
Stunt Double (Sylvester
Stallone): Mark De Alessandro

## Camera and Electrical Department

Camera Operator: Franco Bruni, John Cardiff
Key Grip: Aldo Colonzi
Best Boy Grip: Bruno Colonzi
Still Photographer: Dave Friedman
Gaffer (Mexico): Mariano Garcia
Gaffer: Luciani Leoni
Director of Photography (Helicopter Unit): Peter MacDonald
Best Boy: Fiorangelo Piocco
First Assistant Camera: Massimiliano Sano
Dolly Grip (Mexico): Salvador 'Apache' Serrano
Chief Grip (Mexico): Salvador Vasquez
Camera Operator (Aerial Unit): Stan McClain

## Casting Department

Casting (Mexico): Jesus Guerrero
Casting Associate: Donna Rosenstein

## Costume andWardrobe Dept

Costume Illustrator: Haleen K. Holt

## Editorial Department

Negative Cutter: Donah Bassett
Assistant Editors: Shelley Brown, Danny Retz, Hilarie Roope, Ron South

Assistant Film Editor (Mexico): Sergio Ortega
Colour Timer: Bob Raring

## Location Management

Location Management: Juan Clemente

## Music Department

Music Recording Consultant: Bruce Botnick
Music Editor: Kenny Hall
Orchestrator: Arthur Morton
Musician (Violin): Mark Berrow
Musician (Oboe): Tom Boyd

## Transportation Department

Drivers: Moe Blay, John Cahill, Donald Collis, Vic Cuccia, Bob Dewitt, Joe Dugan, Kendall A. Reed, Michael Stevenson
Driver Captains: Jon Carpenter, Russell Hoverson
Transportation Coordinator: Terry Collis

## Other Crew

Accounting Assistant: Teri Abastado
Crew (Helicopter Unit): Frank Batt, John Campbell, Mario Cisneros, Hugh Forn, Kevin Griffith, Steve Harding
Pilots (Helicopter Unit): Tom Gehrke, Harry Hauss, Karl A. Wickman, Ross Reynolds

Mechanics (Helicopter Unit): Bruce Eidahl, Barry Wall, Steve Stephenson, Robert Mickey
Body Building Coach: Franco Columbu
Security Officer: Gary Compton
Production Secretary: Violet Crane
Production Controller: Charlie Davidson
Production Accountant: Jim Davidson
Archery Consultant: Joe Ellithorpe
Production Assistants: Eric Feitshans, Steve Kilfoy
Assistants to Executive Producer: Jeanne Joe, Linda Lawrence
Presenter: Mario Kassar
Production Coordinator: Richard Liebegott
Knife Designer: Jimmy Lile
Production Accountant (Mexico): Norah Lozano
Technical Advisor: Tony Maffatone
Security Officer: Tony Munafo
Accounting Assistant: Edwin L. Perez
Assistant to Sylvester Stallone: Susan Persily
Production Assistants: Nigel Rick, Bill Cody
Weapons Specialist: Frank Rousseau
Script Supervisor: Jeanne Scott
Unit Publicist: Ken Sylvia

Production Secretary (Mexico): Concepcion Taboada
Assistant to Executive Producer: Ceci Vajna
Accounting Assistant: Marichu Walker
Production Coordinator: Anna Zappia
Financial Services: Frans J. Afman

Film Dedicated to Cliff Wenger Jr.

# 5

# COMMANDO

## (1985)

*Silver Pictures*

**Director:** Mark L. Lester
**Producer:** Joel Silver
**Screenwriters:** Steven E. de Souza, from a story by
Steven E. de Souza, Jeph Loeb
and Matthew Weisman

*C*OMMANDO is one of the most influential films of
the eighties. Produced by Joel Silver – who was
responsible for many Hollywood action movies of the
period, including *Lethal Weapon* (1987) and *Die Hard* (1988)
– and written by Steven de Souza, it took Arnold
Schwarzenegger's career in a new direction. Prior to
*Commando*, the former Mr Universe had made several films
including *Conan the Barbarian (1982), Conan the Destroyer*
(1984) and *The Terminator* (1984), but – as the actor himself
admitted – this was the first time he was allowed to portray a
normal human being with emotions.

Two different writers – Matthew Weisman and
Joseph Loeb III – had already worked on the story before it
was given a final polish by Steven de Souza. Originally the
central character of Colonel John Matrix was to be an out-of-
condition ex-Special Forces soldier (played by Nick Nolte),

who had turned his back on his previous military career and had opted for retirement. But in the end the producers chose Arnold Schwarzenegger, and his Austrian accent was explained away by a line of dialogue which established that Matrix had been brought up in Germany.

The central theme of the story – that Matrix's daughter had been kidnapped and he was being forced to carry out an assassination – was retained, but de Souza added some over-the-top action sequences to fit Schwarzenegger's image, and also some memorable James Bond-style quips. Indeed, when it was reviewed by Barry Norman on BBC 1's *Film 85* programme, the presenter said that it wasn't really a clone of *Rambo* (as many critics at the time claimed) but rather more like 'a super-violent James Bond film'.

The director was Mark Lester, who was given the job after Joel Silver met him at a party. Lester had made nine previous features but none could be described as blockbusters. The musical score was by James Horner, who was later to become an Oscar-winning composer, but at that point was best-known for writing the scores for *Star Trek II: The Wrath of Khan* (1982) and *Star Trek III: The Search for Spock* (1984). Horner's soundtrack for *Commando* was especially memorable as it employed a number of steel drums.

The film opens with a shot of a garbage truck reversing down a street on the outskirts of Los Angeles early one morning. Two of the crew are riding on the back, including a bald, heavily-built African American man named Cooke (Bill Duke). Inside a nearby house, Lawson (Drew Snyder) has just woken from his sleep by the noise of the vehicle. How can this be happening, as it is Tuesday? His wife suggests that they must have changed the bin collection schedule.

Without bothering to dress, Lawson rushes outside in his nightclothes carrying some black bags inside a couple of bins (this was in the happy days before the advent of recycling!).

'I was afraid you'd miss me!' he says.

Instantly he is cut down by bullets from MAC-10 sub machine guns carried by the two operatives.

Later that morning, Cooke is in a car showroom where he is shown a brand-new Cadillac Deville Sedan. This scene was filmed in a real car showroom (Casa De Cadillac) in Ventura Boulevard in Sherman Oaks, Los Angeles.

'I know what you are thinking', says the salesman, Forrestal (Michael De Lano). 'No leather, right? Believe me you don't want leather – it's hot and sticky, and it cracks' (a strange assertion to make, since vinyl upholstery is actually hotter and stickier than leather and cracking can be prevented by using conditioning cream). He invites Cooke to start the engine. It purrs beautifully.

'Know what I like best about it?' asks Cooke. 'The price.' Without further thought, he drives the car (a 1985 Cadillac Eldorado) at the salesman, knocking him down and killing him, then going straight through the showroom window and into the street. It's an exciting scene, but total fantasy. If you were intending to kill someone without being caught, this would probably be the dumbest way to do it! If Forrestal had done anything other than stand directly in front of the car the plan wouldn't work. The broken glass would probably puncture the tyres (in fact, for this scene the showroom's usual window had to be replaced with special safety glass). Plus, of course, there would be scores of witnesses.

The action moves to a marina in San Pedro, near Los Angeles. Bennet (Vernon Wells), wearing a wool cap and casual jacket, boards a motor vessel and sets out to sea. But he is being observed by Cooke, who waits until the boat is well clear of the quayside and then presses a radio-controlled detonator, blowing the ship to smithereens. Bennet was originally played by another actor (whose identity has never been revealed), but he proved unsuitable in the role and was replaced by Australian actor Vernon Wells after just one day's shooting. This explains why Wells's outfit appears to be too tight, as it was originally designed for a smaller actor. Wells himself described his look in the film as being like 'Freddie Mercury on steroids'.

The next scene shows extreme close-ups of a very muscular man. First we see his feet, then his upper arms, and finally his face. These shots were apparently inspired by Leni Riefenstahl's Nazi propaganda films and – according to director Mark Lester – convey the image of an invincible man emerging from the forest. These are the first glimpses in the movie of Colonel John Matrix, played by Arnold Schwarzenegger who some years before had set himself the goal of becoming the world's most perfectly developed man. Matrix is wearing a tight-fitting vest, and his body is gleaming with sweat as he carries a huge log on his left shoulder which he then puts down and chops with an axe. The log in this scene was a hollow dummy, as even a strongman like Schwarzenegger couldn't carry such a weight.

As he continues with his task, he sees someone's reflection in the shiny axe head. He turns round to find his beloved daughter Jenny (Alyssa Milano) and hugs her. The titles then start over some footage of Matrix enjoying life as a father as the two eat ice cream at an outdoor café. Then

Matrix crosses a bridge with Jenny clinging to his back. Next there is a scene of the two fishing, and then one of them splashing about in a swimming pool. All these shots convey the impression of the normal family life Matrix is now enjoying, in contrast to the violence of his past life as a Special Forces soldier.

As the titles end, Jenny makes sandwiches for the two of them. 'What's in this?' says Matrix after the first bite.

'You don't want to know,' replies Jenny

As the two eat their sandwiches, Matrix looks out the window and spots a helicopter approaching. He can hear the 'whump... whump... whump' sound of its rotor blades as it gets closer.

Jenny is anxious as she sees the chopper on approach. 'What's that Army helicopter doing?' she asks. She is worried that the military have come to take her father back to war, but Matrix reassures her he's not going anywhere. The helicopter used in this sequence was a civilian Bell Jet Ranger painted in fake US Army markings, and was the very same one used in *Lethal Weapon* two years later (for which it wore a red and white civil scheme).

The helicopter lands outside Matrix's hilltop home (filmed at Chapman Ranch, Mount Baldy, California), and three soldiers jump out – namely General Franklin Kirby (James Olson) and Privates Jackson (Bob Minor) and Harris (Mike Adams), who both carry M-16 automatic rifles.

Kirby implores Matrix to come out of the house but the ex-Special Forces soldier sneaks up on him from behind, pistol in hand. Kirby tells Jenny that he wants to speak to her father alone and, as the two walk, the General explains that someone has been killing members of his former Special Forces unit. Lawrence, Forrestal and Bennet are now dead, and he must be next. He is going to leave Jackson and Harris to protect him while he goes back into town to coordinate matters with the local police. He climbs back into the Jet Ranger and flies off. Jenny feels anxious and asks her father: 'Is it bad?' But her dad reassures her that he is not leaving.

Suddenly Matrix realises that an assault is imminent. Although it appears he has some kind of sixth sense, it is later revealed that he smelled the attackers who were upwind of him. Matrix dives to the ground as a volley of fire hits the two soldiers guarding him. Harris is killed instantly and Jackson is badly wounded.

Jackson and Matrix get into the house and lie on the floor. Jenny is told to go to her room and hide while Matrix realises he needs to get a rifle from his tool shed. Quickly he dashes across the roof to the hut and uses a PIN code to open a secure gun locker, from which he retrieves a Heckler and Koch HK91 automatic rifle. Meanwhile, Jenny is in her bedroom hiding under her bed where she sees the boots of one of the attackers.

Running back to the house across the roof, Matrix opens the external bedroom door and the dead body of Jackson nearly lands on him. Bearded bad guy Diaz (Carlos Cervantes) is sitting in the kitchen, and tells Matrix they now have Jenny. If he wants to see her alive again, he must cooperate. Matrix looks out the window and sees a Mercedes saloon and a truck departing downhill at great speed. Jenny must be in one of these vehicles.

'You're going to cooperate, right?' says Diaz.

'Wrong,' replies Matrix as he shoots him in the forehead at close range.

Matrix races outside to discover that his car (a 1974 Chevy Blazer 4x4) has been disabled by having its ignition wiring ripped out (the easiest way to disable a car of that era would be to take off the distributor cap and remove the rotor, but it is not clear what the bad guys have actually done). The car can't be started, but that doesn't deter Matrix who decides to freewheel downhill to catch the villains (this is actually possible, as the brakes and steering would still work manually without power assistance – though a lot of muscular effort would be required to steer and brake the car). Matrix pushes the car downhill and then jumps in. His plan is to go in a straight line while the baddies have to negotiate a zig-zag route with hairpin bends. In this way he hopes to catch up with them.

To achieve this stunt, a path was cleared through the forest to enable the Blazer to career downhill in a straight line without hitting anything.

Eventually Matrix's Blazer crashes, and he scrambles clear just before the vehicle bursts into flames (another action movie cliché, as cars in films always explode after crashing). He starts to fight the gang. At first it looks as though Matrix has the upper hand, as he has tremendous strength and is obviously highly skilled in unarmed combat, but he is soon overpowered by sheer weight of numbers. As he is being held down, the supposedly dead Bennet arrives in his field of view, a grin on his face.

'Ever since you threw me out of your unit, I've waited to pay you back. Know what today is, Matrix? Pay Day.' Immediately Bennet fires a gun at him.

Some time later, Matrix awakens and realises he has been shot with a tranquilliser dart. He can see several bad guys, including Bennet and an old acquaintance Arius (Dan Hedaya), the deposed President of Val Verde who wants

Matrix to return to the South American country to kill its current President, Velasco.

'Val Verde' is a fictional South American country which was the creation of screenwriter Steven de Souza who realised he needed to invent an imaginary state which could be used in film and TV productions without any fear of diplomatic or legal repercussions. The name was first used in *Commando*, and has since popped up in a number of action films including *Die Hard 2* (1990).

Bennet then reveals that he faked his own death in the hope that General Kirby would lead him to Matrix. 'You will do exactly as I tell you,' he tells Matrix.

'Fuck you!'

At this point Jenny is brought into the room, bound and gagged, and Matrix is told that if he cooperates and kills Velasco then Jenny will be returned to him unharmed.

Meanwhile General Kirby and a squad of soldiers have returned to Matrix's house and have discovered the bodies of Diaz, Harris and Jackson. One Jet Ranger helicopter is parked on the ground outside the house, while a second is hovering in the air nearby.

A little later, Bennet drives Matrix to Los Angeles Airport accompanied by Sully (David Patrick Kelly) and Henriques (Charles Meshack). He tells the ex-Special Forces Colonel that if he doesn't hear from either of his colleagues then Jenny will die. Matrix asks Bennet how much he is being paid for this operation, and he reveals that he was offered $100,000 but – on discovering that the job involved Matrix – he said that he would do it for nothing.

As Matrix is led to the airport buildings he turns and screams 'I'll be back, Bennet,' repeating his famous line from *The Terminator.* Sully then pushes some currency into

Matrix's breast pocket, which he says is beer money which will 'give us more time with your daughter'. Matrix is furious at his impudence:

'You're a funny guy, Sully. That's why I am going to kill you last.'

Matrix and Henriques board the airliner which is to take them to Val Verde – a Western Airlines DC-10 – and are given seats 7A and 7B in First Class. The flight attendant (Julie Hayek) asks him if he has any 'interior luggage', and he quips 'just him' – pointing at Henriques. Curiously, Henriques takes the window seat and lets Matrix sit next to the aisle: something that no-one trained in security matters would ever do.

Matrix is told that the flight time to Val Verde is 11 hours, which means it must be 5,500 miles from Los Angeles. However, the variant of DC-10 used by Western Airlines only has a range of 3,800 miles, so there would have to be a refuelling stop.

As the main door closes, Matrix asks for a blanket and pillow and, as soon as it arrives, he swiftly breaks Henriques's neck in one quick move with his left arm without attracting any attention. The 'Director's Cut' of this sequence shows that the 'neck breaking' was actually achieved in two steps – a sudden, backward blow with the left hand to knock out Henriques, followed by a twist of the neck (using both arms) to break it. These moves were suggested and approved by a military expert who was present on the set. However, the edited version of this shot – which appears on some DVD releases and TV versions – implies that the fractured neck was caused solely by Matrix's first backward blow as the twisting motion is not shown.

Matrix then props up the villain's head with a pillow and covers his body with a blanket to make it look as though he is just sleeping. He also tells the flight attendants not to disturb his friend as he is 'dead tired'. This is one of many Bond-style quips in the film.

As the aircraft taxies to the runway, Matrix gets up from his seat. One of the flight attendants tells him he can't do this, but Matrix claims to be 'airsick' and makes his way to the toilet. Once there, he steps into the adjacent one-person lift in the galley area and descends to the cargo hold in the lower level. There, he makes his way to the front of the plane, entering the nose-wheel compartment via a hatch. By this point the DC-10 is hurtling down the runway on its take-off run. Matrix climbs down the nose-wheel leg and holds on, just above the rolling wheels. To film this scene, a mock-up of the lower nose section of a DC-10 and its undercarriage leg was attached to a camera truck which drove down the runway at high speed while a stuntman stood in for Schwarzenegger. The rig included hydraulics to lift the leg skyward, simulating take-off.

As the plane lifts off and climbs beyond the threshold of the runway, Matrix jumps from the nose-wheel leg, falling about 500 feet into marshland – the water cushioning the impact. This would be an impossibility, as the water is only waist deep and – in reality – Matrix would have suffered fatal injuries from such a stunt. This shot was achieved using a dummy which was dropped from the nose-wheel leg, and received much praise at the time for its realism.

Having survived the fall without a scratch, Matrix makes his way back to the airport buildings and sets the counter on his electronic watch to 11.00 hours, giving him an indication of how long he has left until Henriques's death is discovered. This idea of the 'ticking clock' also appears in another of Joel Silver's action movies, *24 Hours* (1984), and was re-used in the long-running Fox TV series *24* (2001-14) which starred Kiefer Sutherland.

Meanwhile, back at the airport terminal, Sully is making a call on a payphone. On the other end of the line Arius (also in a public call box, by a marina) is pleased to hear his report, and tells Jenny that his father 'appears to be cooperating'. He informs her that she 'will be back with him soon', asking 'won't that be nice?'

'Not as nice as him smashing your face in,' replies Jenny.

On the other end of the line, Sully hangs up and then spots flight attendant Cindy (Rae Dawn Chong) finishing a call on another payphone. He starts to harass her.

'Sounds like you need a date.'

'I don't. You're really bugging me.'

The diminutive Sully suffers from 'small man syndrome', as he thinks he is devastatingly attractive to women and is not put off. He continues to follow Cindy into the airport car park while puffing on a cigarette. Eventually Cindy tells Sully to leave her alone and the gangster departs, rather disconsolate. 'You fucking whore', he mutters.

But Cindy's problems aren't over. As she prepares to get into her car, Matrix grabs her from behind while promising that he doesn't want to hurt her. He rips out the passenger seat of Cindy's car, a red 1965 Sunbeam Alpine IV convertible, and gets in just as Sully is leaving in his own car, a yellow Porsche 911. The Sunbeam Alpine was a British sports car produced by the Rootes Group from 1953 to 1955, and again from 1959 to 1968. It was actually the first vehicle driven by Sean Connery in a car chase in a Bond movie, as one featured in *Dr No* (1962).

Matrix and Cindy follow Sully to a shopping centre, where the gangster ascends to a higher level in an escalator as Matrix explains that his daughter has been kidnapped. He wants Cindy to go after Sully and pretend she is interested in him. Initially Cindy complies with his request and follows Sully into a restaurant, where the criminal intends to meet a colleague to negotiate a drug deal. The shopping centre used in the film was the Galleria in Sherman Oaks, and the restaurant (Kirwins) was created especially for the production.

Matrix looks at his watch timer – which reads 9.40 – as Cindy approaches a security guard. It is clear that at this stage she doesn't believe Matrix's story and thinks he may be a psycho. The security guard listens to Cindy's tale and calls up his colleagues by walkie-talkie. Soon two pairs of guards close in on Matrix from different directions, intent on apprehending him. Meanwhile, Sully spots Cindy and approaches her, thinking she may be interested in him after all.

Suddenly a fight breaks out between Matrix and the security guards. Despite being outnumbered four to one, the fit, strong ex-Special Forces man is more than a match for his poorly-trained opponents. Unfortunately the commotion is witnessed by an amazed Sully, who races to the nearest 'phone box to tell his bosses what has happened. Before he can make his call, Matrix uproots the box from the floor, breaking the connection. For this scene a lightweight balsa wood phonebox was constructed.

Now Matrix is involved in a fight with six security guards and is still getting the better of them. In the commotion, the gangster who was doing business with Sully gets shot by a security guard and falls off a balcony, spilling dollar notes everywhere. This is witnessed by Cindy, who realises in in an instant that Matrix must be telling the truth. As one security guard tries to shoot Matrix, Cindy pushes him down a staircase.

Sully makes his escape in a glass lift. Matrix uses a string of linked sausage balloons as a makeshift rope to swing onto the roof of the elevator. This stunt was carried out by a diminutive stunt performer, using a hidden cable inside the balloons, and was seamlessly edited into footage of Schwarzenegger standing on top of the lift. Despite Matrix's heroic efforts, Sully still escapes and drives off at high speed in his Porsche, pursued by Matrix and Cindy in her Alpine. After a furious car chase which starts in the streets of Los Angeles and ends in the more rural Mulholland Drive, Matrix knocks Sully's Porsche onto its left side.

He grabs the little gangster and hangs him upside down by his left foot over a cliff edge, saying that the 'only thing that matters now is gravity'. Despite Schwarzenegger's tremendous strength, it was impossible for him to hold Sully in the manner depicted in the film so he was suspended from a crane using a hidden cable.

Sully pleads for his life saying that Matrix needs him to find his daughter, but Matrix says that isn't true. He jangles a key fob with some attached keys in Sully's face (it is actually keys to a motel room which he has retrieved from Sully, though this is not obvious on initial viewing of the film).

Matrix then speaks to Sully:

'Remember I said I'd kill you last? I lied.'

Matrix drops Sully, who falls a great height and hits the ground, dying instantly, prompting another classic quip when Cindy asks what has happened to him: 'I let him go'. He then rights the rather bashed Porsche, and the two of them drive back to LA. As they head back to the city, Matrix shows Cindy a picture of his daughter.

As this is happening, Arius, Wells and Jenny arrive at the deposed dictator's villa (which is supposedly on an island off the coast of California, though this is not explained at this point in the film). In reality, the villa and adjacent military compound scenes were filmed in the Hearst Castle and adjacent grounds at San Simeon near Los Angeles, a location that has been used in many Hollywood films. Some scenes set in Arius's property were also filmed at the Harold Lloyd Estate at 1740 Green Acres Drive in Beverley Hills.

As Jenny is locked in a bedroom, Matrix's digital watch shows 7:57 as he and Cindy arrive at the 'Sunspot' Motel in LA. This was not a real hotel, but a set created for the film. Matrix jumps out and Cindy follows him.

'What are you doing?' says Matrix.

'Helping you get her back,' says Jenny. By this point in the film, Cindy has been totally converted to Matrix's cause.

Matrix uses the key he recovered from Sully to enter the motel room. Suddenly a large Cadillac convertible driven by another of Arius's henchmen – Cooke – parks outside. Thinking quickly, Matrix messes up the bed and unbuttons Cindy's blouse. He then goes into the bathroom, closes the door and turns on the shower just before Cooke knocks at the door. The heavily-built gangster is surprised to see Cindy.

'Where's Sully?'

'In the shower.'

'Who are you?'

'Room service.'

Matrix then emerges from the bathroom and fights Cooke. This is probably the best-staged fight in the film, and is reminiscent of those found in the early Bond pictures – particularly the well-known scrap between Sean Connery's 007 and Robert Shaw's SPECTRE baddie 'Red' Grant in the confines of a railway carriage compartment in *From Russia with Love* (1963).

Cooke holds his own against his opponent and reveals that he is an ex-Green Beret. In fact, Matrix is probably one as well, since this is the name given to the US Army Special Forces and he wears the unit's belt buckle throughout the film.

The two former soldiers' fight spills into the adjoining bedroom via a connecting door (which is the norm in American hotels and motels), and eventually Cooke dies when he accidentally becomes impaled on a sharp piece of wood.

Matrix and Cindy then search Cooke's car and the flight attendant finds an invoice from Patria Enterprises for 'Type 4 fuel for an amphibian aircraft'. An amphibian aircraft is a type of flying boat which has retractable landing gear to enable it to operate from both sea and land. The most famous amphibian aircraft would probably be the Consolidated PBY Catalina, which was manufactured in both amphibian and flying boat versions and used by the RAF and the US Navy during WW2. The British Short Sunderland, by comparison, was only ever made as a flying boat and lacked an undercarriage, though beaching gear (i.e. wheeled trolleys) were manufactured to enable it to be hauled up a slipway. However, amphibian aircraft don't require special fuel as they have the same engines as landplanes, so this plot point is incorrect.

Later, Matrix and Cindy arrive at the Patria Enterprises facility. The gate is locked with a padlock and chain, but Matrix breaks in and discovers that their warehouse is filled with assorted munitions destined for Val Verde. A 105mm lightweight howitzer can be seen in the background as Matrix hides under an armoured vehicle (a WW2 vintage M5 Stuart light tank).

Matrix encounters an employee who he beats up and puts in a cupboard. Then Cindy finds some documents supposedly giving the coordinates of Santa Barbara (a coastal town near LA). There is also a photo of an amphibian aircraft (a WW2 vintage Grumman Goose), and paperwork indicating a refuelling stop in San Pedro.

The pair return to the car, where Matrix announces they are 'going shopping'. Soon afterwards they arrive at 'Surplus City', where Matrix uses an excavator to 'ram raid' the facility. 'Surplus City' was a genuine retail unit, though an extra section was built on by the filmmakers to depict the hidden gun room at one side.

Matrix grabs a shopping cart and starts piling weapons into it. He also opens a power-operated door, which gives him access to a hidden safe room containing even more powerful weapons including machine guns and a four-barrelled M202 FLASH (Flame Assault Shoulder Weapon) 66mm rocket launcher. Another weapon visible in the background is a FIM-43 'Redeye' heat-seeking surface-to-air missile, the less-effective predecessor to the famous FIM-92 'Stinger'. Cindy returns to the car, but as Matrix is about to leave two armed cops arrive with weapons drawn.

'Don't even think about it,' says one of them (a popular clichéd line of dialogue in action movies).

The two policemen take Matrix away in a police van as the soldier looks at his watch, which reads 5:02. He tries to tell the cops what has happened and that they should contact General Kirby, but they don't believe him.

As the van stops at traffic lights Cindy (who has seen what has happened) draws up alongside them in the deceased Cooke's convertible (a 1976 Cadillac Eldorado). She looks at the cops and flirts with them, giving them the idea she may be a hooker. As the police van draws away, one of the cops looks in the rear view mirror and sees Cindy standing up.

'I think she has got something for us,' he says. He thinks she is about to flash her breasts.

Suddenly Cindy puts the large M202 four-barrelled rocket launcher on her shoulder and fires, but she is holding it back-to-front and a missile hits a lamppost behind her. The cops are shocked at the explosion, but before they have time to react Cindy fires again. This time the launcher is the right way round and an M74 round strikes the van, flipping it over. However, the recoil knocks Cindy over and she lands in the back seat (this is an error, since rocket weapons like the M202 and the wartime bazooka don't have any recoil).

The van's crash frees Matrix, and he runs toward's Cindy's car. How he escaped being burned alive by the incendiary warhead of the M74 rocket fired by the M202 launcher (the most likely outcome of Cindy's actions) is never explained.

'Where did you learn to do that?' says Matrix as he jumps into the passenger seat of the convertible. 'I read the instructions', replies Jenny.

Back at Arius's villa, the deposed dictator asks Wells how long it will be before Matrix arrives in Val Verde, and his henchman replies that it will be just two hours. He wonders if Matrix is going to cause any problems, but Wells reassures him that as long as he has his daughter he will not give him any difficulties. As the two villains discuss these matters, Jenny is still locked in her bedroom wondering if she could escape.

As Jenny is planning to break out, Matrix and Cindy have arrived at the pier where the amphibian aircraft is moored. The seaplane is a Grumman G-21 Goose, a small flying boat with twin 450 horsepower Pratt and Whitney R-985 Wasp Junior engines and a high wing, which first flew in 1937 and saw extensive service in WW2 with the US Navy and the British Fleet Air Arm. The Goose was used as a light transport and for air-sea rescue work, and could even carry small bombs or depth charges under its wings for anti-submarine patrol duties. The example used in the film, US civil registration N143DF, was destroyed in a hangar fire in 1999.

Cindy – who has been training as a private pilot – is not impressed, and calls it a 'canoe with wings'. As the pair board the aircraft, two soldiers drive up the pier in a Jeep and open fire with automatic weapons. As Cindy starts the aircraft's two engines, Matrix returns fire with his Uzi submachine gun. The soldiers are hit, and the Jeep goes over the side of the jetty into the water.

The Goose taxies away from the wharf and Cindy opens the throttles as the aircraft makes its take-off run. She isn't confident the seaplane is going to become airborne before it hits some obstacles, but Matrix reaches up and pushes both engine throttles 'through the gate'. This gives maximum power, and the Goose unsticks from the water and soars into the sky.

Back on the mainland, in a military control room, General Kirby tells one of his aides to keep monitoring the radio frequencies for any clue as to Matrix's whereabouts. At the same time, a coastguard operator (Bill Paxton) warns Cindy that her aircraft is entering the San Miguel gunnery range and that she must alter course. Matrix tells Cindy to stay on course, but to go low to avoid detection by radar. Bill Paxton is best known for playing Private Hudson in *Aliens* (1986), but also appeared in two other movies with Arnold Schwarzenegger – namely *The Terminator* (1984) and *True Lies* (1994).

In the meantime, Jenny has come up with a plan. She removes the door handle and uses it as a tool to prise away some small planks of wood which have been used to seal off the patio window. Once she has done that, she can escape.

Nearby, one of Arius's men is boasting about how 'cutting a little girl's throat is like slicing through butter'. Bennet tells him to put the knife away and shut up. He then complains to Arius about how his men are not really that tough, and how both Matrix and him could kill them 'just like that'. He then predicts that Matrix will return to kill Arius regardless of whether Jenny is alive or dead, and that he is the only person who can protect the deposed dictator. Bennet clearly hates Matrix, but it is never made clear in the screenplay what the Special Forces Colonel did to incur his wrath. Dialogue early in the film establishes that Bennet was thrown out of Matrix's unit, but the reason for this is never revealed.

As the sun rises, the Grumman Goose touches down in the water off the coast of Arius's island, and Matrix gets into a dinghy with all his weapons and equipment. Meanwhile, the DC-10 has landed in Val Verde and the passengers get off the aircraft – including an obviously dead Henriques on a stretcher. Arius's men see the body, notice the absence of Matrix, and realise he must still be in the USA. These Val Verde airport scenes were filmed at the old terminal at Long Beach Airport, California.

As the villains 'phone Arius to report what they have found, Matrix comes ashore in his dinghy and prepares for action. He puts on a tactical vest and takes as many weapons as he can carry including a pistol, knives, an automatic rifle, M67 grenades, a Claymore mine, and the mighty M202 four-barrelled rocket launcher we saw earlier.

Matrix approaches the villa and does a recce using binoculars. He then kills a guard with a knife as he prepares his attack. Arius has now received word that he wasn't on the plane, so he tells Bennet to kill Jenny.

As Bennet is on his way to murder her, Matrix sets up an M18 Claymore mine. Such weapons are usually detonated by a command wire, but the (fictitious) version shown in the film is radio-controlled, triggered by a hand-held switch. After killing the guard in the tower, Matrix detonates the Claymore, resulting in an enormous explosion which devastates the barrack blocks. This again is a case of 'Hollywood Science', as real Claymores are pure anti-personnel weapons which project steel balls at advancing enemy soldiers and don't cause huge orange fireballs.

On his way to deal with Jenny, Wells hears the explosions and seems genuinely pleased. 'Welcome back, John. So glad you could make it.' A moment later, he discovers Jenny has escaped and breaks through the remaining planks of wood blocking the French window.

Meanwhile Matrix is conducting a single-handed war against the garrison defending the installation and appears to be winning. First he destroys an entire truck load of soldiers with his missile launcher, and then he blows up a gate. As the battle rages, Jenny succeeds in contacting General Kirby using the radio in the Grumman Goose (which has the call-sign WX448) and asks for back-up.

Back at the villa, Matrix has become a one-man army as he decimates Arius's troops with his automatic rifle and M67 hand grenades. Eventually Matrix is chased into a large garden shed. He shuts the door behind him and takes off his vest. He has been wounded – though not fatally – on the right side of his abdomen, the famous 'flesh wound' of action movies. This is another popular Hollywood action movie cliché – any wound that does not involve a broken bone is a 'flesh wound' which can be 'cured' by removing the bullet (usually by an alcoholic, struck-off-the-medical-register doctor who has been temporarily sobered up with black coffee) and then stitching up the area or even just cauterizing it with a red-hot poker. After such treatment the hero makes an instant recovery and is soon fit for action, when in reality such a wound would take months to heal (during which time there would be considerable temporary disability).

The shed is surrounded by five soldiers, who riddle it with automatic fire. Nobody could survive this intense barrage. After expending considerable ammunition the soldiers kick open the door, but Matrix is nowhere to be seen. Suddenly the resourceful former Special Forces soldier swings down from the rafters and kills his attackers. One is despatched with a garden fork. Another two have the tops of their heads sliced off with deftly thrown circular saw blades (an impossibility, as the skull is too tough). One more is attacked with a long knife.

The 'Director's Cut' DVD and Blu-Ray has a longer, more graphic version of this scene in which one soldier has his arm amputated above the elbow. The script had a scene in which Matrix removes the disembodied arm and smacks the soldier with its hand, but this shot was scrapped as it was considered too horrific.

Matrix captures the most powerful of the attackers' weapons – a mighty M60, 7.62mm light machine gun – and runs across the roof, cutting down more soldiers with bursts of fire from his weapon.

This image of a very muscular guy stripped to the waist firing an M60 from his hip also appears in *Rambo: First Blood Part II* (1985), and was probably the reason that *Commando* and *Rambo* were perceived as direct competitors. Another resemblance between the two films was that the characters of General Kirby in *Commando* and Colonel Trautman (Richard Crenna) in the *Rambo* films were very similar.

Eventually Matrix has killed off all the defending troops except Bennet, and concentrates on hunting down Arius who he swiftly despatches after a brief gun battle. By this time, Jenny has made her way to the boiler room where she is found by Bennet. The boiler room was a real facility found on the Fox lot. As Matrix approaches him, Bennet holds a gun to Jenny's head and threatens to kill her. But Matrix talks him into dropping the gun and releasing the girl, then engaging in hand-to-hand combat with fists and knives.

The two soldiers battle each other, and at one point Bennet is thrown against an electrical control panel and briefly electrocuted. But he shrugs it off and continues to battle Matrix. The fight becomes more desperate, so Bennet grabs a pistol which he points at Matrix, threatening to shoot him 'between the balls'. As he is about to pull the trigger, Matrix throws a length of pipe at him which goes through his chest and into a steam duct behind. Bennet dies clutching the pipe as Matrix makes another Bond-style quip: 'Let off some steam, Bennet'.

The crisis over, Matrix walks onto the beach, carrying Jenny as General Kirby's men arrive in three helicopters – two Jet Rangers and a Bell UH-1 Huey. They are followed by the Grumman Goose (piloted by Cindy) which makes a perfect sea landing.

'Did you leave anything for us?' asks Kirby as he dismounts from his helicopter.

'Just bodies.'

Kirby suggests that Matrix might like to reform his unit, but the ex-Special Forces soldier declines the offer. It is implied that he and Cindy are going to start a relationship, with his new partner becoming Jenny's stepmother. Now reunited, the three board the Goose and fly off as the end credits roll.

The film was released on 4 October 1985 and was number one at the box office in the USA for three consecutive weeks. Eventually it made over $57.5 million against a budget of $10m.

In view of the film's financial and critical success, a sequel has been considered many times over the last three decades, but none has yet been made – in contrast to the *Rambo* franchise, which currently runs to four films. However, in 2010 Fox announced plans to remake the film with David Ayer directing and Sam Worthington as Matrix. The new production is reportedly to have a more realistic approach.

One popular misconception is that the 1988 movie *Die Hard* was originally to feature Arnold Schwarzenegger reprising his role as John Matrix, instead of Bruce Willis as John McClane. Some years ago, Steven de Souza denied this account completely, though it must be said that such a movie *could* have been made as the character of John Matrix would have fitted into *Die Hard*. Although Arnold Schwarzenegger never played John Matrix again, it must be noted that his character in *Predator* (1987) – 'Dutch' Schultz – is very similar to Matrix.

The fact that only one *Commando* movie was ever made has probably helped it to achieve its status as a cult classic, and one of the quintessential action movies of the eighties.

## *Commando* (1985)
## Production Credits

Director: Mark L. Lester
Screenplay: Steven E. de Souza
Story: Joseph Loeb III and
Matthew Weisman

### Cast

John Matrix - Arnold
Schwarzenegger
Cindy - Rae Dawn Chong
Arius - Dan Hedaya
Bennett - Vernon Wells
Major General Franklin Kirby -
James Olson
Sully - David Patrick Kelly
Jenny Matrix - Alyssa Milano
Cooke - Bill Duke
Lawson - Drew Snyder
Leslie - Sharon Wyatt
Forrestal - Michael De Lano
Jackson - Bob Minor
Harris - Mike Adams
Diaz - Carlos Cervantes
Soldier - Lenny Juliano
Henriques - Charles Meshack
Western Flight Attendants -
Chelsea Field, Julie Hayek
Latin Man - Hank Calia
Cates - Walter Scott
Biggs - Greg Wayne Elam
Mall Security Guard - George
Fisher
Officer in Galleria - Phil Adams
Girl in Bed at Motel - Ava
Cadell
Boy in Bed at Motel - Mikul
Robins

Vega - Branscombe Richmond
Fred - Matt Landers
Daryl - Peter Du Point
Kirby's Driver - Tom Simmons
Intercept Officers - Bill Paxton,
Richard D. Reich
Val Verde Heavies - John
Reyes, Billy Cardenas, Edward
Reyes
Woman Officer - Vivian Daily
Young Guerrilla - Thomas
Rosales Jr
Guerrilla - Ronald C. McCarty
Police Officer - Jim Painter

### Producers

Producer: Joel Silver
Associate Producers: Matthew
Weisman, Joseph Loeb III
Co-Associate Producers:
Stephanie Brody, Robert
Kosberg

### Music

Composer: James Horner

### Cinematography

Cinematographer: Matthew F.
Leonetti

### Film Editing

Film Editors: Glenn Farr, Mark
Goldblatt, John F. Link
Casting: Jackie Burch
Production Design: John Vallone
Set Decoration: Robert Gould

## Make-up Department
Make-up Artists: Joe McKinney,
William Turner
Hair Stylist: Joe Zapata

## Production Management
Unit Production Manager:
Larry Kostroff

## Second Unit Director or Assistant Director
Second Assistant Editor: K.C.
Colwell
Second Unit Director: Bennie E.
Dobbins
DGA Trainee: Karen Gaviola
First Assistant Director: Beau
E.L. Marks
Additional 2nd Assistant
Director: Brad Yacobian

## Art Department
Set Dresser: Craig Baron
Lead Man: William D. Derham
Propmaker Foreman: Bruce Di
Valerio
Construction Coordinator: Cal
Di Valerio
Construction Painter: Ron
Esposito
Set Dresser: Douglas Forsmith
Production Painter: Jaymes
Hinkle
Production Illustrator: Nikita
Knatz
Greensman: Mark Lapotsky
Property Master: Doug
Madison
Set Designer: Dan Maltese

Assistant Property Masters:
David Quick, John M. Shenk,
Tom Shaw Jr
Construction Foreman: William
Boyd

## Sound Department
Re-Recording Mixers: Don J.
Bassman, Kevin F. Cleary,
Richard Overton
Foley Recordist: Gary Bolger
Special Sound Effects: Frederick
J. Brown
ADR Mixer: Kevin Carpenter
Sound Editor: Richard Corwin
Foley Artist: Evelyn Dutton
Stereo Sound Consultant
(Dolby): Jim Fitzpatrick
Sound Recordist: Craig Heath
Sound Editors: Pieter Hubbard,
David Ice, Michael Corrigan,
William Hartman
Cable Person: Brent Johnson
Production Sound Mixer: Don
Johnson
Foley Artist: Margie O'Malley,
Gail Ganley Steele
ADR Editor: Glad Pickering,
Ronald Sinclair
Assistant Sound Effects Editor:
Michelle Pleis
Supervising ADR Editor: Hank
Salerno
Boom Operator: Jules Strasser
Sound Re-Recordist: Tim Webb
ADR Recordist: Vic Zaslav

## Visual Effects

Matte Artist: Jim Danforth
Visual Effects Supervisor: Alan
G. Markowitz

## Stunts

Stunt Performers: Michael
Adams, Bruce Paul Barbour,
Simone Boisseree, May Boss,
Jophery Brown, Tony Brubaker,
Jerry Brutsche, Richard E.
Butler, Roger Callard, Carl
Ciarfalio, Justin De Rosa, Vince
Deadrick Sr, Leon Delaney, Nick
Dimitri, Bennie E. Dobbins,
Richard L. Duran, Stephanie
Epper, Diamond Farnsworth,
George Fisher, Buddy Gilyard,
Sandra Gimpel, Bob Harris, John
Hock, Larry Holt, Jeff Jensen,
John M. Johnson, Harold Jones,
Steve Kelso, Kimberley King,
Joel Kramer, William T. Lane,
Lane Levitt, David Le Bell, Gary
McLarty, Tom Morga, Jeff
O'Haco, Jeff Ramsey, Larry
Randles, Mario Roberts, Ronne
Rondell Jr, Thomas Rosales Jr,
Rick Sawaya, Ben Scott, John
Sherrod, Tony Snegoff, Frank J.
Sparks, Ceci Vendrell, Michael
M. Vendrell, Greg Walker,
Rock Walker, Richard Warlock,
Jerry Wills, Brayton W. Yerkes,
Spiro Razatos
Stunt Double for Arnold
Schwarzenegger: Peter Kent,
Joel Kramer

## Camera and Electrical Department

Dolly Grip: Mark Averill
Best Boy: Lloyd Barcroft, Patrick
Blymyer
Second Assistant Camera: Doug
Beal
Second Company Grip: John
Donnelly
Best Boy (Electric): Bob Ellis, Ed
Thompson
Lamp Operator: Frank Tobin,
Robert Fiore
First Assistant Camera: John R.
Leonetti, Tony Rivetti
Key Grip: John Linder
Still Photographer: Bruce
McBroom
Camera Operator: Michael St
Hilaire
Steadicam Operator: Joe
Valentine
Dolly Grip: Dave Wachtman
Camera Technician: Ryne Niner

## Casting Department

Casting Associate: David
Gonzales
Extras Casting: Jim Green, Carl
Joy
Casting Assistant: Billy Da
Mota

## Costume and Wardrobe Department

Costumer (Women): Kathie
Gale
Costumer: Enid Harris
Costume Supervisor: Bob Harris

**Editorial Department**
Assistant Film Editors: Paul Anderson, Carrie Ellison, Jospeh Guresky
Negative Cutter: Jack Hooper
Apprentice Film Editor: David Janson
Head Colour Timer: Jim Schurman
Supervising Editor: Howard Kunin

**Location Management**
Location Managers: Robert Decker, John Panzarella

**Music Department**
Assistant Music Editor: Thomas A. Carlson
Vocal Effects Advisor: Raechel Donahue
Special Music Consultant: Danny Goldberg
Music Producers: Jay Gruska, James Horner
Orchestrator: Greg McRitchie
Music Editor: Ken Runyon
Music Scoring: Mixer Dan Wallin

**Transportation Department**
Transportation Coordinator: Whitey Ellison
Transportation Captain: Wayne Morris
Drivers: Ken Bellanca, Duke Busby, John Hood, Joe Rand, Julio Salazar, Robert Sweet, Joe Tremblay, Mike Wacker, Cary Kelley
Transportation: James Nordberg

**Other Crew**
Production Assistant: Anthony Blake Brand
Craft Service: Dennis Chase
Helicopter Pilot: John Gamble
Assistant Auditor: Debbie Gaudio
Production Accountant: Larry Hand
Caterer: Paul Hibler
Police Coordinator: Fred Inman
Grumman Goose Pilot: Herb Johnson
First Aid: Howard Keys
Assistant to Arnold Schwarzenegger: Anita Lerner
Production Coordinator: Richard Libegott
Publicity Coordinator: Andrew Lipschultz
Helicopter Pilots: Peter McKernan Sr, Ross Reynolds, Michael Tamburo, Al Cerullo, Charles A. Tamburo, Peter McKernan Jr
Production Assistant: Steve McNichols
Production Secretary: Lisa Meechan
Assistant to Mark L. Lester: Leslie Paonessa
Apprentice Location Managers: George Parra, Cliff Taylor
Assistants to Joel Silver: Ron Rotholz, Mary C. Thomas

Production Associate: Elaine K. Thompson
Script Supervisor: Marion Tumen
Martial Arts Specialist: Michael M. Vendrell
Digital Distribution: Tyler Atkinson
Teacher: Arlene Singer
Knife Design: Jack Crain
Military Consultant: Jason Cant

Aerial Coordinator: Charles A. Tamburro

**Special Effects**
Special Effects Coordinator: Henry Millar
Special Effects: Doug Hubbard, Henry Millar, Jay King, Mike Millar, John Peyser, Richard Thompson, Roger Lifsey, Bill Mattox

# 6

(1986)

*Silver Pictures*

**Director**: George P. Cosmatos
**Producers**: Menahem Golan and Yoram Globus
**Screenwriter**: Sylvester Stallone

AS mentioned in the chapter on *Rambo: First Blood Part II* (1985), Sylvester Stallone's career really took off with the first *Rocky* film in 1976 and has continued – with various peaks and troughs – until fairly recently. He is best remembered for the *Rocky* and *Rambo* franchises – which in combination totalled 11 films – but there is one movie that is often overlooked in any assessment of his career, and that is the action picture *Cobra* which premiered in 1986.

In 1974, former advertising copywriter Paula Gosling wrote a crime thriller called *A Running Duck* about an innocent advertising executive – Clare Randall – being pursued by hitmen after inadvertently witnessing an assassin preparing for action. The book, which was published in 1978, was a success and was later released in the USA under the revised title *Fair Game*.

A few years later, Warner Brothers decided that the book would form the basis of an excellent action thriller and invited Sylvester Stallone to write a screenplay as well as play the lead role. In the event Stallone threw out most of Gosling's material, and instead drew on portions of a screenplay he had already written for *Beverly Hills Cop* (1984) in which he also hoped to star as the lead, Axel Foley. As scripted by Stallone, that movie would have had a dark feel with lots of action. Eventually the producers rejected Stallone's draft and went for a much more light-hearted approach, with Eddie Murphy in the lead role.

This had an impact on *Cobra,* which became a much harder and more violent action picture than would be expected from reading Paula Gosling's book. Very few of Gosling's original ideas survive in Stallone's script, which retains several of her character names, some situations and little else. In addition, while Gosling's novel is told from the point of view of her lead character – advertising executive Clare Randall – the screenplay centres around Stallone's character, maverick policeman Marion Cobretti (the 'Cobra' of the title).

My own view (after reading Gosling's original novel) is that the film is a lot better than the book (which at times is too intellectual for its own good), and *Cobra* is essentially a reboot of *Dirty Harry* (1971), the gritty action picture which – along with *Bullitt* (1968), also set in San Francisco – redefined the American cop movie. There are many similarities in the themes of both *Dirty Harry* and *Cobra.* Both feature a maverick cop armed with a powerful weapon who can't play by the rules and is good at killing psychos. Both films have scenes in which the hero comes into conflict with the bureaucrats of the Police and Legal Departments, who are obsessed with correct protocols and criminals' rights. Ironically, one of Cobretti's chief antagonists in the film,

Detective Monte, is played by Andrew Robinson who gave such a brilliant performance as the psychotic serial killer Scorpio in *Dirty Harry*. Incidentally, Cobra's partner – Tony Gonzales – is played by Reni Santoni, who was Inspector Harry Callahan's sidekick, Chico, in the earlier picture.

The film was directed by George Pan Cosmatos, a Greco-Italian who started off his career making Italian films and later helmed *The Cassandra Crossing* (1976) and *Escape to Athena* (1979), the latter being one of the oddest WW2 movies ever made with its casting of Roger Moore as a German officer! In 1985, Cosmatos directed Sylvester Stallone in the second Rambo movie, *Rambo: First Blood Part II*, and it was this which led to his assignment as the director of *Cobra*.

The producers were Menahem Golan and Yoram Globus, who had set up the Cannon Group some years before and were responsible for a large number of Hollywood action movies – particularly those featuring Charles Bronson and Chuck Norris.

The film begins with a close-up of artwork of a cobra's head, with a voice-over from Sylvester Stallone: 'In America there's a burglary every 11 seconds... an armed robbery every 65 seconds... a violent crime every 25 seconds... a murder every 24 seconds... 250 rapes a day'. As the voice-over concludes, the camera pulls back to reveal that the cobra's head artwork is painted on the white handgrip of a black 9mm Colt National Match pistol. The gun then points towards the camera against a red background. This whole sequence is very similar to the title section of the second *Dirty Harry* film, *Magnum Force* (1973), which opens with a voiceover from Clint Eastwood on the merits of the.44 Smith and Wesson Magnum revolver: 'You're looking at a '44 Magnum, the most powerful handgun in the world. One shot from this would blow your head clean off your shoulders. Are you feeling lucky?' as a black gun swings towards the camera against a red backdrop.

The action then shifts to a shot of a character on a motorbike riding against the rising sun. The motorbike and rider appear black against the red sky, maintaining a visual continuity with the title sequence. Then there is a jump cut to a group of individuals holding an axe in each arm, which they clink together above their heads. A blazing cauldron is in the background.

Meanwhile, the motorcycle rider (Marco Rodriguez) drives up to the King supermarket and parks his bike. He looks sinister with his dark glasses, moustache, woolly hat and dark casual jacket. Quickly he brings out a Remington 870 pump action shotgun from under his coat and starts to slaughter the shoppers.

Within minutes, a large number of police officers arrive at the supermarket accompanied by a Bell Jet Ranger helicopter and several vehicles. Police hostage negotiator Detective Monte (Andrew Robinson) attempts to defuse the situation. Monte is a very different character from Scorpio in *Dirty Harry*, as this time he is the smartly-dressed consummate bureaucrat with jacket, shirt, tie and glasses. He could quite easily be a politically-correct policeman in 21st Century Britain with the current emphasis on risk assessments, high-viz jackets, recognising people's rights and treating matters in a 'sensitive' way. As the negotiations appear to be getting nowhere, Captain Sears (Art La Fleur) decides to call in 'The Cobra' – the nickname of policeman Marion Cobretti (Sylvester Stallone).

The supermarket gunman proves to be a real psycho, because he lets one of the hostages go free and then shoots him in the back as he is running to safety. The man falls dead among some Christmas trees and other decorations, thus establishing that the movie takes place around Christmas time, just like many other Hollywood action movies of the period including *Lethal Weapon* (1987) and *Die Hard* (1988).

Help is soon at hand, as Cobretti arrives in his highly distinctive car – a dark grey 1950 Mercury. The vehicle is in immaculate condition, and highly customised with a personalised numberplate (AWSOM 50). The car was actually owned by Stallone, but three other expendable 'stunt double' Mercurys were created for the production. Cobretti has a number of distinctive trademarks. He likes wearing dark clothes – black leather gloves, V-necked top, jacket, blue denim jeans, and cowboy boots – and often has a match between his lips (though he doesn't smoke). It is interesting that Cobretti wears mainly black clothes throughout the movie, suggesting that he is a 'dark' character though on the side of the law. This is a reversal of the usual rule in cowboy movies in which the good guys wear white and the bad guys wear black.

While Cobretti makes his way into the supermarket, the psycho fires twice, screaming that what he is doing is 'the way of the new world'. As Cobretti ponders over a suitable strategy to deal with the criminal, he opens a can of Coors beer, drinks a few swigs and then throws away the half-empty can to make a noise and attract fire. Gradually, Cobretti works his way round the shelves and picks up a microphone with a curly lead which is connected to the supermarket's PA system. Immediately he antagonizes his opponent: 'Hey, dirtbag! You're a lousy shot. You wasted a kid for nothing, so I think it's time to waste you'. Cobretti bursts through a door and confronts the psycho, who is holding a family at gunpoint and is threatening to blow up the supermarket. Cobretti replies nonchalantly that he should just go ahead, as he doesn't shop there: 'Just relax, amigo. If you want to talk, we'll talk. I'm a sucker for big conversation'. But the psycho refuses and asks for the TV cameras to be brought in. Cobretti says he can't do that: 'I don't deal with psychos. I put them away'.

'I'm no psycho; I'm a hero of the New World!' replies the killer. 'You're a disease. I'm the cure', replies Cobretti, who then throws a knife at the killer's chest and blasts him with a few rounds from his customised Colt handgun before releasing the hostages. 'You're a disease. I'm the cure' (or sometimes 'Crime is a disease, I'm the cure!') is Cobretti's catchphrase in this movie, again linking it with the *Dirty Harry* movies which all had their own catchphrases such as 'Go ahead, make my day' from the fourth *Dirty Harry* movie, *Sudden Impact* (1983), and 'You're shit out of luck' from the last in the series, *The Dead Pool* (1988).

As Cobretti makes his way out the supermarket and the hostages are taken away, the TV newsmen try to interview him as Monte criticizes his use of hard-line methods. One TV reporter points out that people are entitled to protection from the law – even criminals – and Cobretti responds by pulling back a sheet and showing the reporter the corpse of one of the supermarket attacker's victims. 'You tell that to his family', he says bluntly.

As the sun is setting over the Pacific Ocean, the action shifts to a beach in Los Angeles where Cobretti is trying to park his cherished classic car. The parking space by the sidewalk isn't big enough, so he simply moves another car forward a few feet by nudging its rear end with his front bumper. The occupant of the car is enraged by his behaviour and jumps out to confront Cobretti, who notices that he is a smoker and pulls the cigarette from his mouth, pointing out that it is bad for his health. He then rips the man's T-shirt, telling him to clean up his act.

Cobretti walks across the road to his apartment, dumping a newspaper in his barbecue. He enters the front door and goes into his flat, making his way to the kitchen where he takes a cardboard pizza carton and an eggbox from the fridge. There is only one slice of pizza left and even that is too much for him, so he simply cuts a small triangle from it with a pair of scissors and starts to eat without bothering to remove his gloves. He opens the eggbox, revealing that it contains a small bottle of gun oil and some weapon tools. As he sits down to eat his pizza and clean his gun, he watches a television programme – a Christmas-themed cartoon. But then Cobretti changes channels to view a TV news programme which is covering the story of the so-called 'Night Slasher' who is terrorising people in Los Angeles. His latest victim is a 22 year old female. Fifteen other people are believed to have been killed by him. His trademark is that he always wears black leather gloves and uses various weapons including a claw hammer, knives, and axes.

A little later, the proprietor of a small, grubby cafe called 'Mugs Up, Coffee Time' is closing down her business for the evening. As she walks to her car she notices an old blue van (a 1970 Ford Econoline) nearby with suspicious looking people hanging about. Quickly she unlocks her car, gets in and locks the door. Almost immediately her car is surrounded by men wearing nylon stocking masks who smash their way in using axes, then kill her.

In the meantime, at the LA Police mortuary a pathologist is carrying out a post-mortem on one of the 'Night

Slasher's victims. He says there is no distinct pattern behind the killings, and Cobretti suggests that perhaps there is more than one killer. His opinion upsets Monte, who points out that pathology is not Cobretti's speciality and that he is reluctant to let him deal with the case.

Cobretti is angry and says that 'as long as we play by these bullshit rules and the killer doesn't, we will lose'. Later, at the LA Police firing range with his buddy Tony Gonzales (Reni Santoni), he suggests that all they can do is wait for another murder to happen again. He then displays his incredible marksmanship with a pistol. This 'police shooting gallery' sequence is another reference to the *Dirty Harry* movies; in this case the second entry in the series, *Magnum Force* (1973).

Meanwhile, the mysterious gang of murderers are committing another dastardly act. Using their van, they drive into the rear end of a silver Volkswagen 1600 'Squareback' station wagon. Socially dysfunctional gang member Nancy Stalk (Lee Garlington) jumps out and goes up to the offside front window of the VW. The VW driver is very upset, asking her 'How could you possibly have hit me? Have you been drinking?' 'Yes', replies Stalk, with a weird expression on her face. Her behaviour alarms the lady, but immediately she is overwhelmed by other members of the gang who surround her vehicle, get into her car and murder her. Not long afterwards, model Ingrid Knudsen (Brigitte Nielsen) is driving her silver CJ-7 Laredo jeep past the two vehicles. Even though she has not seen the murder taking place, she spots the odd-looking gang leader, twigs that something is amiss, and realises she has to exit the area as quickly as possible. Unfortunately the leader of the gang – the 'Night Slasher' himself (Brian Thompson) – sees her numberplate and memorises it.

Later, the Los Angeles police arrive at the scene of the murder but the gang have long gone. Gang member Nancy Stalk – who actually works for the LA Police – uses their computer system to get the name and address of the driver of the jeep. She discovers that she is Ingrid Knudsen, living at 3111 Fourth Street, Santa Monica 90405.

The next scene is set in a parking lot in front of an LA tower block as Cobretti polishes the roof of his beloved car while he awaits the arrival of his colleagues. Gonzales, Monte and Captain Sears soon arrive in their cars, and the four officers confer. Sears points out that Cobretti knows every 'sicko' in Los Angeles, and he gives him instructions to 'shake them down, do what you do'. Monte, however, cautions him about not 'wasting the wrong guy' as he has apparently done before.

Once Monte has left, Gonzales – halfway through munching a chocolate bar – tells Cobretti he would like to celebrate when this is all over by punching a hole in Monte's chest. Cobretti comments that he is 'too violent', and it is all down to his consumption of sugar.

This is another recurring theme in the film, as Cobretti is into healthy eating while everyone around him enjoys scoffing junk food. Cobretti berates Gonzales over his diet, saying that he should be eating things like 'prunes, raisins, fish and rice'. This is a case of art imitating life, as Stallone was himself a fitness fanatic who ate healthily and trained hard to develop a powerful physique for his many action roles.

The next scene is set in a photographic studio where Ingrid is doing a photo shoot. Former Danish model Brigitte Nielsen – who was only 22 when she made the picture – had previously starred in *Red Sonja* (1985) and *Rocky IV* (1985).

At the same time, Cobretti is investigating the rougher parts of LA, including checking out people who are sleeping rough in cardboard boxes. He also visits tattoo parlours, as the 'Supermarket Killer' had a highly unusual tattoo on his wrist. Meanwhile, the 'Night Slasher' is sharpening his very distinctive curved knife on a carborundum stone in preparation for his next assault. The knife was made specially for the film by craftsman Herman Schneider, and incorporated several spikes in addition to a razor-sharp curved blade.

The 'Night Slasher' and his gang are waiting inside their van in an underground car park beneath the photographic studio. Ingrid asks a security guard to escort her to her car, and her photographer Dan (who is desperate to get her into bed) also offers to walk her to her vehicle. In Paula Gosling's original novel, Dan was the name of the female heroine Clare's boyfriend.

As Dan and Ingrid are making their way to the car, the security guard finds Ingrid's handbag in the studio and goes back down in the lift to give it to her. By this time Ingrid has reached her Jeep and realised that she has forgotten her bag. As she makes her way back to the lift to return to the studio, the gang exits their vehicle and attack Dan. One gang member tries to hit Ingrid with an axe, but accidentally cuts through a water pipe instead. Dan is then killed and Ingrid runs towards the elevator, desperately pressing on the lift button repeatedly. Suddenly the lift door opens and the security guard arrives, telling Ingrid to get out of the way so he can shoot at the attackers. But he is overwhelmed by sheer weight of numbers, and is then killed when the gang drive their blue Ford van at the lift. A gang member emerges from the vehicle wearing a stocking mask, but Ingrid is hiding. Suddenly the sound of police sirens is heard, and the gang have to leave the area rapidly.

The next scene is set in Los Angeles Central Hospital, where Ingrid has been given an intravenous tranquilliser. She is feeling drowsy. Cobretti is standing to the right of the hospital trolley while Gonzales is sitting to her left.

Gonzales points out that they are really two nice guys, but they are here to ask some bad questions. He asks her if she has had any threats or odd 'phone calls in the last few weeks. She says 'no', but then remembers the 'creepy guy' she saw in the underpass earlier that evening.

Cobretti is interested to hear this, and realises that the attack on her must be connected with what she witnessed in the underpass earlier that evening. He asks what time this was, and Ingrid says it was about 10pm. Cobretti is also curious as to what it was about the odd guy that scared Ingrid, and she responds that it was 'the way he looked at me'. He asks Ingrid if she saw anything else, and she mentioned that she saw three people in total.

Meanwhile the 'Night Slasher' is sharpening his knife again as Nancy Stalk arrives. She points out that Ingrid knows his face, and so she must be killed before she can give evidence. The 'Night Slasher' dyes his hair dark brown to alter his appearance.

Back at police headquarters, an artist has prepared a sketch of the 'Night Slasher' based on Ingrid's description. Cobretti says that she will have to be moved to a safe house the following day. Gonzales mentions to Cobretti as they are leaving how nice looking she really is, and Cobretti pretends not to have noticed.

Later, Cobretti parks his 1950 Mercury car behind the big saloon on the road outside his flat. This time the owner of the saloon has left him plenty of room to park, having learned his lesson. As he is checking mugshots and fingerprints on his personal computer, the 'Night Slasher' arrives at the Los Angeles Central Hospital with the intention of murdering Ingrid. He goes up an escalator as Ingrid rests in bed and then attacks a cleaner in a storeroom, stealing his uniform, ID badge, and glasses. Suitably disguised, the 'Night Slasher' enters a lift but is soon joined by a female phlebotomist who complains about him using that particular lift, saying that he should be using the service elevator instead.

As Cobretti is checking fingerprints on the police records, the 'Night Slasher' ascends in the hospital lift, hiding his fearsome large, sharp knife behind his back. He is prepared to murder the phlebotomist if necessary, but fortunately she gets off at an intermediate floor after telling him that in future he should use the correct elevator.

While Cobretti is working, he receives a 'phone call from Gonzales who is in the police office. Cobretti asks him what he is doing there, and he says he got a call from HQ saying that he was wanted at the office. Cobretti realises that he has been deliberately called away from guard duty at the hospital by a bogus call in order to make life easier for the bad guys, who are clearly intent on murdering Ingrid. Suddenly two gang members arrive at Cobretti's apartment. Both are wearing stocking masks. Cobretti shoots one immediately and narrowly misses the second. He chases the second villain and fires at him as he runs down the fire escape, causing him to fall to his death. Cobretti runs to his car, gun in hand, and drives as fast as he can to the hospital. In the meantime, back at the hospital one of the nurses is checking an elderly patient and finds her lying dead amongst bloodstained sheets. She screams and, as she does so, the 'Night Slasher' (who is hiding under the bed) grabs her leg.

The 'Night Slasher' then tries to stab Ingrid in her bed, but she is not there as she is emerging from the en-suite bathroom. As Cobretti races to the hospital in his car, the 'Night Slasher' is trying to get at Ingrid, who has locked herself in her bathroom. The 'Night Slasher' batters on the door – it is only a matter of time before he gets in. He then takes out his large knife and starts smashing the door to pieces with its massive, razor-sharp curved blade. Ingrid manages to escape through a second door, which gets her into a cupboard next to the bathroom from where she runs into a main corridor and sets off the fire alarm, causing large numbers of people to appear. As they all arrive, Ingrid hides, meaning that the 'Night Slasher' realises that he cannot now carry out his mission and decides to escape. Cobretti arrives and hugs Ingrid.

Although the hospital sequence is very exciting, it was a cliché even in 1986. Both *Bullitt* (1968) and *Black Sunday* (1977), to give just two examples, contain similar scenes where a hitman arrives at a hospital with the intention of killing a wounded witness.

Later, at a briefing back at police headquarters, Cobretti explains that he thinks that the bad guys must have a person on the inside working for the police department. Monte refuses to accept his assessment. This again is a familiar action movie trope – a 'mole' inside the department who is feeding information to the bad guys. The idea features in numerous action movies such as *Bullitt* (1968) and *Day of the Jackal* (1973), plus TV series such as *The Professionals* (1977-83), *Spooks* (2002-10) and *24* (2001-14).

Afterwards, at LA Central Hospital Cobretti and Gonzales interview Ingrid once more. She is convinced that the 'Night Slasher' is going to get her eventually. Cobretti is eating an apple, still wearing his trademark gloves. Police officer Nancy Stalk has been assigned to the case.

As Cobretti leaves the building by going down an escalator he talks to Monte. He points out that three policemen were assigned to guard Ingrid at the hospital, but two were taken off duty. Why was this so? However, Monte is still hostile and is unwilling to listen to what Cobretti has to say.

Cobretti and Ingrid set off in the policeman's car as Gonzales and Nancy follow in a light grey saloon. They haven't gone very far before a brown pickup truck drives out of an alley and crashes into Gonzales and Nancy's car, putting it out of action. Then two villains drive up in a grey saloon and open fire on Cobretti's vehicle with a pump-action shotgun. The detective accelerates rapidly and fastens his harness. Cobretti's car doesn't have normal seatbelts – instead, it has four-point harnesses as used in racing cars and fighter aircraft. A very exciting high-speed car chase follows in which Cobretti's souped-up 1950 Mercury is sandwiched between the pickup truck behind and the grey saloon in front. The bad guys in the pickup put two rounds into the boot of Cobretti's car, but the policeman responds by doing a 180° handbrake turn which enables him to spray the pickup with 9mm submachine gun fire. Cobretti uses a very unusual weapon in the film: a Finnish Jatimatic 9mm submachine gun, which was only introduced in 1983 and has a futuristic appearance.

The pickup explodes and crashes. Cobretti's car and the grey saloon then go down a narrow alley side-by-side, and the chase continues in a multi-storey car park where Cobretti's car jumps off the first level. Both cars are battered wrecks by this time, although they are still capable of moving. Next, the bad guys blow up two fuel tankers which are situated across the road, but Cobretti manages to drive between the flaming vehicles. He then uses his car's nitrous oxide injection system to accelerate away from the scene rapidly, and then the vehicle flies off the ground as it jumps over a hump-backed bridge.

Nitrous Oxide ($NO_2$) injection is a system for boosting the performance of piston engines for short periods using a cylinder of 'laughing gas', which is piped into the carburettor or fuel injection system. It was used in the final stages of WW2 to boost the performance of fighter planes, and one aircraft which used it to great effect was the De Havilland Mosquito night fighter.

By now Cobretti's Mercury is chasing the villains' car, and the action moves to the Los Angeles docks where Cobretti's car rolls over. Although it is very battered, it ends up standing on all four wheels and Cobretti helps an uninjured Ingrid out of the car. There is a continuity error at this point, as the villain's grey sedan can be seen already smashed into a boat – the scene in which it crashes into the vessel having disappeared during the editing process.

Back at police HQ, Cobretti repeats his theory that there is a whole army of killers out there rather than just one man, but Monte still doubts this. Cobretti wants to take Ingrid out of Los Angeles as he feels she will be safer in the country, but the others are sceptical about this idea. Monte and Cobretti argue, as Monte feels that he is merely using Ingrid as bait.

Shortly afterwards, Cobretti takes Ingrid out of the city in a pickup truck while Gonzales and Nancy follow. The car heads out of the city onto country roads. As they are heading away from the city of Los Angeles, Cobretti and Ingrid have a chat in the car. She wonders why the police cannot simply 'put away crazies'. Cobretti replies that she should 'tell it to the judge. We put them away – they let them out!' As they drive into the country, a motor bike can be seen parked at the side of the road, hinting at what is to come.

Later, the two-vehicle convoy stops to refuel at a gas station. As their cars are being filled up, Gonzales chats with Ingrid as he scoffs Coke and junk food. He remarks that Cobretti looks like 'something from the 50s', but is great at catching psychos as part of the so-called 'zombie squad'. Afterwards, Ingrid has a chat with Cobretti and discovers that his first name is Marion. Cobretti felt this name was not a suitable one for a policeman, so he prefers to be known by his second name. He says that he wanted a 'harder' name, and jokes that a suitable one might be 'Alice'. This sequence may be a reference to one of the earliest action movie stars, the great John Wayne, whose real name was Marion Mitchell Morrison but felt he had to change it to something that sounded more macho.

Meanwhile, the gang is preparing for further action, and there is another shot of them clinking axes together. A deleted scene (which is available to view on YouTube) reveals that the gang normally carries out a number of rituals before each murder, including the clinking of axe heads together and the breaking of mirrors.

The action then cuts to a shot of the two police vehicles crossing the girder bridge near the Cross Roads Motor Court in San Remos (the name is fictional, as the rest of the film was shot in the foundry town of Piru). Ingrid and the police officers eat in a cafe. Ingrid has French fries with a massive quantity of tomato ketchup, and Cobretti picks up a large plastic model of a multi-layered burger, joking that she should maybe think of eating this instead.

'Do you have a life preserver? Because your French fries are drowning', he jokes as Ingrid eats. At the same time, Nancy is on the payphone.

Ingrid asks Cobretti what he does to relax, and he replies that he looks for trouble. She asks him if he ever gets involved, and he mentions that no one could ever put up with the way he lives. 'What if you do find someone?' she enquires.

Meanwhile, the gang of bad guys are tooling up for action and are preparing their motorcycles and weapons. By this time darkness has fallen, and Ingrid has gone to sleep. Nancy is using the payphone outside the motel when she is disturbed by Cobretti. She claims to be checking things are okay at home, but Cobretti is suspicious: 'Why didn't you use the 'phone in a room?' She replies that she was forced to use the payphone because the 'phone in her own room was unserviceable. She also says that she thinks he is doing a great job.

A few miles away, the gang of motorcyclists is driving towards San Remos with headlights blazing. Cobretti realises that a battle is imminent and prepares his weapons. He assembles his submachine gun, looks out a few Mk 2 hand grenades, and carries out essential maintenance on his gun. His Jatimatic submachine gun has an unusual feature, as it comes with a shoulder holster which can accommodate both the weapon and spare magazines.

Ingrid can't sleep, and asks him whether they will see each other when all this is over. They then kiss, and Ingrid says it would be a very good idea for them to meet up again after the current crisis is over. Stallone and Nielsen were an item at the time of filming and later married, although there marriage only lasted for two years between 1985 and 1987.

As the sun rises that morning, the motorcycle gang approach San Remos. Cobretti emerges from the motel with Ingrid. Gonzales is already outside and says 'good morning'. Cobretti mutters that it would be safer to go upstate. They notice that Nancy has disappeared. Suddenly the gang arrives on motorbikes. Cobretti tells Ingrid and Gonzales to get inside the motel as quickly as possible. He notices Nancy in the distance, talking to the bad guys and giving them instructions as the gang's motorcycles cross the girder bridge. Inside the motel, Cobretti and Gonzales break some windows and shoot some of the arriving motorcyclists with their handguns. A gang member appears at the skylight of the room. Cobretti kills him with a burst from his Jatimatic, and the bad guy falls through the skylight. Then a motorcycle drives through a window and its driver is almost immediately killed by Cobretti with another burst from his gun. Cobretti and Ingrid run outside as Gonzales is shot.

Cobretti tells Ingrid to take the wheel of their pickup truck as he fires at the approaching gang members. He throws a grenade and, as it explodes, he jumps onto the flat bed of the truck as they are chased by a bunch of motorcyclists. He opens fire with his submachine gun and mows down many of the gang members. One of them jumps onto the back of the truck and fights with Cobretti, who throws him off the front end of the vehicle, causing him to be run over. Ahead of them is a roadblock of burning cars, but Cobretti tells Ingrid not to panic and to simply drive as fast as possible through the middle of the obstruction. The pickup makes it, but is seriously damaged: the bonnet flies up, the vehicle skids, and Cobretti is thrown off the back of the truck. He lands on the ground, apparently uninjured. Cobretti and Ingrid then run away on foot. Cobretti pauses momentarily to throw another grenade and blows up another motorcycle. He then kills two more gang members with machine gun fire. Ingrid runs into a nearby foundry, followed closely by the 'Night Slasher'. She bangs on the window of an office inside the plant, where there is a security guard on duty. Before the guard can act, Nancy arrives and shoots him. Then the 'Night Slasher' himself arrives. Cobretti places a grenade on the main switchgear of the plant and – as some gang members arrive – he uses the laser sight of his submachine gun to shoot the grenade, causing it to explode and taking out the two bad guys. He then turns on a stop-cock, incinerating another of the gang with burning gas. Cobretti continues to battle the remaining criminals in the foundry. One sniper tries to shoot Cobretti, but misses and accidentally hits a fuel drum over his head causing him to get soaked in petrol. From an overhead gantry, Cobretti strikes a match – the same one he often carries between his lips – on the side of his Colt automatic. He drops the lit match, causing the villain to burst into flames. (One wonders if Cobretti habitually carries a match between his lips just in case he encounters a criminal soaked in petrol who he can easily incinerate!)

Nancy tries to shoot Ingrid, but Cobretti fires first and kills her. Now the 'Night Slasher' is the only gang member left alive. He pulls out his knife in his right hand, and carries a sawn-off shotgun in his left. 'Let's bleed, pig. Do you want to go to hell with me? We kill the weak so the strong survive, pig. You can't stop the new world; we are the future.'

Cobretti puts the laser sight of his submachine gun on the head of the 'Night Slasher'. 'You're history', says Cobretti.

'You won't do it, pig!' screams the 'Night Slasher', 'Murder is against the law. You will have to take me in. Even I have rights. They'll say I'm insane. The court is civilised – isn't it, pig?'

'I'm not', replies Cobretti. 'This is where the law stops and I start.' Then Nancy – who has apparently been wounded, but not killed – jumps on Cobretti, making him drop his gun. He then engages in a hand-to-hand fight with the 'Night Slasher'. He tries to stab Cobretti, but the policeman manages to push him back and hangs him on a moving hook which carries him into the flames of the foundry, where he is incinerated. Cobretti and Ingrid leave the foundry as police and TV crews arrive.

Gonzales has been wounded but is still alive, and is on an intravenous drip as he waits to be taken away in an ambulance. Cobretti asks him if he needs anything, and he says that he would kill for some gummy bears. Captain Sears is pleased at the outcome, saying that he did a 'hell of a job' and is welcome to have a transfer from the zombie squad if he wants it. Cobretti asks if his car can be replaced, and the police chief replies that he would like to do it but it is not in his budget. Monte is satisfied with the outcome, though he feels that a more 'subtle' approach could have been used. He hopes there are no hard feelings. Cobretti agrees to shake his hand, but then punches him. 'No hard feelings, pal', he says. He's offered a lift, but opts to get home on one of the motorcycles with Ingrid as a pillion passenger.

The original cut of the movie came in at 2 hours 10 minutes, but extensive pruning of the picture took place prior to release. Some of these extensive cuts were made in order to remove violent scenes, and the final version of the film was just 83 minutes long. Another reason the film was shortened was to increase its chances of being a financial success, as it was directly competing with *Top Gun* (1986) and more showings per day were then possible.

This makes it one of the shortest feature films ever made. (By the way, the record for the shortest cinema feature would probably be held by the Marx Brothers classic *Duck Soup*, 1930, which ran for only 65 minutes. Other very short films include *The Mummy*, 1932, at just 73 minutes; *Corpse Bride*, 2005, at 75 minutes, and *Meet the Spartans*, 2008, at 86 minutes. By contrast, the longest film ever made – according to *The Guinness Book of Records* – is *The Cure for Insomnia*, 1987, which is 85 hours long.) Despite the extensive last-minute editing, *Cobra* was moderately successful in commercial terms, making $160 million against a budget of £25m.

In 1995, Paula Gosling's book *Fair Game* was made into a film of the same title starring Cindy Crawford and Adam Baldwin. Although *Cobra* and *Fair Game* were based on the same book, they are two completely dissimilar films. *Fair Game* was panned by the critics and was not a great success, costing $50m to make but taking just $26m at the box-office. In my view, *Cobra* was a far better movie. Though reviled by critics, it has become a cult classic and it is my opinion that it deserves recognition as one of the best action pictures of the eighties.

## *Cobra* (1986)
## Production Credits

Director: George P. Cosmatos
Screenplay: Sylvester Stallone
Original Novel: Paula Gosling

### Cast

Lt Marion Cobretti - Sylvester Stallone
Ingrid Knudsen - Brigitte Nielsen
Sgt Tony Gonzales - Reni Santoni
Detective Monte - Andrew Robinson
Night Slasher - Brian Thompson
Cho - John Herzfeld
Nancy Stalk - Lee Garlington
Captain Sears - Art La Fleur
Supermarket Killer - Marco Rodriguez
Security Guard - Ross St Philip
Chief Halliwell - Val Avery
Dan - David Rasche
Low Rider - John Hauk
Prodski - Nick Angotti
Waitress - Nina Axelrod
Policemen - Joe Bonny, Roger Aaron Brown
Innocent Bystander - Bradley Bovee
Supermarket Kid - Kevin Breslin
Father of Blonde Girl - John Cahill
Night Guard - Malik Carter
Woman in Car - Louise Caire Clark

TV News Reporter - Christine Craft
Janitor - Gregory Cruz
Nurses - Deborah Dalton, Dorothy Meyer, Karen Kondazian
Dr Demopoulos - Harry Demopoulos
Killers - Scott Dockstader
Murdered Waitress - Laura Drake
Garage Bystander - Ken Hill
Internal Affairs Men - Arthur Kassell
Sketch Artist - Fed Lucky
Apartment Killers - Robert Martini, Jim Wilkey
Killers - Joe Masino Jr, Joe Stone
Supermarket Clerk - Paul Monte
Commissionaire Reddesdale - Bert Williams
Reporters - Leslie Morris, Clare Nono, Steve Lentz, Glenda Wina, Michael Bersad, Joe Fowler, Helen Kelly
Hospital Visitor - Brian Edwards
Policewoman - Julie Hampton
Suspect in Custody - Kurt V. Hulett
Extra - Ron Jeremy

### Producers

Executive Producer: James D. Brubaker

Producers: Yoram Globus,
Menahem Golan
Associate Producer: Tony
Munafo

**Music**
Composer: Sylvester Levay

**Cinematography**
Director of Photography: Ric
Waite

**Film Editing**
Film Editors: James Symons,
Don Zimmerman

**Production Design**
Production Designer: Bill
Kenney
Art Direction: Adrian Gorton,
William Ladd Skinner

**Set Decoration**
Set Decorator: Robert Gould
Costume Design: Tom Bronson

**Make-up Department**
Make-up Artists: Steve
Abrums, Leonard Engelman
Hair Stylist: Lola Kemp, Barbara
Lorenz

**Production Management**
Unit Production Manager:
Mary Ellis

**Second Unit Director or
Assistant Director**
First Assistant Director: Duncan
Henderson
Second Assistant Directors: Eric
Jewett, Janet Knutsen
Second Unit Director: Terry
Leonard
Third Assistant Director:
Seanna McPherson

**Art Department**
Assistant Art Director: Cathryn
Bangs
Set Dresser: Max E. Brehme
Leadman: William D. Derham,
Doug Forsmith
Property Master: Louis Fleming
Assistant Property Master: Kurt
V. Hulett
Set Designer: David Klassen
Prop Maker: Frederick Lietzman
Illustrator: Fred Lucky
Assistant Art Director: Gayle
Simon
Construction Coordinator:
Michael J. Smith
Stand-by Painter: Jane Stewart
Paint Foreman: Ward Welton
Third Broom Props: Paul
Breuninger
Painter: D.A. Zingelewicz

**Sound Department**
Supervising Sound Editor: Fred
J. Brown
Sound Editor: Jay Wilkinson,
Michele Sharp, Teri E. Dorman
Foley Artist: Evelyn Dutton

Sound Mixer: Michael Evje
Sound Recordist: Stanley B. Gill
ADR Editor: Avram D. Gold
Sound Editor: Joseph A. Ippolito
Re-Recording Mixer: Michael
Minkler, Rick Kline, Gregg
Landaker
Boom Operator: James McCann
Sound Re-Recordist: Gary F.
Ritchie, Bob Nichols II
Foley Artist: Margie Denecke
Assistant Sound Editor:
Michelle Pleis
Utility Sound Technician:
Frederick Talmage
Technical Director of Sound:
Donald C. Rogers

**Special Effects**
Special Effects: Philip Cory
Assistant Special Effects: Jim
Schwalm, David Simmons, Ken
Speed, Ray Svedin
Special Effects Assistant: Hans
Metz

**Stunts**
Stunt Performers: Bradley
Bovee, Dave Darling, Mark De
Alessandro, Scott Dockstader,
Richard Epper, Corey Eubanks,
Debbie Evans, Joe Finnegan,
Terry Jackson, John Michael
Johnson, Tracy Lynn Keehn,
Paul Lane, Lane Leavitt, Mike
McGaughy, Gary McLarty,
Branscombe Richmond, Kerry
Rossall, Mike Ronyard, Ben
Scott, Mike Tillman, Penny

Barndt, Diane Kay Grant, Jeff
Langton, Terry Leonard,
Denney Pierce, Larry Randles
Stunt Coordinator: Terry
Leonard
Stunt Double (Sylvester
Stallone): Mark De Alessandro
Stunt Driving Double (Sylvester
Stallone): Corey Michael
Eubanks
Stunt Double: Terry Jackson
Precision Driver: Greg
McMickle
Stunt Driver: George A. Sack Jr

**Camera and Electrical
Department**
Grip: Danny Boldroff
Key Grip Best Boy: Steve
Boldroff
Chief Lighting Technician: Carl
Boles
Still Photographer: Dave
Friedman
First Assistant Camera: Roger
Gebhard
Grip: Jack Glen, Howard
Hagadorn
Second Assistant Camera: Larry
Hezzelwood, Christopher Ishil
Assistant Video Engineer: Ian
Wayne, Michael J. Hogan
Electrician: Keith Pallant,
Richard L. Jordan
Key Grip: John London
Additional Photographer: Nick
McClean
First Assistant Camera: Richard
A. Mention

Camera Operator: Rick Neff
Video Engineer: Tim Prince
First Assistant Camera: Tony
Rivetti
Camera Operator: Mike St
Hilaire
Electricians: Jeff Stanman, Eddie
Taylor
Best Boy Electric: Ken Tosic
Dolly Grip: Donald Whipple Jr
Camera Operator (Second
Unit): Stephen St John

## Casting Department
Casting: Joy Todd
Casting Assistant: Henry Alford
Voice Casting: Barbara Harris
Extras Casting: Susie Johnson
Casting Assistants: Cynthia
Rothkopf, Sally Stiner

## Costume and Wardrobe Department
Costumers: Robin Borman,
Linda Henrikson, Murray Lantz,
Michael J. Long

## Editorial Department
Assistant Editors: Carmen
Baker, Paul Cichoki, Gregory
Gerlich, Marty November
Negative Cutter: Donah Bassett
Colour Timer: Bob Raring
Apprentice Editor: Markus
Schau

## Location Management
Location Managers: Robert H.
Lemer, Laura Sode

Location Assistant: Janice Polley

## Music Department
Electronic Music Engineer: Dan
Bates
Music Editor: George Brand
Musicians: George Doering,
Sylvester LeVay, Norman
Ludwin
Music Supervisor: Robin Garb
Additional Orchestrator:
Thomas Pasatieri
Supervising Music Producer:
Spencer Proffer

## Transportation Department
Office Driver: John Armstrong
Transportation Coordinator:
Edward Arter
Driver: Michael W. Broomer
Transportation Captain:
Michael Brum
Sylvester Stallone's Driver: John
Cahill

## Other Crew
Assistant to James D. Brubaker:
Tina Arter
Production Associates: Laurie
Allison, Lucy Mardonovich,
Maggie Martin, Paul Monte,
Anthony Poll, Franklin A.
Vallette, Marcel Brubaker,
Susan Brubaker, Bruce Carter
First Aid: James Ealy
Publicist: Tom Gray
Technical Consultant: Joseph R.
Hessekiel

Production Consultant: Bill
Wells
Production Coordinator:
Richard Liebegott
Craft Service: Veria Loomis
Randall, James Lorimer
Technical Advisor: Tony
Maffatone
First Assistant Accountant:
Lynn C Marchionno

Assistant to Sylvester Stallone:
Susan Persily
Assistant to George P.
Cosmatos: Anna M. Perron
Script Supervisor: Hope
Williams
Production Accountant:
Cynthia Wise

# 7

# ALIENS

## (1986)

*Brandywine Productions*

**Director**: James Cameron
**Producer**: Gale Anne Hurd
**Screenwriter**: James Cameron

*A*LIENS is one of that rare breed – a sequel which is better than the original. It is generally accepted by film critics and the general public alike that most sequels are inferior to the film they follow as they generally have weaker scripts, smaller budgets, and a poorer cast. But there are a few sequels which buck this trend, including *Aliens, The Godfather: Part II* (1974) and *The Bride of Frankenstein* (1935). I would also include the three *Rambo* sequels (1985, 1988 and 2008), which are discussed elsewhere in this book.

The original *Alien* (1979) – directed by Ridley Scott – was highly acclaimed though only moderately profitable (some accounts state that it only made a profit of $4m), and it was one of a number of science fiction films which were greenlighted following the unexpected success of *Star Wars* in 1977. *Alien* can be regarded as a tense, claustrophobic thriller, a science fiction film, or a horror movie. Its sequel, *Aliens,* took off in a different direction, as it can be considered a 'science fiction action movie' or a 'war movie in space'.

A sequel to *Alien* was originally considered as far back as 1979 – following the original film's release – but it was never proceeded with, largely because the first movie had never made huge profits. In 1983, though, the film was given the go ahead by 20th Century Fox, with a script to be written by budding filmmaker James Cameron. At the time Cameron was largely unknown, as his first big film – *The Terminator* (1984) – was about to enter production. Originally it was to be shot in Toronto in 1983, but shooting was postponed for nine months to allow its star Arnold Schwarzenegger to complete work on *Conan the Destroyer* (1984). This nine month recess didn't give James Cameron enough time to direct another film, but it did allow him to write much of the screenplay of *Aliens*.

The easy option would have been for Cameron to write a film which was more of the same (as most sequels are), but instead he went off on a different tack, incorporating the US military in the future – a subject that had interested him for years. One inspiration for the screenplay was Robert Heinlein's 1959 novel *Starship Troopers*, which featured the 'Mobile Infantry' armed with futuristic rifles and wearing mechanical exoskeletons ('powered suits') to increase their strength. Although the 'Colonial Marines' in Cameron's screenplay don't wear powered exoskeletons, it is likely that this idea was the inspiration for the 'power loader' which plays such an important role in the plot of *Aliens*. It is interesting to note that *Starship Troopers* was itself made into a film in 1997 (which was directed by Paul Verhoeven), though 'powered suits' were not featured as they were thought to be too difficult and expensive to realise with contemporary special effects technology.

Cameron's screenplay was thus a war movie set in the future, and as the Vietnam War had only ended about a decade earlier there were many subtle references to this conflict in the screenplay – particularly the notion that a heavily armed force with superior weapons and technology can be defeated by a primitive (but more determined) enemy. Studio executives summarized the desired plot to Cameron in just three words – 'Ripley and soldiers' – and he then came up with the movie's tag-line 'This Time It's War', which was used in promotional posters.

*Aliens* is thus best remembered for its many exciting scenes where soldiers battle aliens with futuristic versions of contemporary firearms. This was, I think, a brilliant decision because firefights involving bullet-firing weapons, flame-throwers and grenades are much more exciting than those using lasers or ray guns, and at Cameron's insistence the rifles and machine guns used in *Aliens* were all based on existing firearms.

The Colonial Marines' principal weapon, the 'M41A Pulse Rifle', was built by cladding a vintage M1A1 0.45in calibre Thompson machine gun in a futuristic-looking casing attached to the front end of a Franchi SPAS-12 shotgun, and then fitting the business end of a Remington 12-gauge Model 870P pump action shotgun underneath the barrel. In the film these weapons don't fire shotgun cartridges, but instead shoot '30mm M309 high explosive grenades'. The M309 can also be used as a normal grenade by pressing the button on the end of each round twice.

The other main firearm used in the film, the 'Smart Gun', was created by dressing a WW2-vintage German MG42 machine gun with motorcycle spare parts, and then fitting a Steadicam camera harness which allowed the gun to be fired while slung from the shoulder.

The producer was James Cameron's then-wife Gale Anne Hurd, who had worked on his previous film *The Terminator* while the executive producers were David Giler, Walter Hill and Gordon Carroll who together had formed Brandywine Productions which had made the first *Alien* film.

One issue was whether Sigourney Weaver would be willing to reprise her role as Ellen Ripley, and there were tentative plans to make a sequel without her. In the end she agreed to star in the film for a reported $1m fee, thirty times what she had been paid for the first movie. One thing that changed her mind was James Cameron's script, which made her character the centre of the story. The screenplay also featured many scenes with guns, something which initially troubled Weaver who was a supporter of gun control legislation, but eventually she was talked round by James Cameron who was fascinated by weapons technology (though himself a supporter of gun control).

Ron Cobb – who was a concept artist for the first film – did some designs for the new feature, while a second artist named Syd Mead, who had worked on *Tron* (1982), *Blade Runner* (1982) and *2010* (1984), was also employed. The basic 1979 Alien design by Swiss artist H.R. Giger (including the Alien eggs, facehuggers and chestburster variants) were retained for the new film. The only changes were that the dome over the Alien's cranium was removed and the facehuggers were more mobile, having the ability to crawl around the ground and leap at people. In addition, a less heavy version of the Alien warrior suit was created from spandex covered with lightweight foam pieces. Twelve of these costumes were made, plus six large animatronic puppets with spindly limbs and tiny waists.

Filming commenced in late 1985 at Pinewood Studios near London. The only location used in the film was Acton Power Station in London, a coal-fired generating plant which had been decommissioned two years earlier and was dressed to represent the colony on planet LV-426. Before filming started, a considerable quantity of asbestos had to be removed from the old building to create a safe working environment.

The film has perfect continuity with Ridley Scott's 1979 original, and begins where the previous film ended with a shot of the *Nostromo's* 'lifeboat' – the *Narcissus* – floating through space. James Horner's music at this point includes references to 'Gayane's Adagio' from Aram Khachaturian's *Gayane* ballet suite, which had also been used in Stanley Kubrick's *2001: A Space Odyssey* (1968). As the *Narcissus* model from the previous film no longer existed, a new six-foot miniature was recreated from photographic references.

Eventually the *Narcissus* is discovered by another spacecraft, and a three-man salvage crew burns its way into the small vessel using a robotic arm fitted with a welding torch and scanning device. After wiping frost off the perspex cover of the sleep capsule they discover Warrant Officer Ripley, who has been in cryo-sleep for 57 years. On her chest is the ship's cat, Jones, who is also unconscious.

The next scene is set in the Gateway Station, orbiting high above the Earth where Ripley is recovering from her ordeal. The Earth in this shot was a nine-foot painting which was converted to a photographic print, scaled down and then retouched, while the Gateway Station was a mixture of miniature work and a glass painting.

A visitor calls to see Ripley. It is Carter Burke (Paul Reiser), a bureaucrat from the Weyland-Yutani Corporation, the company which owned the now-destroyed *Nostromo*. Burke is carrying Jones, the ship's cat, who is overjoyed to see Ripley and starts purring. Burke warns Ripley that she should expect some temporary disorientation and muscle weakness. He also mentions that she had been in hyper sleep for 57 years until she was recovered by the deep space salvage team.

Suddenly Jones hisses. Ripley clutches her chest and thrashes about, knocking over a glass of water before calling for the nurses. She looks down at her torso and sees an expanding bulge as what appears to be an Alien chestburster prepares to pop out. Suddenly she wakes up. She has just had a bad dream. She speaks to a nurse on a black-and-white TV monitor, and the nurse asks if she wants something to help her sleep. But Ripley declines, as she feels she has slept enough and instead opts for a cuddle with Jones.

The next scene shows Ripley sitting in a garden, but it is soon revealed to be a hologram which Ripley switches off. Burke arrives and informs Ripley about a forthcoming hearing concerning the loss of the *Nostromo*. Ripley asks if there is any news about her daughter, Amanda Ripley McLaren. Burke tells her that she died two years before at the age of 66. Ripley looks at a photo of her daughter, which shows a woman who is clearly in her sixties (this was actually a photo of Sigourney Weaver's real mother, Elizabeth Inglis). As she looks at the picture, Ripley remembers that she had promised that she would be back home for her daughter's 11th birthday.

The next scene is set at the hearing which has been convened to discuss the loss of the *Nostromo* 57 years before. In the UK this would be called a board of enquiry. Ripley is frustrated, because the hearing has been going for a full three-

and-a-half hours already and yet no progress appears to have been made.

The hearing has been called to discuss the loss of the *Nostromo*, an M-class starfreighter, due to the detonation of its engines – an action initiated by Ripley. The cost of this vessel is estimated at $42 million in adjusted dollars. Ripley sticks to her story that all the other members of the crew were killed by a single unstoppable alien creature with acid blood, but no-one seems to believe her tale of the tragic events which unfolded after the crew of the *Nostromo* investigated a derelict spaceship on the planet LV-426. Once again Ripley repeats her account, but she is not believed. It is pointed out to her that no trace of the alien organism was found in the *Narcissus*, but Ripley points out that this was because she blew the creature out of the airlock.

Eventually Ripley loses her temper. She explains that her fellow (now deceased) crew member Kane saw thousands of alien eggs inside the derelict spaceship, and if 'just one of these things get down here it will be the end of all this, this bullshit that you think is so important. You can just kiss all of this goodbye', she says, brandishing a sheaf of papers for effect.

Eventually the panel comes to the conclusion that Ripley displayed questionable judgement when handling the situation and is therefore unfit to hold a flight licence. For this reason her licence is to be suspended indefinitely, although no criminal charges are to be brought against her. She is to be released on six months' probation, with a monthly review.

As the hearing comes to a conclusion and the members of the board leave the room, Ripley approaches Van Leuwen (Paul Maxwell) – the head of the review board – and suggests that, at the very least, the company investigates planet LV-426 (which is now known as Acheron). Van Leuwen responds that there is no need to do this, as people have been living there for over 20 years without any problems. These colonists (known as Terra Formers) are turning the atmosphere of the planet into one suitable for humans by using devices known as 'atmosphere processing stations'. He describes them as 'Shake and Bake' colonies.

The next scene is set on planet LV-426 and shows a barren, windswept landscape. A painted sign indicates that the colony is known as *Hadley's Hope*, and that it has a population of 158. Scenes set on the planet surface were achieved using a combination of large miniatures and full-size studio sets, with a painted sky backdrop, at Pinewood Studios.

An eight-wheeled vehicle (actually a 1/6 scale radio-controlled miniature) drives past the colony buildings, while a second is covered by a tarpaulin to give some protection from the harsh weather. Inside the building, technicians are discussing the use of what they term a 'mom-and-pop survey team', as they have been asked to investigate a particular grid reference on the map. As the technicians are carrying out their work, two children are playing in the building – namely Rebecca Jorden (Carrie Henn) and her brother (Christopher Henn).

Later an eight-wheeled wheeled vehicle traverses the landscape of LV-426. In the back of the tractor are Rebecca and her brother, while her father and mother are in the front. The two parents have been instructed to check out a location, and are amazed to discover a huge horseshoe-shaped spacecraft that no-one has noticed before. The derelict spacecraft was a large 12-foot miniature made of Styrofoam and plasticine, and was the only prop which was reused from

*Alien* as it had been discovered intact in Hollywood in outdoor storage, belonging to Bob Burns. Because it had been lying outside for several years, it required some cleaning and restoration before it could be featured in the new film. All the footage of the derelict spaceship for *Aliens* was filmed in Hollywood and added to the foreground action (involving actors) by back-projection.

The two adults decide to investigate the strange alien ship, entering through a hole in the side. Both don goggles before venturing outside, while telling their children to stay in the vehicle for safety. Later, their mother returns to the vehicle saying that she needs to put out an emergency call. Newt looks out the door of the vehicle and sees her father lying on the ground, his head covered with a facehugger. She screams.

Back at the Gateway Station Ripley is deep in thought, cigarette in hand. Her reverie is interrupted by two visitors arriving at her door. It is Carter Burke again, this time accompanied by Lieutenant Gorman (William Hope) of the Colonial Marines. When Ripley discovers who is calling she slams the door in their face, but Burke pleads with her to let them in and mentions that contact has been lost with the colonists on LV-426. Hearing this information, Ripley relents and opens the door.

Burke explains that although the problem may be caused by something as simple as a downed transmitter, the authorities are not taking any chances and are sending a military force to investigate further. Gorman reassures Ripley that she will not be going in with the troops. Furthermore, the Colonial Marines have been trained to deal with situations like this. But they would like Ripley to come along as an adviser.

Burke applies further pressure to Ripley to influence her decision. He is aware that she is currently working in the cargo docks as a power loader operator, but if she was willing to go on the mission he could arrange to get her reinstated as a flight officer. However, Ripley still refuses to be involved with the mission. Burke gives her his card so that she can contact him if she changes her mind.

That night Ripley has another nightmare and wakes up screaming. She goes to the restroom, where she splashes some water on her face. Ripley's bathroom in this sequence was created using a toilet from a British Airways Boeing 707 airliner, which was being scrapped at the time the film was being shot.

Ripley calls Burke on the videophone and he answers groggily, rubbing sleep from his eyes. It is obviously the middle of the night. Ripley gets straight to the point: 'You are going to destroy them? Not to study, not to bring back, but to wipe them out?'

Burke replies: 'That's the plan. You have my word on it'.

'Alright, I'm in.' Ripley terminates the call and then glances at Jones: 'And you, you little shithead – you're staying here'.

Some weeks later, a military troop-carrying spaceship – the *USS Sulaco* – is travelling through space as it approaches LV-426. This shot was achieved using a six-foot miniature against a blue screen. Curiously, the spaceship is shaped like a pulse rifle and was only detailed on one side. The camera pans through the interior of the vessel, revealing personal lockers, pulse rifles and machine guns in racks, smart bombs, and a dropship which looks a bit like an AH-64 Apache helicopter gunship but with the troop-carrying capacity of a CH-53

Super Stallion chopper and the firepower of an F-4 Phantom jet. Art Director Peter Lamont dressed the set with old vending machines and helicopter engines. The undercarriage legs of the drop ship came from scrapped RAF Avro Vulcan bombers, while the skids were flare trays from RAF English-Electric Canberras.

Suddenly the hypersleep pods open and the inhabitants – twelve colonial marines plus Ripley and Burke – emerge coughing and spluttering after their three-week sleep. For budgetary reasons only four of these sleep pods were constructed, but their apparent numbers on screen were multiplied by the simple expedient of using strategically-placed mirrors. Similarly, the transparent lids of the pods were opened using invisible wires instead of expensive hydraulic mechanisms.

The leader of the colonial Marines, Sgt Apone (Al Matthews), sticks a cigar in his mouth and starts ordering his troops about. This is one of the great clichés of military films, as they usually feature a tough drill sergeant who is very hard on his troops during training yet who comes to earn their respect when he shows his mettle in combat. 3,000 actors were auditioned in the UK for the roles of just 12 Marines, but in the end most of them were played by American actors. One notable exception was Private Crowe, who was played by English stuntman Tip Tipping.

As the Marines recover from their long hypersleep they walk to their lockers to retrieve their uniforms and kit, while some of them do exercises to get their muscles warmed up. Some of the Colonial Marines are female, an accurate prediction of what did happen in the American and British military establishments some years later. Nowadays we are all quite used to the idea of female soldiers, pilots and sailors, but this was quite ground-breaking stuff in 1986. Among the female Marines is Private Vasquez (Jenette Goldstein), who has a powerful physique. Private Hudson (Bill Paxton) asks her if she has ever been mistaken for a man and she replies with the perfect *non-sequitur*: 'No, have you?'

After doing some exercises and getting dressed, the Colonial Marines (plus Ripley and Burke) enjoy breakfast together. The meal consists of orange juice, scrambled eggs, coffee, and cornbread. As breakfast is coming to a close, Hudson asks Bishop (who had piloted the ship during the previous three weeks) to do the so-called 'knife trick'. This involves Hudson putting one hand, palm down on the table, fingers spread with Bishop's hand on top.

Bishop then stabs his knife onto the table on either side of each of Hudson's fingers, getting faster and faster until he has attained a staccato beat. This sequence was done for real, and actor Lance Henriksen had to practice for weeks to get up to a satisfactory speed. All the same, the apparently rapid motion was achieved by filming the sequence with an under-cranked camera.

After performing this feat Bishop notices a tiny cut on one finger, but instead of exuding red blood it secretes a white substance which looks rather like latex glue. Ripley, who is sitting next to him, notices this and recoils from him angrily. She hadn't been informed that there was an android amongst the crew and is very wary of such creatures after her experiences with Ash on the *Nostromo*, who eventually went berserk.

Bishop says he prefers the term 'artificial person' rather than android. Burke tries to resolve the situation by explaining to him about Ripley's previous negative experience on the *Nostromo*. Bishop is sympathetic and asks what kind of android was involved, and it is explained that it was a 'Hyperdyne Systems 1282 model'. Bishop concedes that this earlier model could be a bit 'twitchy', but reassures Ripley that such an occurrence would be impossible nowadays as he is fitted with behavioural inhibitors which would prevent him from harming a human being or indeed allowing a human being to be harmed by his inactions – statements which appear to have been influenced by Isaac Asimov's well-known 'Three Laws of Robotics'. Bishop then offers Ripley some cornbread and she responds by knocking the plate out of his hand, telling him to stay away from her.

Later, the Colonial Marines receive a briefing from Lieutenant Gorman and Ripley, who is dismayed at their arrogant, overconfident, gung-ho perspective. Burke explains that all contact has been lost with the colony and that a 'xenomorph' may be involved. Ripley then gives an account of what happened after the crew of the *Nostromo* discovered some alien eggs aboard a derelict spaceship on LV-426 during their encounter 57 years earlier.

However, the Marines appear very unimpressed and Vazquez in particular looks bored, saying that she only needs to know one thing – where they are. With her right hand she then mimics the trigger of a gun being pulled.

Ripley is perturbed at the Marines' attitude, saying that she hopes they are right. Hudson then asks how he can 'get out of this chicken shit outfit'. Apone reprimands him for his insolence, and Gorman then points out that Ripley's account is available on disc and that all the Marines should read her report. He wants the soldiers to get ready for action and have a tactical database simulation ready by 08.30. All ordnance is to be loaded onto the dropship, which is to be prepared for action.

As the *Sulaco* orbits LV-426, smart bombs are loaded onto the dropship using devices called 'Power Loaders'. These are powered exoskeletons which fit over the body of an operator and serve the same function as forklift trucks. Ripley offers to operate one, as she is qualified in their use.

The loading complete, the Marines – plus Ripley, Burke and Bishop – board an armoured personnel carrier (APC) which drives up a ramp into the cargo hold of the dropship. The APC used in the film was specially created for the production by modifying an obsolete Hunslett ATT77 aircraft-towing tractor which was obtained from London's Heathrow Airport. The original vehicle was used for moving aircraft which could be as large as a Boeing 747 and consequently was fitted with a powerful 635 hp engine and a considerable amount of lead ballast, which gave it a weight of 72 tons – more than a wartime Tiger tank. Part of the conversion work to make it into an APC involved the removal of this ballast to reduce the weight, though even after reconstruction it still weighed 27 tons which meant that it could only be driven on strengthened surfaces. Although it was capable of speeds of up to 30 miles an hour, with the ballast removed, it was only used in a few shots and many of the scenes in the film featuring the APC were achieved using a 1/6 scale radio controlled miniature and model landscapes and buildings. Another problem with the full-size APC was that it had very little room inside and could only carry three troops so, for scenes in which it is supposedly carrying ten Marines (who then jump out), some of the actors had to hide behind the vehicle and then make their way to the front as though they had exited through a door.

As the *Sulaco* continues to orbit LV-426, the troops strap themselves in and the dropship falls rapidly out of the belly of the spaceship as it heads towards the surface of the planet. Hudson appears to enjoy the experience and says they are on the 'express elevator to hell'. As the troops continue their journey towards the planet's surface, Gorman is asked about his combat experience and he explains that he has been on 38 simulated missions and only two actual combat drops (including the current one!). The other Marines groan at this admission of gross inexperience, but Hudson remains his usual cocky self, boasting about the tremendous weaponry which the Marines possess including smart bombs, tactical nuclear weapons, rifles, machine guns, and knives.

By now the dropship has entered the atmosphere of the planet and is flying low over the colony. Ripley glances at a monitor and sees a grainy monochrome image of the atmosphere processing plant, which looks a bit like a cooling tower of a power station. All the grainy video footage in the film was shot by James Cameron using a home video camera.

In a graceful movement the dropship lands outside the colony, drops its ramp, and the APC trundles out. Nowadays such a sequence would be achieved using CGI, but relatively old-fashioned effects techniques were employed in some shots in *Aliens*. For this scene the dropship was flown on wires using a technique invented in Hollywood by Howard and Theodore Lydecker in the early 1940s, in which three wires were employed. Two of these were guide filaments and a third one was used to pull the model along. For the scene of the APC driving away from the dropship, a 1/6 scale radio-controlled miniature of the vehicle was used in the foreground, while the craft in the background was 1/12 scale giving a forced perspective effect, resulting in greater depth and enabling a smaller model landscape to be used.

As the dropship flies off to land at another location nearby, the Marines jump out of the APC and take up positions, forming into two squads. The first attempts entry into the complex, while the second takes up flanking positions. Hudson uses crocodile clips to bypass the electronic lock, enabling the Marines to enter the complex.

All the Marines carry television cameras on their helmets, enabling Ripley and Burke to view their progress on monitors back in the APC. As the troops enter the complex they notice signs of a recent battle involving small arms fire and explosive charges. On Hicks's screen Ripley notices a large hole in a metal grille which forms the floor. The hole seems to extend through several levels suggesting that it has been caused by acid blood.

Gorman drives the APC into the complex through the South Lock, and Ripley and the others go into a medical lab where they find six face huggers in large lidded glass jars filled with fluid. Burke takes a closer look at one of them and it moves towards him as though to attack. It appears that two of them are alive while the other facehuggers are dead. Suddenly the Marines see something on their motion tracker and get a quick impression of someone (or something) moving across the corridor. Ripley investigates and, after crawling down a duct, discovers a rather bedraggled-looking nine year old who is concealed in a hidey-hole with a few belongings. Gorman tries to question her to obtain some information, but he gets nowhere as he lacks the necessary people skills. Ripley has a more gentle approach and gives her some hot chocolate. This then forces Ripley to wipe around the girl's mouth, and she ends up cleaning her whole face.

Meanwhile, Hudson and Burke are using equipment in the complex to scan for personal data transmitters (PDTs) which had been surgically implanted under each colonist's skin, enabling them to be tracked. As they continue with this work, Ripley is making some progress with her attempts to establish a rapport with the little girl and discovers that although her name is Rebecca Jorden she goes by the name of Newt. Only her brother calls her Rebecca. Ripley tries to reassure Newt that everything is going to be okay and says that the soldiers are here to protect her, but she says that they won't make any difference.

In the Med-Lab, Bishop is dissecting a facehugger. In the original *Alien* a similar dissection scene was achieved using a horseshoe crab and oysters. This time round the equivalent scene was created using stomach tripe from cattle which was rolled out flat. As Bishop continues with this work, Hudson lets out a whoop of joy as he has discovered the colonists' tracking devices. They are all in the processing station at Sub-Level Three.

Sgt Apone tells his troops to saddle up and get ready to travel to the atmosphere processing plant. A miniature shot then follows, showing the APC travelling to the processing plant, and then the troops disembark. Initially they get off at Level One and then travel down a staircase to Sub-Level 3. Back in the APC, Burke, Ripley and Gorman are viewing their progress on the monitor screens. They notice a weird alien honeycomb which is rather like a hive and is presumably made out of some kind of secreted resin. Much of the hive was created using a hanging foreground miniature to save money.

Ripley asks about the type of ammunition the Marines possess and Gorman says that they use '10mm armour piercing caseless ammunition'. Ripley quickly points out that these rounds could puncture the cooling system, resulting in a nuclear explosion, and Burke quickly realises that what she says is correct so Gorman gives instructions that there is to be no firing in the present location. All magazines have to be collected, rifles slung and no grenades are to be used. The only permitted weapons are flame units.

Apone collects ammunition from all the troopers, but Vazquez manages to retain a magazine for her Smart Gun while Hicks (Michael Biehn) holds onto his sawn-off shotgun which he describes as being reserved for 'close encounters'. Biehn had previously played Kyle Reese in *The Terminator*, and replaced James Remar who had already done a week's filming as Hicks. Fortunately some of the existing footage of Remar as Hicks (which was shot from behind) could still be used, as both actors wore the same costume.

The Marines continue to move into the alien hive and discover some hatched Alien eggs which must have contained facehuggers. Suddenly they find a female colonist (Barbara Coles) who has been cocooned by aliens. Although she appears to be dead, she starts to move and the Marines realise that she is very much alive. Unfortunately she doesn't have long to live, because within a minute a bulge starts to appear in the centre of her chest and a facehugger pops out. The facehugger design was very similar to that used in the first film, although proper arms were added.

As the facehugger writhes about, the Marines realise that they have only seconds to act. Apone orders a flame unit to be brought up, and the hideous creature is incinerated. Unfortunately the smoke, flame and noise wakes up all the aliens who are hiding in the hive, and they start to attack the soldiers. Corporal Dietrich (Cynthia Scott), the squad's medic, is lifted off the ground by an alien and attacked. Hudson notices movement on his tracker but can't see anything. Apone tells his Marines to use their infrared visors, but these prove useless for detecting the aliens.

Ripley realises that a disaster is about to happen and tells Gorman he must pull his team out immediately, but the inexperienced Lieutenant appears to be frozen with indecision. 'Let's Rock!', cries Vazquez as she opens fire with her powerful Smart Gun. The heavy-calibre rounds prove highly effective against the aliens, but each 'kill' results in a large quantity of acid blood splashing in all directions, wounding some of the Marines. Gorman tells Apone to lay down suppressive fire with the flamethrowers and fall back to the APC, but the slaughter continues.

As Gorman continues to panic, Ripley secures Newt into her jump seat in the APC using a safety cage and makes her way to the driving position. As Ripley starts up the vehicle and moves forward, Newt releases herself from her safety cage and crawls into what she thinks is a safe place. Ripley drives the vehicle as fast as possible and, as it lurches from side to side, Gorman is knocked unconscious, preventing him from interfering with Ripley's actions. Meanwhile, the carnage continues and Drake is killed by a splash of acid blood.

Eventually Ripley drives the APC as close as possible to the location of the Marines, and the surviving soldiers make their way into the vehicle. Just as they are about to close the sliding doors of the armoured car, an alien appears and tries to make its way inside. Hicks responds by placing the muzzle of his pump-action shotgun inside the mouth of the alien and pulling the trigger. The alien's head explodes, the troops manage to get the door closed, and Ripley gets the vehicle moving again. This scene, though apparently simple, proved difficult to film as Michael Biehn kept missing the alien's mouth every time he poked his gun forward.

Eventually James Cameron solved the problem by reverse filming so Biehn only had to place the nozzle in the alien's mouth and then withdraw it. One alien tries to smash through the windscreen of the APC but Ripley brakes suddenly, making the creature fall to the ground in front of the vehicle. She then drives forward, crushing the monster beneath the chunky tyres of the armoured car. Driving as fast as she can, Ripley crashes through the door of the complex and onto the causeway. Burke tells her to slow down, as she is burning out the transaxle.

Safe for now, the surviving Colonial Marines take stock of the situation. Apone and Dietrich's life trackers are still working, so it can be assumed that they have not been killed outright but have been cocooned by the aliens and will shortly be visited by facehuggers. Crowe, Frost and Drake are dead.

Vazquez suggests a possible solution – namely rolling some canisters of CN20 nerve gas into the complex, as the Marines brought seven canisters of this weapon with them. However, Ripley believes that tactic may be risky and she's not even sure that nerve gas will be effective against the alien lifeforms.

Instead, Ripley suggests taking off from the dropship and then nuking the site from orbit. Burke objects to this plan, as the installation has 'a certain dollar value'. Ripley simply responds that they 'can bill me', but Burke is adamant that the alien represents an important species and that 'we don't have the right to exterminate it'. He also says that he cannot authorise the destruction of this particular species in the current circumstances.

Ripley responds by pointing out that she believes that Corporal Hicks has authority in this situation, as it is a military operation. Hicks agrees with her, and asks for the dropship to return so that they can nuke the site from orbit as he believes that is it is the only option. 'It's the only way to be sure.'

Some distance away on the surface of LV-426, the pilot of the dropship – Corporal Ferro (Colette Hiller) – tells Private Spunkmeyer (Daniel Kash) to prepare for takeoff. Spunkmeyer has discovered some sticky goo on the ramp of the dropship, but she is totally uninterested as they have a job to do. A few moments later, the survivors of the military mission are standing around the APC awaiting the arrival of the dropship. Corporal Hicks throws a flare to guide the pilot.

Suddenly an alien warrior appears in the cockpit of the dropship. Ferro tries to draw her pistol, but she is not quick enough. The alien kills her and the dropship crashes and explodes, damaging the atmosphere processing plant as it rolls along the ground. On the surface, Ripley and her colleagues are forced to run for their life and the APC is destroyed. This scene was achieved by flying the model of the dropship on wires, and then using the resulting footage as back projection material behind the actors.

Newt says that everyone needs to get back to the complex as they (the aliens) mostly come at night. The Marines close metal shutters in all the windows as Hicks reviews the weapons and other equipment they have salvaged from the APC. They have only four pulse rifles, with just 50 rounds each (a pulse rifle's magazine normally contains 97 bullets). They also have 15 M40 grenades and two flamethrowers, one of which works (although half-empty) and one which has been damaged. They also have four UA-571C robot sentry guns with a few hundred rounds for each weapon.

Hicks explains that it will be 17 days before the expedition is declared overdue. However, Hudson panics and says that they 'won't even last 17 hours'. Ripley takes a more pragmatic view and points out that Newt survived far longer than that with no weapons and no training. As she says this, a helmeted Newt salutes the troops. Ripley then tells Hudson that she is sick of his bullshit and he needs to get his act together if they are all to survive. She tells Hudson to get on a computer terminal and call up some kind of floor plan of the complex. Bishop says he's going to the medical lab.

After viewing a floor plan on a computer terminal, Ripley identifies a tunnel that the aliens are using to travel between the atmosphere processing plant and the control centre. She realises that it will be possible to seal off some corridors by welding doors shut and then covering two others with the four automatic sentry guns.

Later, the Marines use their small welding torches to seal off some doors, and they set up pairs of sentry guns in two different corridors. The UA-571C remote sentry gun was one of James Cameron's most brilliant ideas. In principle it is similar to the American Vulcan Phalanx 20mm, 6,000 rounds per minute close-in weapon system (CIWS), which is a shipborne radar and computer-controlled gun turret which automatically fires on any missile or aircraft which comes within range. It is installed on most U.S. Navy warships, and after the 1982 Falklands War the British Royal Navy fitted this weapon to its frigates, destroyers and aircraft carriers to combat the threat posed by anti-ship missiles. In reality, the sentry guns were based around WW2 vintage German MG42 machine guns.

After setting up a pair of sentry guns, Vazquez tests them by throwing a metal case in front of them, shouting 'fire in the hole' to warn of the forthcoming test. Within a couple of seconds the sentry guns open fire and blast the case to smithereens. ('Fire in the hole' is a phrase which dates back to the 19th century mining industry to signify an imminent detonation.)

As the Marines are preparing their defences, Hicks gives Ripley a tracking device so that she can find him anywhere in the complex. Later Ripley tries to put Newt to bed in the medical lab, but the little girl is scared. Her mother used to tell her that there were no real monsters, but she now realises that there are. So why do people say things like this? Newt asks Ripley if she has children. Ripley says she has a daughter but that she is 'gone'. She reassures Newt that she will be in the next room and will be able to see her on a TV monitor.

Later, Ripley reviews the situation in the Med-Lab. She calculates that at least 100 colonists will have been cocooned (as the population of Hadley's Hope was 158 and it can be assumed that some were killed outright while others were cocooned), so Ripley wonders who is laying all the eggs. Bishop suggests that it must be something they haven't seen yet, possibly even an 'Alien Queen'. Ripley asks Bishop to ensure that the two live facehuggers are eventually destroyed, but he points out that Burke gave specific instructions that they should be preserved.

Afterwards, Ripley confronts Burke over the issue. He claims that the facehuggers are worth billions to the bioweapons division of the Weyland-Yutani company. Ripley points out that it would be impossible to get a dangerous organism through quarantine, particularly one which led to the death of 157 colonists. Ripley accuses Burke of sending some colonists to the derelict ship without giving them warning of the dangers that might be involved. Burke simply says it was a 'bad call', and adds that he thought that she would be smarter than this. Ripley merely replies that she is happy to disappoint him. Suddenly Hicks reports that the motion trackers have detected aliens coming through one of the tunnels covered by the sentry guns. Both guns open fire and their rounds kill many of the aliens, but they rapidly run out of bullets and soon both ammunition cans are empty.

At that point Bishop gives everyone some bad news. Because of damage to the atmosphere processing plant caused by the crash of the dropship, the unit is undergoing emergency venting and will blow in just four hours. The blast will be equivalent to a 40 megaton nuclear weapon, with a 50km blast radius.

Ripley suggests that the only remedy is to activate the second dropship on the *Sulaco* and fly it down to the surface of the planet by remote control. Unfortunately it would not be possible to do this from their current location, but there is a solution to this problem which is highly dangerous. Someone must travel to the location of the radio dish while carrying a portable terminal. Bishop volunteers to carry out this task, involving him crawling through a metal conduit to the uplink. It will be a very perilous mission, and there would not be much time to spare. Bishop agrees to do it as he believes he is the best person for the job (though he'd prefer not to, saying that 'I may be synthetic, but I'm not stupid').

In the meantime, the aliens are advancing down another corridor covered by the remaining pair of sentry guns. The weapons open fire and kill many of the creatures. Eventually one gun runs dry, and the other stops with just 10 rounds left in its ammunition box. But it has succeeded in driving off the creatures, which are unaware of the perilous ammunition situation.

As there are now only a few Marines left, Hicks shows Ripley how to use a pulse rifle, including the powerful grenade launcher mounted underneath the main barrel. By this time Gorman has recovered from his concussion and apologises to Ripley for his indecision, but she tells him to just forget about it. Carrying her pulse rifle on its shoulder strap, Ripley goes to the medical lab where she finds Newt under a bed fast asleep. She slips off her rifle, puts it on top of the bed, and gets under it to sleep beside Newt. Meanwhile, Bishop has arrived at the location of the uplink and is operating a small portable keyboard. Above him the dish aerial starts to rotate and changes its orientation in response to Bishop's input on the keypad. On the *Sulaco*, the second dropship starts its engines and prepares to make its journey to the planet's surface.

Back in the Med-Lab, Ripley awakens and immediately notices that two glass jars are lying on their sides on the floor a few yards away, having discharged their contents. She realises immediately that the two live facehuggers have escaped from captivity and are somewhere in the lab seeking out their prey... which can only be her and Newt! She wakes up the little girl, telling her that they are both in trouble.

Suddenly a facehugger jumps at Ripley, who manages to fend off its attack by turning the bed on its side and trapping the facehugger behind it. Part of this scene was achieved very simply by reverse filming in which the facehugger was pulled rapidly from behind using a wire. Ripley looks for her pulse rifle but it is now outside the lab, the doors of which have been locked. In an effort to attract attention she waves at the television camera, but in the control centre Burke simply turns off the monitor so that no-one is aware of her plight.

Back in the Med-Lab, Newt suggests that Ripley breaks the glass. Quickly she picks up a chair and tries to smash the pane, but it is too tough. Newt says that she is scared, and Ripley replies: 'Me too'. Suddenly, Ripley has an idea. She pulls a cigarette lighter from her pocket, flicks it on, and holds it under the heat detector on the ceiling of the lab. Within seconds the fire alarm starts and sprinklers activate. Back in the command centre, Hicks orders Vasquez and Hudson to meet him as quickly as possible in the Med-Lab to find out what's happened. Arriving at the lab, Hicks breaks the glass with a burst from his pulse rifle and then smashes through. The first facehugger threatening Newt is killed with several pulse rifle rounds and then Hicks, Vasquez and Hudson manage to pull another off Ripley before it can impregnate her. On a count of three, the Marines rip the creature off Ripley, uncoiling the tail round her neck, and throw it against a wall. Immediately Vazquez destroys it with a well-aimed burst from her pulse rifle.

The recovering Ripley explains that Burke was behind this near-disaster. Later in the command centre, she gives an explanation of what she believes Burke's plan was. He planned to ensure that herself and Newt were impregnated by facehuggers, and then intended to smuggle the frozen bodies through quarantine. In order for the plan to succeed all the surviving Marines would have to die, and Ripley suggests that this would have been achieved by sabotaging the cryogenic sleep chambers and then ejecting the bodies into space.

Hudson is appalled at this revelation and threatens Burke, saying that he's 'dogmeat'. Burke denies everything, and claims that it is nothing but Ripley's paranoid fantasies. However, Hicks takes command of the situation and decides to kill Burke immediately. Unfortunately, Hicks is unable to carry out his plan because the power is suddenly cut.

Hudson's tracker shows that there is movement all over the place, and the aliens appear to be approaching the command centre. Vazquez seals the door with her hand welding torch, as the tracking devices shows the aliens are only 20 metres away. Ripley cannot understand why this has happened because she thought she had covered every angle. So how are the aliens managing to approach them?

As the Marines prepare to repel the invading aliens, Hicks asks them to use short controlled bursts from their pulse rifles to conserve their limited ammunition. Eventually Ripley realises that the aliens must be making their way towards them in the space above the ceiling. Hicks removes a ceiling panel and looks into the space, only to be confronted with a mass of moist, squirming aliens making their way towards the humans. This highly effective shot was achieved by holding the camera upside down, which makes the aliens look as though they're sticking to the ceiling.

Hicks jumps down to warn everyone but, within seconds, several aliens burst through the ceiling prompting the Marines to open fire. Ripley suggests a retreat to the Med-Lab before killing an alien herself with a short burst of fire. Unfortunately, in all the confusion no one has bothered to keep an eye on Burke, who has retreated through the only exit and then sealed the door from the other side.

Hudson dies a hero, taking down several aliens before his demise, while Vazquez dispatches two of the creatures using the 30mm grenade launcher on her pulse rifle. Meanwhile, Ripley bangs on the door, asking Burke to open it. But on the other side, the company bureaucrat encounters an alien warrior who attacks him.

Newt and Ripley escape from the command centre via some ducting, followed by Hicks, Gorman, and Vazquez who kills another alien with her rifle. As Bishop reports that he will arrive at the complex in 16 minutes, Vazquez runs out of rifle ammunition and has to use her pistol to defend herself. The handguns used in *Aliens* were unmodified Heckler and Koch VP70s which had a futuristic appearance.

By now Gorman and Vazquez are trapped in a conduit with aliens on both sides and no bullets left. As the monsters close in, Vazquez pulls out a 30mm grenade and presses hard twice on the button on top, arming the weapon. The munition explodes, killing Gorman and Vazquez and taking two aliens with them. Unfortunately the shock wave blows Newt down a chute, and she splashes into some water in the level below. The only way that Ripley can save her is by cutting through some metal grill flooring above her, and she exhorts Hicks to do this as quickly as possible. Just as it looks as if she's about to be saved, an alien warrior rises from the water behind Newt and carries her away.

Ripley wants to go after Newt because, as she tells Hicks, 'they don't kill you'. But he points out that there is nothing that she can do at that moment, and they have to concentrate on escaping. The two of them get into a lift. Hicks presses the button to close the door, but before this can happen an alien warrior appears in the doorway. Hicks kills the alien with his pulse rifle, but the acid splashes all over him and starts to burn its way through his metal breastplate. Quickly Ripley unfastens the armour plate and it crashes to the ground just before the acid eats its way through it.

With 26 minutes to go before the complex explodes, the dropship arrives and Ripley and Hicks board it. As soon as she gets aboard, Ripley arms herself with a new pulse rifle. She slaps in a full magazine, which gives her 97 rounds, and also tapes an M240 flamethrower to the gun, creating a devastating combination weapon. She also loads the under-slung grenade launcher with four 30mm grenades, slings a bandolier over her shoulder, and tapes a tracking device to her rifle. She now has just 19 minutes left before detonation.

Ripley discovers that Hicks' first name is Dwayne, and she in turn reveals that her forename is Ellen. Using the tracker fitted to her gun as a guide, she enters the alien nest firing short bursts from her flamethrower to keep any hidden aliens at bay. She cannot find Newt, who is nearby in a cocoon. But then an alien egg in front of the child opens and a facehugger emerges. Newt screams and Ripley hears the noise. Just in the nick of time she fires a short burst at the alien egg, killing the face hugger.

Then she starts to pull Newt out of her cocoon and, as she makes her way to safety, she discovers that she is standing in a field of alien eggs. As she looks up she sees a long oviduct discharging eggs which is attached to a huge version of the alien creature, which Ripley realises must be the Queen.

Two alien warriors emerge from different directions to tackle Ripley, but she fires a burst from her flamethrower over the eggs and makes her intentions clear to the Queen. If she is attacked she will flame the eggs, destroying many of the facehuggers. The Queen understands the threat and signals the two alien warriors to retreat.

The Alien Queen was created by Stan Winston from designs by James Cameron. Two stuntmen were inside the costume to work the four limbs, and the longer two were operated by means of devices like ski poles. In addition, five puppeteers and four technicians operated mechanisms which worked by various means including wires, Bowden cables, and hydraulics. The Queen had to be suspended from wires, as it could not stand upright by itself. For some scenes a smaller puppet operated by rods was used.

Ripley slowly backs away from the field of eggs but then suddenly opens fire with the flamethrower destroying many of them. She also uses her pulse rifle to good effect and kills the two warriors. Finally she fires all four 30mm grenades from her pulse rifle at the Queen's oviduct, and then throws her bandolier of grenades into the flaming cauldron. All the eggs have been destroyed, and it looks as though the Queen is going to be engulfed by the flames. But, as Ripley withdraws, the big alien tears her body away from the oviduct, becoming a terrifying 14-foot fighting warrior.

Carrying Newt, whose arms are around her neck, Ripley makes her way to the lift and ascends to the higher level where Bishop is going to pick her up in the dropship. But he is not there! She has no bullets left in her pulse rifle, her flamethrower is almost exhausted, and she is out of grenades. Meanwhile, the Queen is ascending in the second elevator – intent on killing Ripley and Newt in revenge for the death of all her offspring. The complex is now in flames and, if the Queen doesn't get them, the inferno will. Just as the Queen is about to arrive, the dropship appears, piloted by Bishop. Ripley and Newt climb on board, and the craft departs at speed as the complex blows up.

Later, back on the *Sulaco*, Bishop and Ripley attend to the injured Hicks who rests on a cot with his head and eyes bandaged. Bishop explains he had to take off to circle, as the platform was unstable. Ripley reassures him that he 'did good'.

Suddenly a drop of acid blood appears in front of Bishop's foot, burning a hole in the floor. Then a spear-like shape bursts out of Bishop's chest. Initially it looks like a face hugger has emerged but, as Bishop is lifted up, Ripley realises that it is the tail of the alien Queen who has somehow managed to get on the dropship before it lifted off. Bishop starts vomiting a white substance (which in reality was milk and yoghurt) as he is pulled up towards the main body of the Queen. As he reaches the Queen's body she uses her arms to rip him into two pieces. The top half of Bishop's body – consisting of his chest, arms and head – falls on the floor.

Once again, Ripley uses her initiative to turn the situation around. She waves her arms to attract the Queen's attention while Newt scampers to safety beneath the grille-like floor. Then, once she knows Newt is safe, she sprints into a nearby bay and closes a metal power-operated door behind her. The alien chases after her and tries to bash her way into the room, but even the powerful Queen cannot break through such a thick metal door. Instead, she turns round and tries to find Newt. Eventually she sees her beneath the grille floor and lifts up a panel to expose her. She is about to grab Newt when a power-operated door opens, revealing Ripley who is now operating a power loader. Sitting within the powered exoskeleton, she is now at least the equal of the Queen in strength.

'Get away from her, you bitch!' she says angrily.

Ripley starts fighting the Queen using her power loader, and soon has the upper hand. At one point the Queen tries to attack her using her extending tongue, which includes sharp teeth and a second jaw, but Ripley repels her by switching on the built-in welding torch which is part of the power loader's equipment.

Rather like the Alien Queen, the Power Loader was suspended from steel cables and required a stuntman inside it (behind Sigourney Weaver) and several off-screen technicians to operate it. A smaller quarter-scale rod puppet was also built for some scenes. The sound effect of the mechanisms operating was apparently the same one used in *Kelly's Heroes* (1970) to depict a rotating Tiger tank turret.

Eventually Ripley grabs the alien Queen and uses remote-control buttons to open some power-operated sliding doors on the floor, which lead into a large vertical airlock. Her plan is to drop the Queen into the airlock and then open the outer doors at the bottom, throwing the creature into space.

Unfortunately things don't go quite to plan and, as the Queen falls into the airlock, she takes the power loader with her. Both go clattering to the bottom of the airlock where they hit the outer doors with a mighty crash. Ripley quickly clambers out of the power loader and climbs up a ladder at the side of the airlock as the Queen tries to follow her. Eventually Ripley reaches the top of the ladder and opens the outer airlock doors. The power loader falls out and eventually the Alien Queen is sucked out as well, screaming as she is discharged into outer space. However, all the air in the loading bay is being sucked out through the airlock and Newt is in danger of being drawn out as well. She is only saved when Bishop grabs her. Eventually Ripley manages to close the outer airlock door, and the pressure in the loading bay returns to normal.

The final scene is set in the hyper-sleep chambers which we saw earlier in the film. The injured Bishop has been placed in one of the capsules with some kind of drip attached, while Hicks is also in one of the chambers. As Ripley and Newt appear to go back into hyper sleep, Newt asks if they're going to sleep all the way home and if it will be safe for them to dream. 'Yes', replies Ripley, 'we can now dream', and she implies that there will be no more nightmares about monsters.

*Aliens* was released in North America on 18 July 1986, and in the UK on 29 August that year. It was the number one film at the American box office for four weeks, and eventually grossed $180m – ten times its budget.

Initially running at about two and a half hours long, 17 minutes of footage were deleted prior to release. The scenes which were cut included the Jorden family's discovery of the derelict ship, Ripley finding out that her daughter had died two years earlier (thus giving her greater motivation to save Newt), and all the shots featuring sentry guns.

In 1992 a 'Special Edition' was released on VHS and Laserdisc which reinstated most of the missing scenes, giving a running time of two hours and 28 minutes, and my scene-by-scene description on the preceding pages is of this longer version.

The film's composer, the late James Horner, was never entirely happy with his score for the movie, as he considered that he had been given insufficient time to complete his work. He was also displeased at the antiquated technical facilities at the EMI Abbey Road studios in London where he had to work. Despite his reservations, the score was nominated for an Academy Award.

*Aliens* was also nominated for six other Oscars including Best Sound, Best Film Editing, and Best Art Direction and Set Decoration. It won two awards for Sound Effects Editing and Visual Effects, while Sigourney Weaver received her first Academy Award nomination for Best Actress.

In 1992 a third Alien film, *Alien³*, premiered. Directed by David Fincher, it opened with the deaths of Hicks, Newt and Bishop – something which upset James Cameron, since much of the plot of *Aliens* was concerned with saving Newt. The film also did not feature any guns, something which apparently was in accordance with Sigourney Weaver's own wishes.

This film was poorly received by many fans, who would have preferred to see more of Newt, Hicks and the Colonial Marines. In the mid-nineties the British fanzine *Dreamwatch Bulletin* (aka *DWB*) published an alternative screenplay for a third *Alien* film which did feature these elements, and was very much like a direct continuation of *Aliens.* Sadly it was never made.

Five years later, another sequel – *Alien: Resurrection* (1997) – appeared, featuring a cloned Ripley (who had died at the end of the previous film) who now had acid blood as a result of her having a combination of human and alien DNA, something which played a key part in the plot.

After this film there were hopes that a fifth *Alien* film – possibly written by James Cameron, directed by Ridley Scott and featuring Sigourney Weaver – would be made, but instead 20th Century Fox chose to make *Alien vs Predator (AVP)* (2004) – directed by Paul W.S. Anderson – to bring together the *Alien* and *Predator* franchises. This new direction in the series dismayed many fans, though James Cameron reportedly preferred it to *Alien: Resurrection.*

A rather dismal sequel – *Alien vs Predator: Requiem* (2007) – followed, and performed poorly at the box office, making just $42m against a budget of $40m. At this stage it might be assumed that the next logical step for 20<sup>th</sup> Century Fox would be a film entitled *Abbott and Costello Meet the Alien and Predator*, but in fact there have been reliable reports that a new film – *Alien 5* – might be produced in 2017 or 2018 starring Sigourney Weaver and helmed by respected director Neill Blomkamp. This movie would apparently follow on directly from *Aliens* and would disregard the events of *Alien³* and *Alien: Resurrection*, resulting in the re-appearance of older versions of Hicks and Newt.

Production paintings which can be viewed on YouTube show an older Hicks with a half-scarred face and opaque cornea (caused by the acid burns he sustained toward the end of *Aliens*). The most recent reports suggest that the film may not be made because of possible conflicts with planned further sequels to Ridley Scott's *Prometheus* (2012), but it will be interesting to see what happens in the years ahead. *Aliens*, though, remains the best of the franchise to date, and is not just one of the best science fiction films of all time but also one of the truly great action movies.

# *Aliens* (1986)
# Production Credits

Director: James Cameron
Screenplay: James Cameron
Based on story material by
David Giler and Walter Hill,
and original characters created
by Dan O'Bannon and Ronald
Shusett

## Cast
Ripley - Sigourney Weaver
Newt - Carrie Henn
Corporal Hicks - Michael Biehn
Burke - Paul Rieser
Bishop - Lance Henriksen
Private Hudson - Bill Paxton
Lieutenant Gorman - William
Hope
Private Vasquez - Jenette
Goldstein
Sergeant Apone - Al Matthews
Private Drake - Mark Rolston
Private Frost - Ricco Ross
Corporal Ferro - Colette Hiller
Private Spunkmeyer - Daniel
Kash
Corporal Dietrich - Cynthia
Scott
Private Crowe - Tip Tipping
Private Wierzbowski - Trevor
Steedman
Van Leuwen - Paul Maxwell
ECA Rep - Valerie Colgan
Insurance Man - Alan Polonsky
Med Tech - Alibe Parsons
Doctor - Blain Fairman

Cocooned Woman - Barbara
Coles
Alien Warriors - Carl Toop,
Chris Webb
Power Loader Operator - John
Lees
Lydecker - William Armstrong
Newt's Father - Jay Benedict
Newt's Mother - Holly De Long
Newt's Brother - Christopher
Henn
Ripley's Mother - Elizabeth
Inglis
Simpson - Mac McDonald
Salvage Team Leader - Stuart
Milligan
Salvager - Tom Woodruff Jr

## Producers
Executive Producers: Gordon
Carroll, David Giler, Walter Hill
Producer: Gale Anne Hurd

## Music
Composer: James Horner

## Cinematography
Director of Photography:
Adrian Biddle

## Film Editing
Film Editor: Ray Lovejoy

## Production Design
Production Designer: Peter
Lamont

## Art Direction
Supervising Art Director: Terry Ackland-Snow
Art Directors: Ken Court, Bert Davey, Fred Hole, Michael Lamont

## Set Decoration
Set Decorator: Christian Sallis

## Costume Design
Costume Designer: Emma Porteous

## Make-up Department
Chief Hairstylist: Elaine Bowerbank
Make-up Supervisor: Peter Robb-King
Special Make-up Effects: Everett Burrell
Creature Effects Crew: Tony Gardner
Assistant Make-up Artist: Melissa Street

## Production Management
Unit Production Managers: Gil Whelan, Mo Coppitters
Production Supervisor: Hugh Harlow

## Second Unit Director or Assistant Director
First Assistant Director: Derek Cracknell
Second Assistant Director: Melvin Lind
Second Unit Director: Stan Winston
Second Assistant Director: Julian Wall

## Art Department
Conceptual Designer: Ron Cobb
Property Master: Berty Hearn
Conceptual Artist: Syd Mead
Production Buyer: Sidney Palmer
Construction Manager: Vic Simpson
Graphics Artist: Janice Body
Draughtsman: Michael Boone
Plasterer: Mick Chubbock
Artistic Supervisor (Miniature Effects): Tony Gardner
Technical Set Dresser: Mark Harris
Supervising Plasterer: Paul James
Art Department Assistant: Simon Lamont
Sketch Artist: Maciek Piotrowski
Draughtsman: Tony Rimmington
Prop Storeman: Colin Thurston

## Sound Department
Dubbing Mixer: Michael A. Cater
Sound Recordist: Roy Charman
Sound Editors: Scott Brose, Deveril Goodman, William Parnell, Peter Horrocks, Jack T. Knight, Alan Paley

Chief Dubbing Mixer: Graham
V. Hartstone
Dubbing Mixer: Nicholas Le
Mesurier
Dialogue Editor: Archie Ludski
Foley Editor: Rocky Phelan
Supervising Sound Editor: Don
Sharpe
Assistant Sound Editor: Chris
Blunden
Re-recording Mixers: Jeffrey
Perkins, Otto Snel
ADR Mixer: Lionel Strutt

**Special Effects**
Workshop Supervisor: Norman
Baillie
Creature Effects Crew: Nigel
Booth, Mark Williams, John
Robertson, Ian Rolph, Matt
Rose, Bill Sturgeon, Willie
Whitten, Stephen Norrington,
Christine Overs, Rick Lazzarini,
Ray Lovell, Lindsay McGowan,
Graham High, Steven James,
David Keen, Trevor Butterfield,
Julian Caldow, Gregory Figiel,
Philomena Davis
Creature Effects Coordinators:
Richard Landon, Shane Mahan
Senior Special Effects
Technicians: Ron Burton, Ron
Cartwright, Michael Dunleavy,
Nick Finlayson, Paul Whybrow,
Joss Williams, Peter Pickering
Creature Effects Coordinator:
Alec Gillis
Special Effects Technician:
Matthew Harlow

Special Effects Supervisor: John
Richardson
Senior Special Effects
Technician: John Morris
Alien Effects Creator: Stan
Winston
Creature Effects Coordinators:
John Rosengrant, Tom
Woodruff Jr
Sculptor: Howard Berger
Miniature Effects Unit: Michael
Burnett
Special Effects: Dave Chagouri
Special Effects Assistant: Simon
Cockren
Video Effects Technician: Simon
Hewitt
Effects Crew (Los Angeles):
Julian Parry
Miniature Effects Assistant:
Tim Turner
Special Effects Technician:
Andy Williams
Model Maker: Steven
Woodcock
Visual Effects Unit
Camera Operators: Michael
Anderson, Leslie Dear
Senior Special Effects
Technician: Jonathan Angell
Mechanical Armature Design:
Doug Beswick
Senior Special Effects
Technician: John Brown
Assistant Director: Paul Frift
Editor: Robert Gavin
Video Effects Supervisor:
Richard Hewitt

Visual Effects Supervisor: Brian Johnson
Assistant Director (Visual Effects): Christopher Knowles
Camera Operator (Visual Effects): David Litchfield
Miniatures Technical Supervisor: Pat McClung
Senior Special Effects Technician: Digby Milner
Process Photographer: Roy Moores
Mechanical Armature Design: Phil Notaro
Camera Operator: Harry Oakes
Art Director: Peter Russell
Construction Manager: Barry Saunders
Visual Effects Supervisors: Dennis Skotak, Robert Skotak, Alan G. Markowitz
Miniature Floor Effects: Brian Smithies
Production Secretary: Sarah Spooner
Process Photographer: Charles Staffell
Unit Production Manager: Paul Tivers
Gaffer: Wally Wheeler
Titles and Video Graphics Design: Tony White
Visual Effects: Larry Arpin, Suzanne M. Benson
Model Effects: Steven Begg
Rotoscope Artists: Martin Body, Andrew Coates
Visual Effects Trainee: Zoe Cain

Optical Camera Operator: Alan Church
Motion Control Programmer: Andrew Elo
Cosmetic Supervisor: Tony Gardner
Model Makers: John Lee, Jay Roth
Matte Artist: Peter Melrose
Optical Compositing: Tim Ollive
Camera Grip: Tony Rowland
Assistant Visual Effects Editor: Adrian Trent

**Stunts**
Stunt Performers: Elanor Bertram, Simon Crane, Sue Crosland, Steve Dent, Stuart Fell, Jazzer Jeyes, Sean McCabe, Eddie Powell, Chris Webb, Bill Weston, Jason White, Tom Delmar, Nick Gillard
Stunt Doubles (Carrie Henn): Kiran Shah, Louise Head
Stunts (Queen Alien): Stuart St Paul, Malcolm Weaver
Stunt Double (Private Frost): Clive Curtis
Stunt Coordinator: Paul Weston

**Camera and Electrical Department**
Camera Focus: Martin Hume, Martin Kenzie
Camera Operators: Shaun O'Dell, David Worley
Still Photographer: Bob Penn
Gaffer: Jack Thetford

Video Operator: Kevin
Brookner
Steadicam Operator: Pete
Cavaciuti
First Assistant Camera: Michael
Condro
Generator Operator: Stewart
Hadley
Focus Puller: Paul Kenward
Special Photographer: Rolf
Konow
Gaffer (Second Unit): Michael
McDermott
Electrician: Pat Miller
Steadicam Operator: Jan Pester
Assistant Camera: Nigel Seal
Video Assist Operator: Chris
Warren

**Casting Department**
Casting (USA): Jane Feinberg,
Mike Fenton
Casting (UK): Mary Selway,
Judy Taylor

**Costume Department**
Costume Supervisor: Tiny
Nicholls

**Editorial Department**
Associate Editor: Peter Bolta
Second Assistant Editor: Simon
Harris
First Assistant Editors: hil
Sanderson, William Parnell
Assistant Editors: Robert
Hambling, Steve Maguire
Editor (Additional Material,
Special Edition): Brian Q. Kelley

**Music Department**
Music Editors: Robin Clarke,
Michael Clifford
Synthesizer Effects: Randall
Frakes, Robert Garret, Ian
Underwood
Orchestrator: Greg Ritchie
Music Recording Engineer: Eric
Tomlinson
Orchestra: London Symphony
Orchestra
Score Re-mixer: Michael J.
MacDonald
Music Pre-dub Mixer: Otto Snel

**Other Crew**
Assistant to Producer: Polly
Apostolof
Production Accountant: Jill
Bennett
Script Supervisor: Diana Dill
Unit Publicist: Geoff Freeman
Original Alien Design: H.R.
Giger
Location Auditor: Jay Roberts
Production Controller: Paul
Tucker
Production Coordinator: Joyce
Turner
Armourers: Simon Atherton,
Andrew Fletcher
Queen Alien Design: James
Cameron
Armour Designer: Terry English
Production Assistant: J.
Randolph Harrison

# 8

# PREDATOR

## (1987)

*Silver Pictures/Lawrence Gordon Productions/
Davis Entertainment*

**Director:** John McTiernan
**Producers:** Joel Silver, Lawrence Gordon
and John Davis
**Screenwriters:** Jim Thomas and John Thomas

ALONG with *The Terminator* (1984) *and Aliens* (1986), *Predator* is one of the three greatest science fiction action movies made in the 1980s. It is best remembered for its stunning combat scenes and remarkable creature design by Stan Winston. If Swiss artist H.R. Giger's striking concepts for *Alien* can be considered the most original space monster in the history of the movies then the Predator must come a close second.

It is interesting to note that the original *Alien*, *Terminator* and *Predator* movies all spawned franchises which continue to this day, each of them with various sequels, remakes and reboots. As previously noted in the chapter on *Aliens*, there have even been two *Alien vs Predator* sequels which have combined two of the franchises.

The story of *Predator* began in 1985. At that time, the fourth *Rocky* film had just been made and a joke was circulating in Hollywood that the only thing left for Sylvester Stallone's character to do was fight an alien. Taking inspiration from this joke, novice scriptwriters Jim and John Thomas produced a 'spec' script (a 'speculative', i.e. unsolicited, non-commissioned script) in which aliens came to Earth to hunt prey for sport. Simple logic dictated that the most challenging opponents would be a group of Special Forces soldiers, and a completed script with this plot – at that point called *Hunter* – was sent to film producer Michael Levy. Eventually the screenplay ended up in the hands of producer Joel Silver, who had just made *Commando* (1985) starring Arnold Schwarzenegger, and he realised it would make an excellent big-budget action movie. Eventually the title was altered to *The Predator* (and later to the shorter *Predator*), and the group of hunter aliens envisaged by Jim and John Thomas was changed to just one creature.

Arnold Schwarzenegger was given the lead role of Major Alan 'Dutch' Schultz, a tough Special Forces commander with an incredible physique. Schwarzenegger's career was really taking off at that point following roles in *Conan the Barbarian* (1982), *Conan the Destroyer* (1984) and *The Terminator* (1984). The only other actor who could have conceivably played the part of Schultz would have been Sylvester Stallone, but he was committed to the series of *Rambo* movies which are discussed elsewhere in this book.

In the mid to late eighties the media made much of the supposed rivalry between Schwarzenegger and Stallone, particularly as *Commando* and *Rambo: First Blood Part II* (both 1985) were perceived as being very similar, competing movies. But in fact the two actors were good friends and, with Bruce Willis, they later set up the series of 'Planet Hollywood' restaurants round the globe.

Most of the other actors who participated in *Predator* also had very muscly physiques. Jesse Ventura (who played Blain) was a former wrestler and weightlifter, while Carl Weathers (George Dillon) was a bodybuilder and athlete whose most famous role to date was as boxer Apollo Creed in the *Rocky* movies. Bill Duke (Mac Eliot), who had previously starred with Schwarzenegger in *Commando*, had an imposing 6 foot 4½ inch frame and a muscular build. The casting of such physically powerful actors was not necessarily inaccurate, because in the US Special Forces (such as the Navy SEALs and Delta Force) there is a tradition of bodybuilding. This is in sharp contrast to the British SAS and SBS, whose troopers – while being very fit – tend to be wiry rather than muscle-bound.

One unusual piece of casting was Shane Black, who played the squad's radioman, Rick Hawkins. The 25 year old had written the screenplay for *Lethal Weapon* (1987), and the producers were keen to have him on the set in case any last-minute script changes were required. In the event, Black's only contribution to the script were the two infamous 'pussy jokes', of which more later. For his role as Hawkins, Black wore a pair of large spectacles and read Sergeant Rock comics to look 'geeky'. It was also originally intended that he wear a red beret to stand out from the other characters. Black declined to do this, but later regretted the decision. Incidentally the red beret is universally recognised as the preferred headgear of airborne troops (hence the reason the 1953 Alan Ladd movie *The Red Beret* is also known as *Paratrooper*). This is one of the major errors in the UNIT costumes in post-2005 *Doctor Who* stories, as the soldiers wear red berets but clearly are not parachute troops.

The production was mainly shot in Mexico at two different locations, namely Puerto Viarta and Pallenca. One problem with the former location was that no-one had realised that the jungle there had deciduous trees and, by the time filming started in the autumn of 1986, the leaves were going brown. The problem was solved by placing branches with green leaves in the foreground of many shots but, despite this, brown leaves can be seen lying on the ground in many scenes.

The director was John McTiernan, who at that point had only made one theatrical feature *Nomads* (1986) but who, the following year, would score a major hit with *Die Hard.* McTiernan later consolidated his position as a competent action director with the third *Die Hard* picture, *Die Hard with a Vengeance* (1995), the submarine movie *The Hunt for Red October* (1990), and the highly-criticised though competently-made *The Last Action Hero* (1993).

The actor originally chosen to play the Predator was Jean-Claude Van Damme, a Belgian celebrity who some tabloid newspapers dubbed 'the Muscles from Brussels'. Van Damme later became an action star in his own right, though some of his later movies were flops – notably *Sudden Death* (1995), which might be described as '*Die Hard* in an Ice Rink'. After just two days filming in the original Predator costume, Van Damme left the movie to be replaced by Kevin Peter Hall, a 7 foot 2 inch Afro-American actor. Van Damme found his costume to be very uncomfortable, and was also concerned at being in a movie where his face would not be seen.

The film opens with an anamorphic version of the 20th Century Fox logo. This was a practical joke on the part of director John McTiernan, who was not permitted to make the film in Panavision as it would have greatly increased the cost of the special effects sequences.

Then, to the accompaniment of Alan Silvestri's music – which beautifully conveys the vastness of space – there is a shot of a star field. The camera tilts down to reveal an odd-looking alien spacecraft traversing the screen. It is noticeable that the craft moves from left to right, since in the world of special effects this is perceived as the 'correct' direction – possibly because most people perceive their past as being to their left and the future to their right. This is the same reason why in *Star Trek* the *Enterprise* always orbits planets in an anti-clockwise direction, since this looks 'right'.

This mother craft ejects a smaller ship containing the Predator, which makes its way into the Earth's atmosphere.

The titles then roll, played out over footage of a Bell 212 UH-1N Twin Huey helicopter coming in to land on a beach in an undisclosed Latin American country as three CJ-5 jeeps drive up. Two other choppers – a second Huey and a civilian Bell 206 Jet Ranger in military livery – are already sitting on the beach on small helipads made from wooden decking.

One of the Huey's passengers, Major Alan 'Dutch' Schaefer (Arnold Schwarzenegger), lights a cigar and jumps out of the chopper accompanied by the rest of his men. The glow of Dutch's lit cigar inside the helicopter cabin was the only piece of CGI in the whole film, as this technology was in its infancy. For safety reasons it wasn't possible to actually light a real cigar inside the fuselage.

Schaefer's arrival is witnessed by Major-General Homer Phillips (R.G. Armstrong). As director John McTiernan has admitted, the 69-year old Armstrong was really too old for the part of Phillips, but the production crew got round this problem by using a lot of suntan make-up to hide his wrinkles. The occupants of the helicopter get into the three jeeps, and the one containing 'Dutch' comes to a halt outside the wooden office where Philips and Dutch's old colleague George Dillon (Carl Weathers) are already waiting.

Phillips tells Schaefer that he and his men are needed to defuse a potentially explosive situation. A military helicopter containing a Cabinet Minister and his aide has strayed off course and crashed on the wrong side of the border, and Schaefer and his squad have to rescue them before they can be executed by guerrillas. Schaefer thinks that such a mission should be a job for the regular army, but Dillon disagrees as he feels that Dutch and his men are the best people for the task.

Curiously, the exact location of the action in *Predator* is never revealed, but it is clear that it is taking place in an unspecified Central American or South American country. If Steven de Souza had been involved in the production, it would probably have taken place in 'Val Verde' (see the chapter in this book on *Commando*). The novelization of the film does mention the events of *Predator* taking place in Val Verde, but dialogue in the sequel *Predator 2* (1990) suggests Guatemala as the location for the action. Similarly it is never specified whether Schaefer's squad is a serving unit of the US Army or just a group of mercenaries with previous US Special Forces experience. The helicopters that take them into battle, for example, are painted in camouflage but don't carry any US markings, and were in reality civilian examples in warpaint.

After the short briefing, Dutch and Dillon greet each other. It is clear that they go back together a long way. They slap their hands together and then engage in some brief macho arm wrestling. Dillon – who now works for the CIA – asks Dutch why he 'passed on Libya', and Dutch replies that his squad are 'a rescue team, not assassins'. In 1986 US President Ronald Reagan sanctioned air strikes against Libya on 15

April (Operation El Dorado Canyon) from British airbases and US Navy aircraft carriers, in retaliation for the bombing of the La Belle nightclub in West Berlin on 5 April which had resulted in the deaths of three people (including a US serviceman) plus 229 wounded. Dillon's comments suggest that there may have been some kind of Special Forces actions against that North African country, perhaps with the intention of assassinating its leader – Colonel Muammar Gaddafi. Dillon concludes his dialogue by announcing that he is going to be taking part in the forthcoming mission to rescue the Cabinet Minister.

The film then cuts to a night-time action shot (filmed day-for-night) of the two Huey choppers flying low over the jungle. Inside one of the helicopters, its cabin lit by dim red light (to preserve night-vision), Blain Cooper (Jesse Ventura) is playing *Long Tall Sally* by Little Richard on a Sanyo cassette boombox strapped to the inside of the cabin. *Long Tall Sally* was first released in 1956, and was originally entitled *The Thing* which coincidentally was also the title of a 1982 John Carpenter movie on which the creator of the Predator costume – Stan Winston – had worked. The song was subsequently covered by other artists, including The Beatles.

As the troopers endure the deafening noise, Rick Hawkins tells Native American soldier Billy Sole (Sonny Landham) one of the first of two 'pussy jokes' in the film. 'The other day I went up to my girlfriend. I said I'd like a little pussy. She said: "Me too; mine's as big as a house"'. However, Billy doesn't get the joke.

As the two choppers make their way over the dense jungle, Blain Cooper is chomping his way through a bag of chewing tobacco. He offers some to his colleagues but they decline, and Cooper says they are a bunch of 'slack-jawed faggots' and that this stuff will turn them into a 'sexual tyrannosaurus': a rather puzzling claim to make, since one of the effects of tobacco consumption can be sexual dysfunction due to diminished blood flow to the penis.

Meanwhile, Mac Elliott (Bill Duke) is passing the time by shaving himself using a blue plastic disposable razor, but without any shaving cream (or even a mirror). Duke came up with this idea himself as a way of making his character stand out, though the razor had to be modified by the special effects department to ensure that he didn't cut himself.

Blain concludes his mastication by spitting out a large brown gob of well-chewed tobacco mixed with saliva onto the floor of the helicopter; behaviour which disgusts Dillon, as some has ended up on one of his boots. He tells Blain he has 'a real nasty habit'. Having reached their destination, the helicopters hover over the trees and the troops quickly abseil down ropes into the jungle. This method of exiting rapidly from a helicopter (also known as rappelling) to minimise exposure to enemy fire was widely used by the US military in Vietnam.

The soldiers plod through the jungle and soon find the wreck of a crashed Huey helicopter up a tree. It looks as though the machine has been taken out by a heat-seeking missile (which would have probably been a Soviet-made SA-7 Grail). Using his highly developed tracking skills, Billy establishes that the occupants of the helicopter were captured by twelve guerrillas and taken elsewhere. They were subsequently followed by six men wearing US Army-issue boots. Soon afterwards, the squad discovers three bodies hanging upside down from the trees. Their corpses have been mutilated, as their skins have been removed. Dutch finds a dog tag on the ground belonging to one of the men, Jim Hopper. He knew the dead men. They were all Green Berets out of Fort Bragg, and he wonders what they were doing here.

Billy works out that there had been a firefight with shooting in all directions, but doesn't understand what happened to the rest of Hopper's men who have apparently disappeared. Mac says it's time for a little pain, while Blain Cooper says it is 'payback time' and uncovers his personal weapon – a General Electric minigun. This wasn't the first time that this particular weapon had featured in a movie, but its use as a field weapon carried by one man was unique.

The story behind the General Electric Minigun is particularly fascinating. In 1862 American Dr Richard Gatling patented his design for a hand-cranked machine gun with six rotating barrels which was mounted on a large wheeled carriage. Some of these early Gatling guns were used in the American Civil War, and were capable of a rate of fire of 400 rounds per minute.

Dr Richard Gatling was qualified in medicine but never practised, and one of his motivations for creating his weapon was that he thought it would actually save lives as smaller armies could then be deployed on the battlefield, ultimately minimising casualties.

By the end of the 19th century, Gatling realised that an electrically-driven version of his design would be capable of very high rates of fire, but the US military were uninterested as they had already started to replace their Gatlings with smaller, lighter, single-barrelled Maxim guns which could fire at a rate of 500 rounds per minute, which was judged to be perfectly adequate.

After the end of the Second World War, US engineers decided to revisit the Gatling gun as they realised its firing mechanism was ideally suited to modern jet fighter aircraft which had a requirement for very high rates of cannon fire in order to destroy an enemy aircraft with a very brief burst lasting just a second or two. To test their theory, they took a 1903 model Gatling out of a museum, fitted it with an electric motor, and discovered it could then fire at 4000 rounds per minute. This discovery lead to the development of the M61 20mm Vulcan rotary cannon, which had a rate of fire of 6,200 rounds per minute and was subsequently fitted to US fighter aircraft from the late 1950s onwards. Updated versions of this weapon are still in use in aircraft such as the F-15 Eagle and F-16 Fighting Falcon.

Later, the General Electric company developed a smaller version of the weapon firing 7.62mm ammunition (known as the Minigun) which was installed on helicopters and fixed-wing aircraft during the Vietnam War. In more recent years, this gun has been fitted to naval vessels to protect them from attacks from speedboats and pirate craft.

The Minigun would not be practical as a field weapon in the manner depicted in the film as – due to its weight, bulk, enormous ammunition consumption and need for a power supply – it is really only suitable for use as a vehicle-mounted gun. Blain carries a backpack filled with bullets but, on account of the Minigun's colossal appetite for rounds, he would only be able to carry enough shells for a few seconds' firing. In addition, he would have to lug a huge, heavy battery pack around with him. In reality, the gun used in the film was powered by an off-screen electricity supply fed through concealed cables.

At this point the audience sees a 'Predator's eye view' of the troops making their way through the jungle, and it appears that the hunting alien sees with some kind of infrared heat vision. At the start of filming, attempts were made to achieve this footage using a real thermal imaging camera, but this proved impractical for a number of reasons. One of them was that the camera was very bulky and had to be attached by short, thick cables to equipment in the back of a truck. To get the shots that would be required by the production, the camera and truck would have to be mounted on a crane. Another problem was that the ambient temperature in the Mexican location was in the nineties, so human bodies did not stand out against background foliage as they were the same temperature. Attempts were made to overcome this problem by hosing down the jungle with ice-cold water, but this did not work so eventually the heat camera effect was achieved by manipulating the colour negative in the processing lab. Thus all shots of the Predator's 'heat vision' in the film are actually altered colour negatives.

Slowly, Dutch crawls to the perimeter of the guerrilla camp and then surveys the scene through his binoculars. As he watches, he sees one American soldier executed by a terrorist with a pistol. Using his initiative, Dutch sees a way to take the defenders by surprise. The rebels are using an old Willys 4x2 pick-up truck, with its rear wheels removed and its back end propped up to turn a water pump via a belt drive. Dutch creeps up to the back of the truck, places a satchel charge and timer in the flatbed, lifts the rear end of the vehicle off the ground and then sends it rolling down the hill out of control towards the guerrilla camp, where it explodes. While the fighters are still disorientated by this unexpected explosion, Dutch's men open fire with automatic weapons.

Schaefer carries an M-16 automatic rifle with an underslung M203 40mm grenade launcher, while Blain Cooper uses 'Painless' – his powerful General Electric Minigun – to great effect to mow down the guerrillas in large numbers.

Some of the guerrillas try to take off in a Huey helicopter and get as far as starting the engine, but their plans go awry when Dutch fires a 40mm grenade from his M203 into the fuselage of the chopper which causes a large explosion. Incidentally, the Huey which appears in this scene is the very same one which was used to depict the crashed example up a tree earlier in the film. The entire rebel encampment – complete with derelict Huey – still exists in Mexico as a tourist attraction.

One fighter tries to overpower Dutch, but he knocks her out and is astonished to discover that she is a female – Anna Gonsalves (Elpidia Carrillo). With the attack over, Dutch searches the guerrilla camp and discovers that the 'Cabinet Minister' was actually a CIA agent. Mac also points out that the troops manning the base included some Russian military advisers. It is obvious that something big was going to happen here. Dutch is angry with Dillon, because he realises he has been duped into attacking a guerrilla camp and wiping it out – thus preventing a military attack on a neighbouring country just over the nearby border – under the pretence that they were rescuing hostages. Dillon attempts to defend his position, saying that they have just stopped a major invasion (though how such a small enemy force could ever constitute a 'major invasion' is never made clear).

His explanation doesn't satisfy Dutch, who claims that he cooked up a story 'to put us in the meat grinder'. At this point, Hawkins interrupts their conversation to point out that aerial surveillance has reported that there are 'guerrillas all over the place' and they need to move out fast. Dillon agrees to this, but says that he wants to take the female guerrilla (Anna) along as a hostage.

As soldiers are arguing we see another 'heat vision' point-of-view shot of the Predator viewing them from the nearby jungle. As the alien watches, Mac spears a scorpion on Dillon's left shoulder with his combat knife and crushes it under his boot, leaving the dead insect on the ground.

As the Predator continues to observe the soldiers from a nearby vantage point, Hawkins tells Billy another pussy joke. 'The other day I was going down on my girlfriend. I said to her "Gee you've got a big pussy. Gee you've got a big pussy." And she said, "why did you say it twice?" And I said, "I didn't".'

Billy is initially puzzled by the joke, so Hawkins explains it to him. He is talking about the fact that his girlfriend's vagina was so big, there was an echo. Suddenly Billy gets the joke and starts laughing. Close nearby, the Predator imitates his laugh but the troops don't hear it. This is another curious feature of this particular alien – he has the ability to recite back anything that he hears, rather like a parrot.

As the troops head off through the jungle, there is another heat-vision point-of-view shot of the Predator finding the dead scorpion and apparently having some sympathy for it, suggesting that the alien is a similar species. This again follows another tradition in monster movies (also seen in the BBC TV series *Doctor Who*), which is that the alien or monster is never fully revealed until well into the story.

Close by, the troops pause for a rest and Mac has a swig from his hipflask. The troops get ready to move out again, but Billy is spooked. Dutch goes up to him to ask what is wrong. He replies that there is something in the trees, but he doesn't know exactly what it is. Although Billy cannot see the Predator, it can see him clearly with its heat vision. Suddenly Anna breaks free and tries to escape through the jungle. Dutch uses hand signals to tell his men to go after her, and she is chased by Hawkins who catches up with her. Hawkins sees a vague shape in the jungle and is then killed with a high-tech energy weapon. The other soldiers arrive, but they are puzzled as to what has happened to their colleague – there is blood everywhere but no sign of his body. Dutch orders his men to carry out a sweep to look for Hawkins' body as the camera tracks up to reveal the trooper's remains in the branches of a tree.

Blain is itching to go into action to avenge his comrade's death. 'Come on, you fuckers! Old painless is waiting', he says as he prepares his Minigun for action. Suddenly, Blain is struck down by an energy bolt from an unseen foe and collapses in a pool of blood. Dutch runs through the jungle and sees the vague shape of the Predator disappearing into the trees, firing his M-16 until he runs out of ammunition. Mac picks up Blain's discarded Minigun and blasts away at the unseen intruder. He is joined by all the other troops, and for a few minutes they blast away at the jungle with every available weapon – expending hundreds of rounds of ammunition plus grenades. The Minigun's fire is so powerful and concentrated that it actually cuts down trees, an effect that was achieved by mounting explosive squibs in the trunks and branches. Eventually the electric Gatling gun runs out of ammunition, and the only sound that can be heard is the electric motor rotating the six barrels at high speed.

One problem facing the film-makers was that the sound of a real Minigun firing at its normal rate of 3,000 to 4,000 rounds per minute was not dramatic enough as it sounded like a buzz-saw or a piece of canvas being ripped. Their solution was to create a sound effect for the gun by multi-tracking the noise of a Browning M2 0.50in cal machine gun firing, to which was added the sound of a whirring electric motor. In addition, the firing rate of the Minigun was reduced to a quarter of its normal rate to make the spinning barrels visible – otherwise the camera would have only recorded a blur.

Dutch examines Blain's body, but can't find any signs of powder burns. He realises that he needs to get on the radio to report what has happened, and also set up defensive positions. The defences include flares and Claymore mines, which are both activated by concealed tripwires.

The M18A1 Claymore mine, to give it its full title, is a directional anti-personnel mine invented by Norman MacLeod and named after a Scottish medieval sword. It is fired by a command wire, and shoots a pattern of metal balls into the kill zone rather like a shotgun.

As they setup their weapons, Dutch reflects on what a good soldier Blain was. At this point in the soundtrack there are a few bars of music which are Alan Silvestri's homage to Aaron Copland's famous 1942 composition *Fanfare for the Common Man*. This particular piece of music became very well-known when a rock version was recorded by the group Emerson, Lake and Palmer (ELP) in 1977. Both the Copland original and the ELP version have since been used many times on television as a stock music track. The original Copland composition was used as the title music for BBC TV Scotland's *Reporting Scotland* news programme in the late eighties and early nineties. Alan Silvestri named his pastiche of Copland's original *Fanfare for a Common Mercenary*.

As the soldiers are preparing their defences, the Predator is resting nearby. Though not killed by the troops' gunfire, he has been wounded and has to de-cloak in order to affect repairs. At this point in the film we still don't see the Predator in his entirety. One of the great clichés of science fiction is that alien monsters are always invulnerable to bullets, although it is not usually explained why this should be so. In *Predator* there is a plausible reason for the alien's resistance to conventional munitions, namely high-tech body armour. The alien's green blood was created very simply by extracting the fluid from fluorescent glow sticks, and the high-tech repair kit which the Predator accesses by flipping open a panel in his body armour was made from veterinary surgical tools.

As the Predator continues with his first-aid efforts, Dillon uses the radio to request an urgent evacuation by helicopter. Unfortunately this is denied because the extraction point has been compromised, and he is told to proceed to another location. Dutch is dismayed at the latest development and says that they are all regarded as 'expendable assets'.

Meanwhile, Mac has been spooked by his encounter with the Predator and says that he got a vague glimpse of the creature running away and offers the opinion that 'nothing on earth' could survive the volley of fire which the troops unleashed. As darkness falls on the troops' temporary encampment and the moon rises, we hear another rendition of Alan Silvestri's *Fanfare for a Common Mercenary*. Suddenly several of the flares and Claymore mines explode as something has triggered the tripwires. While the soldiers prepare to defend themselves, Mac is aware of a creature crawling through the jungle towards them and successfully kills it with a knife, although he is dismayed to discover he has in fact murdered a wild boar. The men then discover that Blain's body is gone – it appears that the Predator came in through the tripwires and took it from under their noses.

Dutch interrogates Anna and then asks her what she saw, but she's clearly traumatised and terrified. He then slices through her bonds to release her, explaining that they are now all in the same boat as the creature is intent on killing every one of them. The men have a chat about what they're going to do. Dillon wants to make for the new exfiltration point about 10 to 12 miles away, while Dutch wants to make a stand where they are. Anna then remembers that the creature that is hunting them was wounded in the recent battle and points to some glowing green blood on the leaves. Dutch makes the observation that 'if it bleeds, we can kill it'. The troops set up some more Claymore mines and also make a net trap for the creature by bending a tree using ropes. Dillon however is sceptical, wondering whether 'this Boy Scout BS is going to work'?

As the soldiers await the next attack, Mac nervously shaves himself with his disposable razor. The men set up tripwires on every tree within a 50 yard radius, ensuring that there is only one way in to the defensive position. Under the stress of waiting for something to happen, Mac cuts his cheek with a disposable razor which then breaks. This was a special effect achieved by drilling a hole inside a disposable razor and fitting a tube filled with fake blood.

Suddenly the rope net containing an invisible assailant is propelled high into the trees. But within seconds the creature breaks free by burning through the lattice using high-tech weapons. It falls to the ground and races away for safety. Mac fires at the retreating creature and throws Dillon an MP5 sub machine-gun. Dillon now opens fire on the alien using two MP5s, one in each hand, but it gets away apparently unharmed while Poncho has been injured by a falling log.

Mac and Dillon head off in hot pursuit of the creature and eventually spot it amongst the trees. Although the Predator is using its cloaking device, its outline can still be seen. At this point in the film, the Predator can only be glimpsed as a vague shape amid the trees. To achieve this impressive effect, an actor was filmed wearing a red suit and mask against the green backdrop of the jungle. Using the same technology used in green screen and blue screen matte work, this footage was used to create a 'hole' in the film image. A second camera then filmed exactly the same moves using motion control camera technology, but with no actor present and using a different focal length of lens. This second batch of footage was then used to fill in the optical 'hole' previously created by the red suit, resulting in the Predator appearing as a vague outline moving through the jungle. In an attempt to get shots of the Predator swinging through trees, a monkey was dressed in a red suit, but the ape became very embarrassed at having to wear the costume and wouldn't perform as desired.

As Mac crawls forward to get into a better position to open fire, three dots of laser light appear on his forehead. He has been targeted by the Predator and almost immediately he is shot. Next the Predator fires an energy bolt at Dillon which amputates his right arm above the elbow, but his MP5 submachine gun clutched tightly in his right hand keeps on firing.

Billy takes off his shirt and slashes his own left breast, but the Predator sees him with his heat vision and kills him with an energy bolt. Dutch fires his remaining M16 rounds at the creature, which returns fire. Poncho is then killed by an energy bolt. Now out of ammunition, Dutch screams at Anna to 'Run! Go! Get to da choppa!' as he crawls through leaves and then runs through the jungle pursued by the Predator. In his haste to get away from the creature, he slides off a cliff and falls down a steep incline into a river. This scene was achieved by having Arnold Schwarzenegger sit on a wooden wheeled bogie – on which an unmanned camera was mounted – which travelled down rails at speed. Dutch falls over the edge of a cliff and splashes into a river, but manages to swim ashore to some muddy ground. However, the Predator is behind him and emerges from the water as he pursues the Major. Dutch crawls ashore, by this time covered from top to toe in mud. At this point the Predator switches off its cloaking device, allowing Schultz to see its true form.

The alien searches for his prey, but is unable to see him with his infra-red vision due to the mud. Dutch realises that he can make himself invisible to the Predator by maintaining a coating of mud over his body. 'He couldn't see me', he mutters to himself.

At last Dutch realises that he now has a chance of defeating the alien as he has discovered a way to make himself invisible to his foe, so he gets to work preparing traps for the Predator using available materials such as tree logs. As the soldier continues with his work, the Predator is busy removing the spinal cord from a victim and blasting off all the remaining flesh using some kind of gas. Meanwhile, Dutch is preparing his traps. He breaks open two 40mm grenades and extracts the gunpowder propellant from them to use as the filling for a couple of 'leaf bombs', while the explosive warheads are employed to make explosive-tipped arrows.

Now he is ready to take on the Predator on what looks like equal terms. As he looks at the moon he starts a fire, screams, and then raises a blazing torch in his right hand as he walks across a fallen log. Some distance away, the Predator looks up astonished at this latest development. Within a few moments he arrives on the scene, swinging through branches. In a concealed position, Schultz sees the Predator walk across a large log, silhouetted against the flames. He fires one of his explosive-tipped arrows, which hits the tree trunk directly in front of the Predator. The alien is not injured but starts to panic, firing blindly in all directions. The resulting blast knocks Dutch off his log, but he manages a soft landing in leaves. Although not wounded, the Predator's invisibility cloak has now been damaged and he is visible. Dutch runs through the jungle, chased by the Predator. He clings to the underside of a log bridging a ravine as the Predator walks on top. To distract the alien, Dutch picks up a stone and throws it some distance. The creature turns round and fires at the location of the stone, while Schultz responds by throwing an explosive-tipped spear at his foe. The Predator has now been wounded – though not mortally – and Dutch is able to follow a trail of its fluorescent green blood spots. Dutch is thrown into the water by the blast of one of his leaf bombs and swims a distance, but then discovers that the water has washed off most of the mud which will make him visible to the creature.

Dutch looks up to find the Predator now looming above him. The two fight. The Predator gets the better of Schultz and then, as the Major lies on the ground exhausted, there is a hiss of gas as the Predator removes his helmet, revealing his true alien form and prompting Dutch to utter one of the most classic Schwarzenegger lines of all time: 'You are one ugly motherfucker'.

For the first time in the movie, we see the Predator's real face which up till now has been hidden by a mask. Originally the producers were going to use a creature with a bird-like head, but John McTiernan was appalled when the first costume arrived on set in Mexico. He realised that the monster that had been constructed simply wasn't realistic or striking enough, and there was a hiatus in filming while he approached Stan Winston who was regarded as one of the world's greatest experts in creature design. Winston had previously designed the skeletal robotic version of *The Terminator* and the Alien Queen in *Aliens* (based on sketches by James Cameron).

Winston's design for the Predator incorporated dreadlocks and a face with moving external mandibles, a suggestion which apparently came from his colleague James Cameron who had always wanted to see an alien with mandibles. Several radio-control units with individual operators were required to work all the different moving facial features, and the revised costume reportedly cost $1.5m. Another unique feature of the costume was the moving gun mounted on the Predator's left shoulder, which looked like a hairdryer and fired energy bolts.

The Predator approaches Dutch, and the two engage in a hand-to-hand fight. The alien appears to be winning, but then Dutch crawls away into a hole in the ground and – as he lies in this depression – he implores the creature to follow him and finish him off: 'Do it. Do it! Kill me! I'm here'. Fortunately the Predator takes the bait and, as he moves in for the kill, Dutch kicks away a branch, causing a large tree trunk to fall vertically on the Predator's head. The creature is badly wounded and bleeding. For the first time he's been seriously injured by a human because he made the fatal mistake of removing part of his body armour. Without his helmet he is vulnerable to attack. Dutch picks up a large rock, intending to smash it against the creature's skull and finish him off, but he hesitates when he realises the true alien nature of his opponent. 'What the hell are you?' he wonders.

The Predator still has one last card to play, though. He flips open a panel on his wrist, taps in a code and then laughs. Dutch twigs that he has set a timing device for a small tactical nuclear weapon. As the creature laughs, realising that he has deprived Dutch of victory in this final battle, the American soldier takes to his heels and runs as fast as possible. Small explosions start in the background and lightning bolts cross the skies as the countdown continues.

In the world of the movies we are quite used to the idea of heroes out-running explosions and fire balls, but this is the first time in cinema history that the hero actually outruns a nuclear blast. Suddenly there's a massive explosion, and the film cuts to the interior of a Huey helicopter where the pilot (Kevin Peter Hall, who also played the Predator) and Major General Paul Phillips, who we last saw at the beginning of the film, witness the atomic explosion. The helicopter comes in to pick up Dutch as Alan Silvestri's *Fanfare for a Common Mercenary* plays for the third and final time in the movie. Covered in dirt, Dutch is still standing amongst blasted trees and clouds of smoke. This scene was filmed in an area which had recently suffered a forest fire. The helicopter lands, Dutch gets in, and as it takes off the Predator's theme plays over the closing titles. The film concludes with shots of all the main cast members accompanied by captions giving their character names and those of the actor who played them. This is a homage to a technique which has been used in many famous war movies, in which there is a 'curtain call' at the end of the movie.

The film was released on 12 June 1987, and was number 1 at the US box office in its opening weekend. Eventually the film made over \$98m worldwide, set against a budget of \$18m. Three years later a sequel – *Predator 2*, set in New York and starring Danny Glover who co-starred with Mel Gibson in all the *Lethal Weapon* films – premiered. This movie did not make as much of an impact as the original, but notably featured a scene near the end (which was in the script of the first film but never shot) in which Glover's character enters the Predator's spaceship and kills him with one of his own weapons. Inside the ship in the background can be seen the Predator's trophies, which include the elongated skull of an Alien Warrior as seen in *Alien* and *Aliens*. This one scene established that the *Predator* and *Alien* movies took place in the same universe and paved the way for the two *Alien vs Predator* movies which were released in 2004 and 2007.

In 2010 a fifth film featuring the Predator creature – *Predators*, directed by Robert Rodriguez – was released. This film was effectively a reboot of the first movie, but set in the future on an alien planet with Adrien Brody's Royce playing an equivalent role to Arnold Schwarzenegger's 'Dutch' Schultz.

A sixth *Predator* movie, called *The Predator*, is scheduled for release in 2018. Interestingly, this is to be scripted and directed by Shane Black who played Hawkins in the first movie. In interviews Black has stated that this new film will be a true sequel to the first one, so it may possibly feature Arnold Schwarzenegger reprising his role as 'Dutch Schultz.

## *Predator* (1987)
## Production Credits

Director: John McTiernan
Screenwriters: Jim Thomas and
John Thomas

**Cast**
Dutch Schultz - Arnold
Schwarzenegger
Dillon - Carl Weathers
Anna - Elpidia Carrillo
Mac - Bill Duke
Blain - Jesse Ventura
Billy - Sonny Landham
Poncho - Richard Chaves
General Phillips - R.G.
Armstrong
Hawkins - Shane Black
The Predator - Kevin Peter Hall
Helicopter Pilot - Kevin Peter
Hall
Executed Hostage - Steve Boyum
Guerilla Soldiers - William H.
Burton Jr, Henry Kingi
Predator Voice - Peter Cullen
Russian Soldier - Sven-Ole
Thorsen
Guerilla Helicopter Pilot - Jack
Verbois

**Production Credits**
Producers: Lawrence Gordon,
Joel Silver
Associate Producers: Beau
Marks, John Vallone
Executive Producers: Laurence
P. Pereira, Jim Thomas

**Music**
Composer: Alan Silvestri

**Cinematography**
Director of Photography:
Donald McAlpine

**Film Editing**
Film Editors: Mark Helfrich,
John F. Link
Casting: Jackie Burch

**Production Design**
Production Designer: John
Vallone

**Art Direction**
Art Directors: Frank Richwood,
Jorge Sainz
Set Decorator: Enrique Estevez

**Costume Design**
Costume Designer: Marilyn
Vance-Straker

**Make-up Department**
Hair Stylist: Bertha Chiu, Carlos
Horcasitas
Mud Make-up Artist: Jefferson
Dawn
Make-up Designer: Scott H.
Eddo
Moldmaker: Adam Hill
Additional Make-up Artists:
Elvira Oropeza, John Rizzo,
James R. Scribner

Special Make-up Effects Artist: Tom Woodruff Jr

**Production Management**
Production Manager: Beau Marks
Unit Managers: Anna Roth, Art Seidel

**Second Unit Director or Assistant Director**
Second Assistant Directors: Tom Archuleta, K.C. Colwell
Second Unit Director: Craig R. Baxley
Assistant Director (Second Unit): Michael Katleman
First Assistant Director: Beau E.L. Marks
Assistant Director (Mexico): Jose Luis Ortega

**Art Department**
Sculptor: Henry Alvarez
Assistant Greensman: Juan Barreto
Assistant Property Master: Benito Cano
Carpenter: Mark Fambro
Production Illustrator: Nikita Knatz
Construction Coordinator: Jesus Labastida
Assistant Greensman: Camilo Litra
Assistant Property Master: Antonio Mata Jr
Property Masters: Antonio Mata Sr, Tommy Tomlinson

Greensmen: Frank Mitchell, Fransisco Ramirez
Assistant Greensmen: Alejandro Ramirez, German Ramirez
Property Gun Master: Michael Papac
Construction Coordinator: Salvador Pena
Production Illustrator: Paul Power
Set Dresser: Macedonio Ramos
Art Director (Mexico): John Krenz Reinhart
Assistant Property Master: Carlos Torres
Assistant Art Director: Theresa Wachter
Property Master: Christopher Gilman
Storyboard Artist: Donald Meyers

**Sound Department**
Foley Artist: Vanessa Theme Ament
Supervising Dialogue Editor: George H. Anderson
Supervising Sound Effects Editor: Richard L. Anderson
Re-recording Mixer: Richard Overton, Kevin F. Cleary, Don Bassman
Audio Programming: David Bifano
ADR Mixer: Kevin Carpenter
Sound Effects Editor: Gene Corso
Assistant Re-recordist: Phyllis Drury

Sound Effects Recording: Ezra Dweck
Stereo Sound Consultant (Dolby): David Gray
Boom Operator: Jorge Gomez
Foley Artist: Ronin Harlin
Re-recordists: Craig Heath, Robert Renga
Dialogue Editor: Cindy Marty
Assistant Sound Effects Editor: Mark Pappas
Special Sound Effects: John Pospisil
Foley Editor: Steve Richardson
Dialogue Assistant: Christy Richmond
ADR Editors: Hank Salerno, Corinne Sessarego, Bill Voigtlander
Sound Effects Editors: Catherine Shorr, Richard Schorr
Supervising Sound Effects Editor: David Stone
Cable Operator: David Sanchez
Sound Mixer: Manuel Topete
Assistant Sound Effects Editor: Jo Van Metoyer
Foley Mixer: J. R. Weston
Dialogue Assistant: Rosemarie Wheeler
Sound Effects Editor: Gary Wright
ADR Recordist: Vic Zaslav
ADR Assistant: Richard Brassaw
Re-recording Engineer: Bill Henderson
Technical Sound Director: Donald C. Rogers

**Special Effects**
Creature Effects Crew: Grant Arndt, Howard Berger
Animatronic Animals: Jim Boulden
Special Effects: Stan Winston, Steve Johnson, James Camomile, Daniel Cordero, Manuel Cordero, Jesus Duran, Paul Stewart, Pedro Gonzalez, Adrian Duran, Margarito Lopez, Alejandro Duran, Magdaleno Rodriguez, Javier Moreno, Fermin Duran
Creature Effects Crew: Screaming Mad George, Eddie Yang, Greg Nicotero, Emilio M. Gonzalez, Robert Kurtzman, Michito Tagawa, Jackie Tischner, Brian Simpson, John Rosengrant, Leslie Neumann, Steve Patino, Shane Mahan, Jacki Lancette
Art Department Coordinators (Creature Effects): Matt Rose, Shannon Shea
Special Effects Supervisors: Laurencio Cordero, Al Di Sarro
Mould Department: Stan Winston, Lindsay McGowan
Concept Artist (Creature Effects): Mitch Suskin
Special Effects Foreman: Bruno Van Zoebreck
Art Department Coordinator (Creature Effects): Steve Mang
Creature Design: William Stout

## Visual Effects

Motion Control Technicians:
James Balsam, Scott Beattie
Special Effects Supervisor:
Michael Bigelow
Design Consultant: Jeff Burks
Effects Animator: Russell
Calbrese
Special Effects: Eric
Chamberlain
Optical Camera: Patrick
McDonough, Richard Lorenzo,
Scott Nicholas, Richard Champa
Location Motion Control: B.
David Green
Visual Consultant: Richard
Greenberg
Visual Effects Producer: Robert
M. Greenberg
Optical Supervisor: Robert Hall
Visual Effects Supervisor: Joel
Hynek
Animation and Rotoscope:
Donald Poynter, Payul D.
Johnson, Harry Venezia
Optical Line-up: Ken Price, Jim
Mini, Laurel Klick
Visual Effects Editor: J.W.
Compare
Motion Control Assistant:
Marco Maldonado
Camouflage Co-Developer:
Eugene Mamut
Design Consultant: Terry
Moews
Inker: Bryan Moore
Animation Camera: Bruce
Morosohk
Animation Supervisor: Robert
Mrozowski
Motion Control Assistant:
Davin Nunez
Thermal Visual Effects
Supervisor: Stuart Robertson
Location Video: David Statin
Matte Artist: Robert Scifo
Production Manager (Visual
Effects): Keith Shartle
Visual Effects Cameraman:
Steve Slocombe
Fabricator (Boss Film): Mark
Yuricich, Mike Smithson
Compositor: Donna Tracy
Rotoscope Supervisor: James
Valentine

## Stunts

Stunt Performers: Gerardo
Moreno, Gregory Barnett,
Bobby Bass, Gary Baxley,
Manuel Benitez, Steve Boyum,
Jophery Brown, Tony Brubaker,
Bill Burton, Steven Chambers,
Doug Coleman, Angel De La
Pena, Alejandro De La Pena,
Leon Delaney, David Drazes,
Dave Efron, Robert Hammond,
Norman Howell, Richard
Humphreys, Sergio Kato, Peter
Kent, Henry Kingi, Joel Kramer,
Mauricio Martinez, Raul
Martinez, Gabriela Moreno,
Noe Rolando Smith, Eric
Valdez, Jack Verbois, Eddie L.
Watkins
Stunt Double (Sonny Landham):
Gregory R. Barnett

Stunt Double (Jessie Ventura): Monty Jordan
Stunt Doubles (Arnold Schwarzenegger): Peter Kent, Joel Kramer
Stunt Double: Brian Kent
Stunt Coordinator: Craig L. Baxley

## Camera and Electrical Department
First Assistant Camera: Robert Agganis
Infrared Camera Operators: Frank Bryson, Pete Sekelick
Gaffer: Warren Mearns, Tony Holtham, Fernardo Calvillo
Thermal Camera: David Eggby
Gaffer (Second Unit): Jim Hunt
Key Grip: Patrick Nash, Juan Iniestra
Second Grip: Grahame Litchfield, Geoffrey Jamieson
Director of Photography (Second Unit): Frank E. Johnson
Best Boys: Gary Scholes, Adolfo Lara, Alleyn Mears
Second Grip: Ian McAlpine
Gaffer
Camera Operator (Second Unit): Carlos Montano
Assistant Camera (Second Unit): Guillermo Moysen, Clinton Palmer
Camera Operator (Second Unit): John Oteri
Dolly Grip: Antonio Ramirez
Key Grip (Second Unit): Richard Randall

Assistant Camera: Mark Sarfaty, Guillermo Rosas
Still Photographers: Zade Rosenthal, Alfredo Ruvalcaba
Director of Photography (Mexico): Leon Sanchez
Assistant Dolly Grip: Pascual Villa
Assistant Camera: Pedro Vazquez
First Assistant Camera (Second Unit): Tim Wawrzeniak

## Casting Department
Extras Casting: Guillermo Castillo, Humberto Johnston
Casting Assistant: Billy Da Mota

## Costume and Wardrobe Department
Assistant Costumer: Maria Antonieta Esquivel
Costume Supervisor: Robert M. Harris
Assistant Costumers: Ismael Jardon, Jaime Ortiz
Costumers (Men): Gary Sampson, Enrique Villavicencio
Costume Supervisor (Men): James Tyson

## Editorial Department
Digital Colour Correction: Brent Eldridge
Assistant Film Editors: Kim Bennett, Bryan Carroll, Mark Elson, Julie Feiner, Carol Fitzgerald, Rudy Freeman, Billy

Meshover, Wille Navarro, John
Nenzel
Colour Timers: Dale E. Grahn,
Bob Hagans
Negative Cutter: Jack Hooper
Apprentice Film Editor: Patty
Kudish

## Music Department
Vocal Effects Editor: Michael
John Bateman
Scoring Crew: Chuck Garsha,
Terry Brown, Walt Borchers
Musician (Oboe Soloist): Tom
Boyd
Orchestrator: James Campbell
Special Vocalization: Peter
Cullen
Violin: Bruce Dukov
Music Scoring Mixer: Dennis S.
Sands
Vocal Effects Supervisor:
Norman B. Schwartz
Musician (French Horn): James
Thatcher
Music Editor: Michael Tronick
Music (Percussion): Tom Raney

## Transportation Department
Transportation Coordinator:
Charles Enzen
Transportation Co-Captains:
Margarito Guttierez, Benito
Villapondo, Mario Ramariz
Transportation Secretary:
Mayaya Gonzalez
Drivers: Manuel Peredes
Marillo, James Nordberg,
Alfonso Paredes

## Other Crew
Dubbing Projectionist: Alex
Algarin
Animal Trainer: Eduardo
Apellaniz
Production Office Liaison
(Mexico): Emilau Arau
Production Auditor: Todd
Arnow
Helicopter Pilots: Peter J.
McKernan Jr, Alejandro
Madrid, Michael Tamburro,
Guillermo Saavedra
Assistant (Mr Davis): Brooke
Brooks
Production Coordinator USA:
Patti Calhoun
Production Assistants: Efren Del
Moral, Guillermo Carreno
Creature Crew: Craig Caton
Knife Design: Jack W. Crain
Development Executive: Riley
Kathryn Ellis
Union Head of Production:
Alejandro Ferrer
Production Coordinator
(Mexico): Emily Gamboa
Technical Advisor: Gary
Goldman
Script Supervisor: Gabriela
Gurrola
Animal Trainer: Miguel Gurza
Mechanical Department
(Creature Effects): David
Kindlon, Wayne Sturm, Brent
Scrivner, Richard Landon
Assistant to John McTiernan:
Carol Land

Assistants to Joel Silver: George Luis, Tamara Smith

Assistant to Lawrence Gordon: Suzanne Nupoff, Sandi Yount, Kellett Tighe

Body Double: Jean-Claude Van Damme

Infrared Consultant: Dr Robert Madding

Publicity Coordinator: Katherine Moore

Script Supervisor: Elizabeth Norton

Production Auditor: Michael Perkal

Production Assistant: Rodolfo Lopez Real

Animal Trainers: Carlos Renero, Hector Zurita

Animal Wrangler: Humberto Gurza

Maintenance Engineer: Ken Stone

Creature Designer: William Stout

Aerial Coordinator and Helicopter Pilot: Charles A. Tamburro

Production Coordinator (USA): Dana Taylor

Production Associate: Elaine K. Thompson

Script Supervisor: Marion Tumen

Assistant Auditor: Gerard Yubero

Special thanks to Brad Naples

# 9

# LETHAL WEAPON

## (1987)

*Silver Pictures*

**Director:** Richard Donner
**Producers:** Richard Donner and Joel Silver
**Screenwriter:** Shane Black

*L*ETHAL *Weapon* – one of the most popular action films of the 80s – was the brainchild of screenwriter Shane Black, who was just 25 when he wrote the script. Black's concept was of an updated version of *Dirty Harry* (1971), featuring a maverick cop living on the edge who is teamed up with a much more conservative partner. In this respect, *Lethal Weapon* can be considered a 'buddy movie' – the origins of which go back to the sixties with films like *Butch Cassidy and the Sundance Kid* (1969).

*Lethal Weapon* is best remembered for its superb action sequences and stunts – some of which though are somewhat unbelievable, with people surviving car crashes and torture without any apparent injury. In this respect, *Lethal Weapon* can be considered a quasi-fantasy film rather than a serious look at the work of the Los Angeles Police Department.

All the same, the film is hugely entertaining with its unique blend of comedy, tragedy and action. One moment the film is dealing with hero Martin Riggs's latest suicide attempt, then all of a sudden there a scene of pure comedy, giving a unique bitter-sweet feel to the whole production. Later films in the series dropped the tragic elements in favour of humour, with detrimental results.

The role of traumatised cop Martin Riggs was given to 30 year old Australian-American actor Mel Gibson, whose career was at its peak at that time following roles in the *Mad Max* series of films and other successes like *The Year of Living Dangerously* (1982) and *The Bounty* (1984), while his partner Roger Murtaugh was played by prolific actor Danny Glover.

Following the rules of 'buddy' movies, the two cops' characters were like chalk and cheese. Riggs was an impulsive, chain-smoking, heavy drinking maverick who lived alone (with his dog) in a dirty, untidy trailer and always dressed scruffily, while Murtaugh was a family man with a wife, three children and a cat who usually wore a shirt and tie and resided in a smart, clean, modern house. Murtaugh believed in following correct police procedures whereas Riggs preferred to shoot first and ask questions later.

The producer was Joel Silver, whose company Silver Films made many of the most successful action films of the eighties, and the director was Richard Donner whose breakthrough film was the supernatural thriller *The Omen* (1976) starring Lee Remick and Gregory Peck. Following this highly successful movie Donner directed *Superman* (1978), starring Christopher Reeve. He also directed much of *Superman 2* (1980), although due to a dispute with executive producers Alexander and Ilya Salkind he was fired from the movie and the remaining scenes were directed by Richard Lester, who subsequently received full directorial credit.

*Lethal Weapon* opens with blue titles (with a 3D effect) against a black background while *Jingle Bell Rock* by Bobby Helms plays on the soundtrack, establishing that the events of the movie take place over the festive period, ending on Christmas Day itself. The title sequence concludes with an aerial view of Los Angeles at night, shot from a moving helicopter. Eventually the camera zooms in on a high building (actually International Tower at 700E, Ocean Boulevard, Long Beach) where a young, beautiful blonde woman – Amanda Hunsaker (Jackie Swanson) – clad in white lingerie (but with exposed breasts), lies on a bed while she ingests white heroin powder and some capsules. The balcony outside her penthouse apartment is festooned with fairy lights and a Christmas tree. Clearly off her head on drugs, she steps off the balcony and falls to her death, landing heavily on the roof of a saloon car.

The next morning, middle-aged cop Sergeant Roger Murtaugh (Danny Glover) is relaxing in his bath at home when his wife and three children enter, carrying a birthday cake – which has just been delivered – covered with candles. It is Murtaugh's 50th birthday. He kisses his kids, and his elder daughter Rianne (Traci Wolfe) says that his newly-grown beard makes him look older. As his family leave the bathroom Murtaugh looks right, sees his reflection in the mirror, and ruminates about how old he must be looking. Murtaugh seems in great shape in this scene, with no flab and well-toned muscles, which is partially explained by Danny Glover's regular workouts for the role and also by the fact that he was only 40 when the film was made and not his character's supposed age of 50.

The film then cuts to a beach in Los Angeles where maverick cop Sergeant Martin Riggs (Mel Gibson) resides in a GMC trailer home. His dog runs up the beach and into his caravan as he lies naked in bed, smoking a cigarette while he watches TV. He decides to get up without dressing (treating cinema audiences to a view of his bare backside) and fetches breakfast from his fridge – a bottle of beer.

Mel Gibson also appears to be in great physical condition in the film, with a flat stomach and bulging muscles, but in a way this is totally unrealistic as one would expect a man who has suffered a mental breakdown (as his character Riggs has) and is smoking, drinking and living on junk food to be in poor shape. The toned, fit bodies of Riggs and Murtaugh aren't representative of real American cops who are sometimes fat and unfit, like many of the general population in the US (an estimated two-thirds of the country's inhabitants are considered to be overweight or obese). But this is just a part of what I term the 'reality gap' in Hollywood movies, in which only people with perfect bodies are shown naked or semi-naked on screen.

As this film was made in 1986, Gibson wears the famous 'mullet' haircut (long at the back, short at the front and sides) which was popular at the time. This hairstyle was specially created for the film by K.G. Ramsey, but in subsequent sequels the actor was progressively 'de-mulleted'.

Back at Murtaugh's house the cop eats a cooked breakfast of bacon and eggs made by his wife Trisha (Darlene Love) before getting ready for work, donning a smart shirt and tie. He carries a gun in a holster fitted to a belt around his waist. Trisha is struggling to prepare the meal, having already dropped an egg on the floor. As he is leaving, Trisha tells him that someone called Michael Hunsaker has been trying to get hold of him on the 'phone for the past three days. Murtaugh is puzzled, because he hasn't seen him for many years.

Meanwhile, Riggs is watching TV on a small portable TV in his caravan. A commercial for the Super Bowl (an annual championship game of the National Football League) annoys him so much that he throws his empty beer bottle at the set, smashing its screen. Then he looks wistfully at wedding photos featuring his late wife Victoria.

'Buy a new one', he mutters. But is he referring to his TV or his wife?

Later, Murtaugh is at the police firing range, wearing safety glasses and ear defenders. He presses a switch to move a paper target away from him on an electric hoist. Once it is a respectable distance away he fires several times, then brings the target back for inspection. He has achieved a good 'grouping' (which in the world of markmanship means that all his bullets have struck home very close together).

As Murtaugh is practising his shooting, Riggs is on his way to the police station in an unmarked squad car when he receives an emergency call. He proceeds to a playground across the road from a school, where there is a report of a sniper shooting at kids. Riggs puts a flashing red light on top of his dashboard, switches on his siren, and drives to the scene of the crime as fast as possible.

When he arrives, a few policemen are there but the SWAT team has not yet appeared and no-one knows what their ETA (Estimated Time of Arrival) will be. Riggs realises he will have to deal with the situation himself, so he asks a policeman what he knows about the shooter. Is he a good shot? Is he shooting at random? And does he have an automatic weapon?

Riggs cocks his Beretta 92F pistol and goes up the steps heading for the shooter, ignoring pleas from a policewoman (Selma Archerd) that he is in the line of fire. As he approaches the sniper's position, the gunman breaks cover and fires at Riggs from an open window with his M14 rifle. Bullets start dancing around Riggs' feet, but the cop simply ignores them and fires several pistol rounds in rapid succession. The bad guy collapses dead. As Riggs turns round and leaves the scene, one of his police colleagues says that he is 'one psycho sonofabitch – but good'. As he descends the steps, a 10-man SWAT team arrives carrying M16 rifles. It is implied that the suicidal Riggs is taking great risks as he actually wants to die.

In the meantime, Murtaugh has arrived at the scene of the suicidal jump from the high building the previous night. Police are interviewing Dixie, a hooker who witnessed the event. He is told that the victim was Amanda Hunsaker, aged 22, with no previous convictions and born in Tennessee. Murtaugh asks about her parents and is told they are Michael and Clare Hunsaker. Murtaugh remembers that he knows them and asks his colleague to find out who has been paying the bills. He then looks at a photo of Michael and Amanda when they were younger, picks up the 'phone and asks the operator for Michael Hunsaker's telephone number.

As Murtaugh is making his enquiries, Riggs is carrying out some undercover work, posing as someone interested in buying a stash of heroin. The transaction is being carried out outdoors in a small plot which is also being used to sell Christmas trees. As Riggs examines the large stash of heroin, the leader of the drug gang (Jimmie F. Skaggs) says he will throw in a Christmas tree for free, and that he can have the best one on the lot. Riggs asks the price and the bad guy says it is '100'. He obviously means $100,000 and not $100, but Riggs proceeds to count out just $100 from the contents of his wallet. The drug dealers are furious, but then Riggs says he has an even better offer – he will take the stash for free and all of them will go to jail. Riggs shows them his police badge (which has the number '6893'), but the drug dealers don't believe it is real and claim he is crazy.

'You wanna see crazy?' says Riggs as he slaps his own face a few times, then pummels the bad guys' faces in turn. As they are reeling from the shock of this strange behaviour, Riggs pulls out his pistol and points it at them. As he does so, he is aware of a gang member (Jason Ronard) in the Christmas trees behind him, turns round and shoots. Eventually Riggs kills three of the gang, with only one surviving.

The last of the villains (Blackie Dammett) grabs Riggs and holds an Astra Terminator pistol to his head, telling the other cops (who have just arrived) to back off. Riggs advises them to shoot anyway, but they are reluctant to open fire. Eventually Riggs uses his martial arts skills to overpower the attacker, and the crisis is resolved.

Afterwards, as the sun is setting, Riggs returns to his caravan and feeds his dog with a turkey sandwich from the fridge. As he watches TV – a Christmas-themed *Bugs Bunny* cartoon – he loads his gun, puts the muzzle to his forehead and then into his mouth, and prepares to shoot himself as he looks at his wife's photo. But he can't go through with it and starts crying.

This was one of the things that made *Lethal Weapon* so intriguing, as it contains a mixture of various elements – a bit of comedy, the interesting relationship between Riggs and Murtaugh, plenty of action, and the tragedy of the death of Riggs's wife which seems to be pushing him towards suicide and making him take incredible risks as well as indulging in self-destructive behaviour.

Back at the LA Police Department, several officers are rehearsing the Christmas carol *Silent Night* while a police psychologist (Mary Ellen Trainor) discusses Riggs's case with his captain, Ed Murphy (Steve Kahan). As she points out, Riggs's wife had died in a car crash only 11 months before, and he may be 'psychotic' (though in fact PTSD would be a more likely diagnosis).

One of Riggs's police colleagues announces that the results of the autopsy on Amanda Hunsaker are now available. As well as heroin she was taking barbiturate capsules which had been doctored with drain cleaner, so she may have been dead even before she jumped. (This is a rather questionable plot point from the scientific point of view, as it would be impossible to put enough drain cleaner in a few tiny barbiturate capsules to cause serious problems. Drain cleaner is usually made from caustic soda, and the very small amount that could be injected into barbiturate capsules would simply be neutralised by stomach acid. On the other hand this scheme might have worked if a highly concentrated poison such as potassium cyanide was used.)

As Murtaugh is pondering over the implications of this news, his colleague Boyette (Grand Bush) tells him that he looks younger *with* the beard. Murtaugh then learns that the condition of the sheets and mattress in Amanda's bed suggests she was with another man before she died. As he is hearing this, he sees Riggs standing nearby. He is wearing scruffy casual clothes and a baseball cap. Suddenly he pulls out a gun. Murtaugh thinks he is a criminal intent on killing police officers and attacks him, but Riggs uses his martial arts skills to throw him to the ground. He then learns that he has just met his new partner.

Later, their unorthodox introduction over, Riggs and Murtaugh are walking in the underground car park at the police station. Murtaugh mentions that he knows that Riggs had seen action with the 'Phoenix' group during the Vietnam War. He is also impressed by Riggs's handgun, which is a 9mm Beretta 92F with 15 rounds in the magazine plus one in the breech. 'That's some serious shit you're carrying', he says. The Beretta 92F used by Riggs throughout the film was the same actual prop gun used by John McClane in *Die Hard* the following year. Murtaugh himself carries an older weapon, a Smith and Wesson Model 19, 0.357 revolver with just six rounds.

Murtaugh is also aware of Riggs' martial arts skills and suggests that he himself should be registered as a 'Lethal Weapon'. This is one of the clichés of action films, in which there seems to be a rule that the title of the film must be mentioned by one of the main characters somewhere, with the most egregious example of this trend being Christopher Walken's line of dialogue about 'A View to a Kill' in the 1985 Bond film of the same name.

Riggs mentions that no-one wants to work with him, as he is either genuinely disturbed or else faking insanity to get a 'psycho pension'. Either way, everyone 'thinks he's fucked'. Murtaugh says that's the way he feels as well. 'God hates me', says Murtaugh, to which Riggs replies 'Hate 'em back; it works for me'.

The next scene is set in the boiler room next to a nightclub owned by a criminal drugs gang (in reality the Ritz Theatre at 6652 Hollywood Boulevard), where the boss Colonel Peter McAllister (Mitchell Ryan) and his chief henchman Mr Joshua (Gary Busey) are having a heated discussion with Mendez (Ed O'Ross). Mendez is unimpressed with Joshua, asking McAllister if he got him at 'Psychos R' Us' (a jokey reference to the 'Toys R' Us' retail chain), but McAllister decides to shock Mendez with a demonstration of Joshua's toughness and loyalty.

He asks for Mendez's cigarette lighter, ignites it, and holds the naked flame under Joshua's exposed forearm for a minute. Joshua doesn't even flinch, though it is rather obvious how this effect was achieved as the flame is actually slightly behind Joshua's arm and is only heating air, not flesh.

Later, Murtaugh meets Mike Hunsaker as Riggs stands in the background. Murtaugh looks at old monochrome photos of him and Mike in military uniform, and tells Mike his daughter was murdered to put pressure on him. He then asks Mike why he tried to get in touch, and he answers that someone told him that Murtaugh was working out here. He was hoping Murtaugh could rescue her before it was too late, as she was involved in drugs, prostitution and making porno videos. Now that Amanda is dead he wants Murtaugh to find the people responsible and kill them, as he owes him a favour.

The next scene is set at a hamburger stand. As the two cops eat, Riggs asks Murtaugh how he 'owed' Hunsaker, and the cop explains how – in Vietnam in 1965 – Hunsaker had saved his life after he took a bayonet in his lung.

Before Riggs has time to think this over, the two cops receive an emergency call. A man is threatening to commit suicide by jumping off a roof, and the two policemen are to get to the scene as quickly as possible and wait for a police psychologist to arrive. However, Riggs chooses to deal with the matter in his own way. He makes his way up to the ledge of the building on the edge of the flat roof, offers the potential 'jumper' a cigarette, and then snaps a handcuff on the man while attaching the other cuff to his own wrist. He then throws away the key, meaning that he is now cuffed to the jumper. If he chooses to fall, he will take Riggs with him. 'You can jump if you want to, but you'd be taking me with you. You would be killing a cop. Do you wanna jump?'

Without further thought, Riggs leaps from the roof, pulling the jumper with him. The camera follows them down but, instead of dying, the two men have a soft landing on a huge blue airbag (like a giant lilo) which the police have just inflated.

This whole scene is very similar to one in the Clint Eastwood movie *Dirty Harry* (1971), in which Inspector Harry Callahan travels up the side of a high building in a cherry picker to confront a potential jumper. After provoking the jumper into assaulting him, Callahan knocks him unconscious, grabs him, and then takes him back to ground level on the descending hoist. The equivalent scene in *Lethal Weapon* may even have been a deliberate homage by screenwriter Shane Black, who intended his film to be an updated version of *Dirty Harry*.

Despite the successful outcome, Murtaugh is furious with Riggs, accusing him of having a death wish. The two cops argue, and Riggs admits that he sometimes considers 'eating a bullet'. He even has a special hollow point bullet earmarked for this purpose. A 'hollow point' bullet has a burrowed-out shape in its tip intended to cause the bullet to expand upon entering the target, thus causing maximum tissue destruction. In fact, the supposed 'hollow point' slug which Riggs plays with at some points in the film is a standard, unmodified bullet.

Murtaugh decides to call Riggs's bluff and offers him his Smith and Wesson revolver. The younger cop accepts the weapon and puts it under his chin, but he doesn't go through with it and withdraws the gun. Handing it back to Murtaugh, he says he is hungry and is going for something to eat.

As Riggs departs in search of a fast food outlet, Murtaugh speaks on the radio-phone to the police psychologist saying that he thinks Murtaugh has a death wish. Later – as the two cops drive off – Murtaugh mentions that he has reached the age of 50 without a scratch. He has a house and a fishing boat. Riggs says he didn't know it was his birthday, and Murtaugh informs him that it was the previous day.

Shortly afterwards, the two cops arrive at a plush house in Beverley Hills to interview a suspect. An electrically-operated gate opens to allow them into the drive of a plush, modern house. As they get out the car they see two young, attractive girls in the dining room who are viewing them through the glass patio doors. The girls appear upset when they realise they are cops. Suddenly a gunman appears and opens fire on the two cops with a Remington 870 Witness Protection shotgun. Fortunately his shots go wide and the two policemen return fire, wounding him. Riggs handcuffs the two girls (presumably hookers) to a tree. Then Murtaugh tells him to read the gunman his rights. As the gunman is helped to his feet, he produces a Walther PPK/S pistol and starts struggling with Riggs. In the ensuing struggle Riggs shoots him, and the villain falls into the swimming pool where he drowns despite the efforts of the two cops to save him.

The next scene is set in Riggs's caravan a few hours later. Darkness is falling as the cop watches an 'Alka-Seltzer' commercial on his TV. Murtaugh arrives. He has calmed down, and thanks Riggs for saving his life. He has also come to invite Riggs to his house for dinner.

Later the two cops arrive at Murtaugh's house, which is decorated for Xmas including exterior lights. Murtaugh's youngest daughter – Carrie (Ebony Smith) – comes out to greet them. She is carried into the house by her father. Once inside, Riggs is introduced to the rest of the family – Roger's wife Trisha, and their three kids including eldest daughter Rianne, who clearly finds Riggs attractive. Trisha has many positive qualities, but cooking skills are not among them and her lack of culinary ability was to become a running joke throughout the series.

As the meal comes to a close, Murtaugh asks Rianne to take three desserts out of the fridge as Riggs tells her she can call him 'Martin'. However, her father is a bit non-plussed about this and insists that she calls him 'Mr Riggs'.

After dinner Murtaugh is showing Riggs his large fishing boat – which is parked on a trailer on his drive – as Trisha is taking out the rubbish. 'Thanks for taking out the garbage', she says sarcastically as Murtaugh shows Riggs all the features of his craft – which include a stash of beer. As Riggs sips from his beer, they consider the latest developments. In particular, why did the gunman apparently murder Amanda Hunsaker and then try to kill them?

As they are pondering over the case, Rianne comes up to them. She is dismayed as she has been 'grounded' for smoking pot in the house, and she wants to go out with a guy. Riggs leaves, telling Murtaugh that he enjoyed the meal but points out that he feels Murtaugh doesn't trust him. 'If you can make it through tomorrow without killing anyone, I'll trust you', says Murtaugh.

Riggs then points out that the only thing he has ever been good at is shooting. In Laos (during the Vietnam War) he had taken out a guy at 1,000 yards range, and claims that 'only 8-10 guys in the world' could have achieved that feat. This revelation may be based on the real-life exploits of US Marine Corps sniper Carlos Hathcock, who the Vietcong referred to as the 'White Feather Sniper' owing to his habit of wearing a white feather in his hat. Hathcock achieved 93 confirmed sniper kills during the Vietnam War, and also held the record for the longest-range sniper kill which was only broken as recently as 2009 in Afghanistan by British Army Corporal Craig Harrison who killed several Taliban insurgents at a range of 2475m using a L115A3 long-range sniper rifle.

As Riggs departs, Murtaugh asks him if he really liked his wife's cooking. 'No', he replies. He was just being polite. Later, on his way home Riggs picks up a young prostitute (Renee Estevev). He offers her 100 dollars. But he doesn't want to have sex with her. He merely wants her to keep him company while he watches *The Three Stooges* on TV in his caravan in 20 minutes time. Little known in the UK, 'The Three Stooges' were an American comedy trio who were active from the late 1920s till the early sixties and made 190 short films.

The next morning, Murtaugh receives a package addressed to him at his house. It contains a School Yearbook for the 'Class of 83' at Palos Verdes School, and Murtaugh is particularly interested in the photos of Amanda Hunsaker and her sister Beverley. The videotape shows the two Hunsaker girls – plus a third female – in a porno film. Murtaugh goes to wake up Riggs in his caravan to tell him about the latest development. He has guessed that the third hooker in the video, Dixie, was the same person who witnessed Amanda's fatal jump.

Later that morning, the two cops are at the police firing range. Murtaugh goes first, sets his target at a medium range, and puts a single bullet through the 'head' of the target. The middle-aged cop is pleased at his prowess with his weapon. Then Riggs follows. Humming loudly, he presses a switch to take the same target as far away as possible and then puts seven rounds into it. When the target is brought forward for inspection it has eight neat holes in it, forming two eyes and a mouth!

Murtaugh is gobsmacked. It makes for an amusing scene, but is pure 'Hollywood Science'. In the world of marksmanship it is possible to have several hits which are closely grouped (i.e. very near to one another), but it is impossible to make a smiley face with bullet holes. This scene is probably inspired by the police shooting range sequence in *Magnum Force* (1973), the second *Dirty Harry* picture, in which Inspector Callahan discovers that a group of suspected vigilante cops happen to be excellent marksmen.

Afterwards, the two cops arrive in their car to interview Dixie at her house. Kids are playing on the sidewalk as they approach the building, which suddenly blows up. After putting out an emergency call, the two cops investigate the wreckage and Riggs discovers the remains of a mercury switch used in bombs. He had not seen one since his days in Vietnam.

Murtaugh chats with the kids and gets some information out of one of them, who is called Alfred (Donald Gooden). He discovers that a man had called earlier to read the gas meter and that he was blonde with a tattoo, just like the one Riggs has on his right biceps. Riggs reveals that this means he must be a former member of the US Special Forces (i.e. a Green Beret).

Later Murtaugh interviews Hunsaker at a clifftop house (at Palos Verdes Peninsula), where Amanda's funeral is being held as Murtaugh waits outside. He is quite blunt with Hunsaker, and tells him that his daughter was killed to stop him talking. Hunsaker reveals that during the Vietnam War he was involved with a CIA-organised outfit called 'Air America', which carried out clandestine flights from Laos as part of operations to stop 'Charlie' (the Vietcong) from bringing heroin into South Vietnam. He claims that some of these former 'Shadow Company' personnel are now engaged in criminal activities involving the importation and sale of heroin. They need his help, as his bank can be used as a front for their illicit activities.

Murtaugh is furious, saying he wants to 'burn down' the organisation, but Hunsaker says they are too big and powerful. Suddenly a Bell Jet Ranger helicopter appears outside the patio window. Standing in the passenger compartment with the sliding door opened, Mr Joshua fires a burst from his Colt XM177 Commando Carbine, killing Hunsaker as Murtaugh dives for cover. The Jet Ranger was a civilian version of the famous UH-1 'Huey' helicopter used in Vietnam, and has made countless appearance in action films starting with the Bond picture *On Her Majesty's Secret Service* in 1969.

The example which appeared in *Lethal Weapon*, with the US civil registration N230CA, was a film star in its own right, having appeared in several blockbusters including *Blue Thunder* (1982), *Close Encounters of the Third Kind* (1977) and *Commando* (1985).

As the helicopter banks away and escapes by flying low over the ocean, Riggs opens fire on it with his pistol – even pausing briefly to change magazines – but it is a futile gesture as the helicopter is soon well out of range.

While the Bell returns to base, Joshua reports to his boss on the radio. His mission has only been partially successful. Though Hunsaker is dead, he had already spoken to the police. His boss, Colonel Peter McAllister, decides that it is time to 'turn up the heat'.

Later, Riggs is prowling the streets of Los Angeles wearing an orange jacket and a baseball cap. He approaches a prostitute with a photo of a girl he is looking for. Suddenly a large saloon car screeches past. Mr Joshua is in the back, and he shoots at Riggs using a Remington 870 shotgun. The cop is hit several times in his chest and is blasted through a plate glass window by the impact of the rounds.

Murtaugh is quickly on the scene and attends to his apparently dead partner. But he is uninjured, as he is wearing a bulletproof vest under his jacket and had apparently set himself up to be 'killed' in order to fool the bad guys – one of the great clichés of action movies.

Riggs points out that the villains now think he is dead, so there is an opportunity to take them down. Then a call comes through on Murtaugh's police car radio. They have to investigate a report of a body. From the description (blond with big dimples), Murtaugh realises it is the guy his elder daughter Rianne is dating. The two cops make their way to Murtaugh's house, where the cop discovers a note which states that his daughter 'looks really pretty naked'. In a flash, Murtaugh realises the drug gang have kidnapped his daughter to put pressure on him. Then the 'phone rings. It is Mr Joshua, who tells Murtaugh he has a very beautiful daughter.

Next, Joshua 'phones the police department, posing as a journalist trying to find out information about a cop who was involved in a shooting incident earlier that evening. Lieutenant McCaskey (Jack Thibeau) answers the 'phone and confirms that the officer involved in the shooting was Riggs and that he is dead.

Back at Murtaugh's house, the two cops discuss their plan to get Rianne back. Riggs wants to do it his way, in which he will 'shoot to kill' and 'won't miss'. Then the 'phone rings again, and Joshua confirms they don't really want Murtaugh's daughter – they just want to know what Hunsaker told him. He gives details of the planned exchange in which they will return Rianne and take Murtaugh. They have to rendezvous the following day at the Dry Lake at Victorville at sunrise (which would be Christmas Day).

The following morning, Murtaugh heads off across the desert in his station wagon. A little short of the agreed rendezvous point, he drops off Riggs who is carrying a Heckler and Koch PSG-1 sniper rifle with a Harris bipod and plenty of ammunition. He runs off to find a suitable place to conceal himself.

Soon afterwards the drug gang arrives in two vehicles: a white Lincoln Town Car stretch limousine and an SUV, escorted by the same Bell Jet Ranger (N230CA) we saw earlier in the film. The villains – consisting of seven heavies plus Mr Joshua – offer to exchange Rianne for Murtaugh, but the veteran cop ups the ante by producing an M26 hand grenade. 'Let her go or we all die', he says.

Some distance away, Riggs is lying on his belly observing the scene through the telescopic sight of his sniper rifle. He is itching to blast the bad guys to kingdom come, but Murtaugh is in the way of a perfect shot. Mr Joshua implores

Murtaugh to surrender as he is outnumbered and outgunned, but the cop refuses.

Joshua shoots Murtaugh, but the cop is only wounded and he tosses his grenade – which is revealed to be just a smoke bomb (a puzzling plot point, since a real M26 is a fragmentation grenade). Riggs also takes out some of the villains with his sniper rifle, and Murtaugh tells Rianne to get into the limo and drive away from the scene. One of the gang climbs onto the windscreen of the limo but is shot by Riggs. At last Riggs has Joshua in his sights, but then someone puts the muzzle of a gun to his head. It is Colonel McAllister – the head of the gang. He calls Joshua on the radio to tell him he has found Riggs.

Meanwhile, Murtaugh is forced to surrender as bullets are striking the ground round his feet. Rianne's escape is also being frustrated by the Bell helicopter, which is banging its skids on the roof of the limo. Eventually Rianne is forced to stop and she is captured.

The next scene is set in the boiler room next to the nightclub owned by the gang (seen earlier in the film), where Riggs is stripped to the waist, his hands over his head and secured to a pipe which is discharging water over him. Mr Joshua tells him that they are going to torture him to force him to reveal what he knows about the pending drugs shipment. His torturer is Endo (Al Leong), who is wielding two chunky jump leads with wet sponges attached which are connected to a car battery.

In the next room Murtaugh is also being tortured with physical blows, and his daughter – wearing just her underwear – is brought into the room and tied up. Endo continues to torture Riggs with the jump leads, but the policeman overpowers him by throttling him with his powerful thighs and then manages to unhook himself from the overhead pipe.

Next door, Colonel McAllister is threatening Rianne, but suddenly Riggs bursts in carrying Endo's body which he throws at the villains. In the ensuing confusion, Riggs finds a knife and frees Murtaugh and Rianne. He then captures a gun and shoots at a gang member on a gantry above – but it is not Mr Joshua.

Riggs, Murtaugh and Rianne make their way into the adjacent nightclub, heading for the door. Riggs is forced to shoot a few gang members to facilitate their escape. Realising the game is up, Joshua retreats from the nightclub, firing off a burst from his automatic rifle and then hijacking a car, firing more rounds at Riggs as he speeds away. A policeman arrives and Murtaugh asks him to call for backup. Riggs doesn't have a car, but he pursues Joshua on foot as he can head him off by taking short cuts only available to pedestrians. A little out of breath, Murtaugh follows Riggs on foot.

Eventually Riggs manages to reach the parapet of a bridge, from where he can fire at Joshua's car with a captured Heckler and Koch MP5 submachine gun. His burst strikes home, and the villain crashes in flames. Amazingly, he escapes uninjured and is pursued along a freeway on foot by Riggs. Unfortunately Riggs is hit by a passing taxi and, although not badly injured, ends up sprawled on a windscreen. As Riggs recovers from this shock, Joshua hijacks a car to get away.

In the meantime, Colonel McAllister is trying to make his escape in a car which he drives out of a garage with a power-operated door. Unfortunately for him, he is confronted by Murtaugh who riddles his car with bullets. After exiting the alley, McAllister's car crashes into a bus and ends up on its roof. As McAllister lies bleeding in his car, surrounded by bags of heroin, the dripping petrol ignites and the car explodes, incinerating the gang leader. Riggs arrives on the scene and says he has to get Murtaugh to hospital to have his wounds treated, but the older cop is more concerned at getting back to his house as Joshua knows where he lives.

Murtaugh's fears are not unfounded, because Joshua is already on his way to the family house. As he drives up and parks his car, he is challenged by two uniformed cops who are sitting in a squad car outside the building with their engine running. Without warning, Joshua shoots them both – causing the car to move forward and hit a fire hydrant, leading to a powerful jet of water rising up into the air. This is again a reference to *Dirty Harry*, which also features a scene where a car hits a water hydrant.

The police guard eliminated, Joshua walks up to the Murtaugh house, fires several bullets through the front door and bursts in. But the house appears to be empty. The TV is switched on and is showing *A Christmas Carol* (1951) with Alastair Sim. Joshua then finds a note which reads as follows:

'Dear Bad Guys, No one here but us Cops.
Sorry. The Good Guys.'

Suddenly, an empty police car drives through the front lounge window of the house. Joshua looks in the driver's window and notices that car's automatic transmission lever is in 'drive', with the accelerator jammed fully open.

This scene alone turns *Lethal Weapon* into a fantasy film rather than a gritty, realistic look at police work. No real police officer would ever come up with this highly dangerous scheme. A far better idea would simply be for Riggs and Murtaugh to conceal themselves in the house with weapons drawn. It is not even an original idea anyway, as it is a direct steal from *The Terminator* (1984) and a similar scene features in the third *Dirty Harry* movie *The Enforcer* (1976).

Suddenly Riggs appears, gun in hand. But he feels he has a score to settle and agrees to Joshua's request for a hand-to-hand fight using martial arts skills. The two former Special Forces men fight on the front lawn, which is becoming a mud bath due to the falling water from the burst fire hydrant, as several police vehicles and a helicopter with a spotlight arrive.

Eventually Riggs triumphs over his adversary. But as he is being taken away by two policemen Joshua breaks free, and Riggs is forced to shoot him (both Riggs and Murtaugh draw and aim their weapons, but only Riggs's gun shows a muzzle flash). This sequence is very similar to the penultimate one in *Die Hard* (1988), in which the apparently dead terrorist Karl comes to life and is shot by Sergeant Al Powell – even down to the fact that both villains have a mop of blonde hair.

The next scene shows Riggs putting flowers on the grave of his late wife Victoria. The inscription on the tombstone reads 'Victoria Lynn Riggs 1953 -1984'. This shot is almost identical to the opening of the Bond movie *For Your Eyes Only* (1981), in which James Bond (Roger Moore) visits the grave of his late wife Tracey who had been assassinated at the end of *On Her Majesty's Secret Service* (1969).

The next film in the series, *Lethal Weapon 2* (1989), established that Victoria had died in a car crash but that this was no accident, having been staged by a hitman. In the first *Dirty Harry* picture it was revealed that Inspector Callahan's wife had been killed by a drunk driver, and that this partly explained his hatred of criminals and what he perceived as the 'soft touch' justice system.

*Lethal Weapon* ends with Riggs visiting Murtaugh's house, where he asks Rianne to give her father the special hollow point bullet (now wrapped in Christmas ribbon) which he has been keeping for the sole purpose of shooting himself. He says he no longer needs it, and it is implied that he has conquered his demons. As he leaves, Murtaugh arrives and Riggs confesses that he's not crazy after all.

The film premiered in the USA on 6 March 1987 and was hugely successful, making $120.2 million at the box office against a budget of $15m. Three sequels followed: *Lethal Weapon 2* (1989), *Lethal Weapon 3* (1993) and *Lethal Weapon 4* (1998). The last three films featured the annoying recurrent character of Leo Getz (played by Joe Pesci), and had a greater emphasis on comedy.

A reboot of the film, featuring a new, younger cast has been mooted, and a TV series based on the four films and with the same characters (but played by different actors) premiered in the USA in the autumn of 2016. In the new version Martin Riggs (Clayne Crawford) is an ex-Navy SEAL who is devastated when his wife (now called Miranda) and her unborn baby die in a road accident on the way to hospital. His partner, Roger Murtaugh, is played by Damon Wayans. On Friday 3 March 2017 the 18-part series premiered on ITV1 in the UK.

As is often the case, though, it is the original film and not the three sequels which is best remembered as one of the greatest action movies of all time.

## *Lethal Weapon* (1987)
## Production Credits

Director: Richard Donner
Screenplay: Shane Black

### Cast
Martin Riggs - Mel Gibson
Roger Murtaugh - Danny Glover
Mr Joshua - Gary Busey
The General - Mitchell Ryan
Michael Hunsaker - Tom Atkins
Trish Murtaugh - Darlene Love
Rianne Murtaugh - Traci Wolfe
Amanda Hunsaker - Jackie Swanson
Nick Murtaugh - Damon Hines
Carrie Murtaugh - Ebonie Smith
Beat Cop - Bill Kalmenson
Dixie - Lycia Naff
Cops - Patrick Cameron, Don Gordon, Gail Bowman, Robert Fol
Drug Dealers - Jimmie Skaggs, Jason Ronard, Blackie Dammett
Policewoman - Selma Archerd
Police Officer - Richard B. Whitaker
Psychologist - Mary Ellen Trainor
Captain Ed Murphy - Steve Kahan
McCaskey - Jack Thibeau
Boyette - Grand Bush
Mendez - Ed O'Ross
Gustaf - Gustaf Vintas
Mercenaries - Paul Tuerpe, Chad Hayes, Chris D. Jardins,

Sven Ole-Thorsen, Peter Du Point, Gilles Kohler, Cedric Adams, James Poslof
Endo - Al Leong
McCleary - Michael Shaner
Patrol Cop - Natalie Zimmerman
Blonde on Bike - Deborah Dismukes
Girls in Shower - Cheryl Baker, Teri Lynn Doss, Sharon K. Brecke
Alfred - Donald Gooden
Alfred's Friends - Alphonse Philipe Mouzon, Shaun Hunter, Everitt Wayne Collins Jnr
Patrol Cop - Lenny Juliano
Plainclothes Cop - Henry Brown
Family Friend - Brian Strohm
Hooker - Teresa Kadotani
Beat Cop - Frank Reinhard
Cops in Car - John O' Neill, Tom Noga
Burbank the Cat - Himself
Sam the Dog - Himself
Policeman - Larry Clardy
Underage Hooker - Renee Estevev
Crime Scene Officer - Conrad Hurtt
Bus Driver - Mic Rodgers
Girl in Black Playsuit - Joan Severance
Fire Rescue Attendant - Chris Tashima
Bartender - Norman D. Wilson

## Production Credits
Producers: Joel Silver, Richard Donner
Associate Producer: Jennie Lew Tugend

## Music
Music: Eric Clapton
Composer: Michael Kamen

## Cinematography
Director of Photography: Stephen Goldblatt

## Film Editing
Film Editor: Stuart Baird
Casting: Marion Dougherty
Production Design: Michael Riva
Set Decorator: Marvin March
Costume Design: Mary Malin
Makeup Artist: Scott Eddo
Hairstyling: K. G. Ramsey
Unit Production Manager: Steve Perry

## Second Unit Director or Assistant Director
Second Assistant Director: Terry Miller
First Assistant Director: Benjamin Rosenberg
Additional Second Assistant Director: William E. Simmons

## Art Department
Assistant Art Director: Eva Anna Andry
Lead Person: Jack Eberhart
Production Scenic Artist: Jimmie J. Hinkle
Labor Foreman: Ron Morales
Property Master: Erik Nelson
Construction Foreman: James Orendorff
Assistant Art Director: Virginia L. Randolph
Construction Coordinator: George Stokes
Art Department Researcher: Leslie Warren-Smith
Scenic Artist: Michael Denering
Swing Gang: Mario Castillo, Oscar Delgadillo, Joyce Gordon, Bob Santaella

## Sound Department
Re-recording Mixer: Dick Alexander
Assistant Sound Editor: Sherrie Bayer Burke
Sound Editors: David M. Horton, Richard Oswald, Bruce Lacey, Milton C. Burrow, Neil Burrow, Gordon Davidson
ADR Editor: Juno J. Ellis
Supervising ADR Editor: Jay Engel
Re-recording Mixer: Les Fresholtz
Assistant ADR Editor: Barbara Gandolfo
Assistant Sound Editor: Dee Dee Goldner
Supervising Sound Editor: Robert G. Henderson
Supervising Sound Editor: Alan Robert Murray

Production Sound Mixer: Bill Nelson
Re-recording Mixer: Vern Poore
Cable Man: Mychal Smith
Assistant Sound Editor: Jim Sparks
Boom Man: Jules Strasser
Foley Editor: Scott D. Jackson
Foley Mixer: Greg Orloff
Foley Artist: John Roesch

## Special Effects

Special Effects: Greg John Callas, Elmer Hui, Thomas Mertz, Bruce Robles, Harold Selig, Jeff Wischnack, Richard Wood
Special Effects Foreman: Joe Day
Special Effects Coordinator: Chuck Gaspar

## Stunts

Stunt Performers: John Alden, Gregory Barnett, Jophery C. Brown, Kelly Collins, Monty Cox, Jeff Dashnaw, Mike De Luna, Steve M. De France, Shane Dixon, David Ellis, Richard Miller Ellis, Donna Evans, Diane Hetfield, Freddie Hice, Billy Hank Hooker, Jeff Imada, Mark Lonsdale, Dana Mackey, Bennie E. Moore Jr, Jim Nickerson, Mary Peters, Chad Randall, Dar Robinson, Mic Rodgers, Ron Rondell, Keith Tellez, Elliott Valderrama, Randy Widner, Glenn Wilder, Steven Burnett, Annie Ellis, Tom Noga

Stunt Coordinator: Bobby Bass
Stunt Pilots: Jim Gavin, R.W. Martin, Karl Wickman
Fight Choreographer: Royce Gracie
Stunt Double (Mel Gibson): Mic Rodgers
Stunt Rigger: Tony Snegoff

## Camera and Electrical Department

Dolly Grip: Kirk Bales
Video Assist: Richmond G. Cogswell
Aerial Photographer: Frank M. Holgate
Electrical Best Boy: Bill King
Rigging Gaffer: Tim McArdle
First Assistant Camera: Geary McLeod
Grip Best Boy: Ron Peebles
First Assistant Camera: Calmar Roberts
Key Grip: Charles Saldana
Still Photographer: John R. Shannon
Panaglide Operator: Stephen St John
Gaffer: Mike Strong
Underwater Photographer: Ronald Vidor
Camera Operator: Richard Walden
Second Assistant Camera: Rick Whitesman, Bess Wiley
Set Lighting Technician: Adam Glick
Additional Camera Operator: Michael Hofstein

Additional First Assistant
Cameraman: Jeffrey Norvet
Camera Trainee: Scott Paperfus

## Costume and Wardrobe Department
Costume Supervisor: Barry
Francis
Costumer: Dallas D. Dornan
Assistant Costume Designer:
Paki Wolfe

## Editorial Department
Assistant Editors: Michael
Greenfield, Billy Meshover
Post-Production: Bernard
Weiser
Location Managers: David
Israel, John Panzarella, Paula
Shaw

## Music Department
Additional Orchestrators: Bruce
Babcock, Chris Boardman
Music Editor: Christopher
Brooks
Music Producer: Steve Chase
Musician: Eric Clapton
Orchestral Recordist: Robert
Fernandez
Additional Orchestrator: Philip
Giffin
Music Producer: James Guthrie
Music Producer/Conductor:
Michael Kamen
Musicians: David Sanborn,
David A. Stewart, Tom Boyd,
Tommy Johnson, James
Thatcher

Orchestrator: William Ross

## Transportation Department
Transportation Captains: Jim
Barbarino, Cliff Hill, Myra Hill
Drivers: Don Cannon, Vernon
Dautenhahan, Ron Kelley, Paul
Tampourios, Dennis Junt

## Other Crew
Technical Advisor: Cedric
Adams
Dialogue Coach: Julie Adams
Unit Runners: Gordon Antell,
Tom Maslow, Michael Alan
Kahn
Production Office Aide:
Matthew Baer
Technical Advisors: Rod
Bernsen, Art Fransen
Production Office Aides: Lauren
Caplan, Leah Dunatchik, Linday
Hirsch
Production Accountant: Jan
Garner
Jiu-Jitsu Advisor: Rorion
Grancie
Production Secretary: Laura
Hoffman
Assistants to Joel Silver: George
Luis, Tamara Smith
Animal Trainer: Alvin Mears
Unit Publicist: Katherine Ann
Technical Advisor ('Jailhouse
Rock'): Dennis Newsome
Weapon Specialist: Michael
Papac
First Aid: Jim Porter
Liaison: Spencer Quinn

Production Office Aide: Jean Paul Riva
Assistant to Jennie Lew: Laurie Ryan
Craft Service: Ron Saffold
Production Office Aides: Debby Shively, Tatum Share, Ellen Wolff, Susan Stern
Associate to Producer: Michael Thau

Production Associate: Elaine K. Thompson
Script Supervisor: Marion Tumen
Technical Advisor: Richard Whitaker
Assistant Production Accountant: Shari Cartun
Development Executive: Riley Kathryn Ellis
Dispatcher: Lynnanne Zager

# 10

# DIE HARD

## (1988)

*Silver Pictures/Gordon Company*

**Director:** John McTiernan
**Producers:** Lawrence Gordon and Joel Silver
**Screenwriters:** Jeb Stuart and Steven E. de Souza

*DIE Hard* isn't just one of the great action films of the eighties; it is probably the best film of its type ever made. Not only has it spawned four sequels (with a fifth in production at the time of writing), but it has had an influence on Hollywood that continues to this day.

At least ten major American films – *Under Siege* (1992), *Under Siege 2: Dark Territory (1995), Cliffhanger* (1993), *Executive Decision* (1996), *Air Force One* (1997), *Passenger 57* (1992), *The Rock* (1996), *Olympus Has Fallen* (2014), *White House Down* (2014), and *London Has Fallen* (2016) – have plots which follow the formula used in *Die Hard*, i.e. one man (who may be a maverick cop or an ex-Special Forces soldier, etc.) takes on a gang of terrorists, kills them off one at a time, and foils their plan. Even the recent series of three *Taken* films (2008-15) starring Liam Neeson may be considered variants of the *Die Hard* formula, albeit with the action taking place in a less claustrophobic environment.

The roots of *Die Hard* go back to 1966 and a Roderick Thorp novel, *The Detective*, which featured a policeman called Joe Leland. In 1968 it was made into a film with Frank Sinatra in the title role, and in 1979 a sequel was published called *Nothing Lasts Forever*. The plot involved anti-capitalist terrorists led by Anton 'Little Tony' Gruber taking over a skyscraper, and Joe Leland's single-handed efforts to thwart their plans. Thorp supposedly got the idea for the book after seeing the film *The Towering Inferno* (1975), and then dreaming about a man being pursued by terrorists through a skyscraper.

It is possible that the origins of the film's plot go back even further. In the movie *Sailor of the King* (1953) – itself a remake of the 1935 John Mills film *Brown on Resolution* – Royal Navy sailor Andrew Brown (played by American actor Jeffrey Hunter) escapes imprisonment in an anchored German cruiser during WW2, makes his way ashore and then, bare-chested, hinders repair work on the German vessel by shooting at the crew with a captured rifle. Despite being faced with superior numbers and firepower, which includes the warship's main armament, Brown delays the Germans' patching of a torpedo hole in the hull long enough to allow a force of British cruisers to arrive and sink the enemy vessel.

One episode of the LWT TV series *The Professionals* also has similarities with *Die Hard*. In *Close Quarters*, written by Brian Clemens and first broadcast by the ITV network on 10 February 1978, CI5 Agent Bodie (Lewis Collins) and his girlfriend Julia (Gabrielle Drake) are forced to take shelter in a house which is then besieged by a gang of German terrorists from the 'Meyer-Helmut Gang' (clearly based on the real-life Baader-Meinhof Gang). The bad guys in *Die Hard* are eventually revealed to be 'common criminals', but in *Nothing Last Forever* they are anti-capitalist terrorists.

In *Die Hard*, John McClane (as the Joe Leland character was renamed) starts off with his own handgun but then steals a submachine gun from a dead terrorist. In *Close Quarters*, Bodie kills the first terrorist with his pistol and then captures a submachine gun from him. Both productions end with a climax on the top floor and Gabrielle Drake's character Julia has red curly hair, just like Bonnie Bedelia. Incidentally, Lewis Collins and Gabrielle Drake were very nearly Mike Gambit and Purdey in *The New Avengers*, as they did a screen test together for these roles. In *Die Hard*, John McClane has a handicap as he has to fight the bad guys in his bare feet. In *Close Quarters* Bodie has an injured right hand which makes it hard to hold and fire a gun, so he has to do everything with his left hand. Bruce Willis incidentally is left-handed, something which isn't always apparent in the film.

In 1987, 20th Century Fox decided to make a film adaptation of *Nothing Lasts Forever*, but with the new title *Die Hard* which had been suggested by screenwriter Shane Black. Thorp didn't like the new title, which was also the name of a type of car battery manufactured by the Sears Corporation, which had been on sale in the USA since 1967. For contractual reasons they had to offer the part of Joe Leland to Frank Sinatra, who by then was 72 years old. Sinatra declined the part, and the role was given to 32 year old Bruce Willis, in a departure from his usual roles. Although Willis is now widely known as an action movie star, prior to *Die Hard* he was best known for starring in romantic comedies like *Blind Date* (1987) and the TV series *Moonlighting* (1985-89) with Cybil Shepherd. Other actors considered for the role of John McClane included Richard Gere, Sylvester Stallone and Burt Reynolds.

It should be noted, though, that the Joe Leland character in Thorp's original novel would have been at least 60 as he fought in WW2 (his exact age is never revealed) and not the young man depicted on screen. Thus the original book, *Nothing Lasts Forever*, presaged the current fad for 'geri-actioners' with relatively old leading men such as Liam Neeson.

For the crucial role of villain Hans Gruber, the producers turned to 42 year old English actor Alan Rickman. Like many leading British thespians, Rickman trained at RADA and was a member of the Royal Shakespeare Company. Though he had done a lot of work in the theatre and on British television, he had never acted in a film before. In casting Rickman, the producers were following a Hollywood trend for using British actors as villains which probably dates back to the 1930s.

The director chosen to helm the project was 37 year old John McTiernan, who had made just two previous features – *Nomads* (1986), featuring Pierce Brosnan in his first leading role, and *Predator* (1987), a science fiction action film which is discussed in detail in another chapter of this book.

The film was produced by Lawrence Gordon and Joel Silver. Gordon was a highly experienced producer who had been President of 20th Century Fox between 1984 and 1986, while Silver specialised in action films such as *Predator* and *Lethal Weapon* (both 1987).

The script was the result of a collaboration between Steven E. de Souza and Jeb Stuart. De Souza had a long career in film and television going back as far as *The Six Million Dollar Man* TV series (1974). He was also the writer of

*Commando* (1985), starring Arnold Schwarzenegger, but has strenuously denied that *Die Hard* was originally going to be a sequel to that film, with the Austrian actor reprising his John Matrix character who would have replaced John McClane.

The film opens with a shot of a Boeing 747 landing at Los Angeles Airport on Christmas Eve, having made the five-hour trip from New York. Policeman John McClane (Bruce Willis) looks tired and stressed from his long journey, and a neighbouring passenger offers him some advice: when he gets to his destination he should take off his shoes and socks and make fists with his toes to unwind. It will refresh him better than a shower or a coffee.

As McClane takes a large soft toy bear out of an overhead locker, the passenger catches sight of his Beretta 92 pistol in its shoulder holster and McClane has to reassure him that he is a cop who has been doing the job for 11 years. A deleted scene at this point includes some mild flirtation between McClane and a flight attendant (Stella Hall). In Roderick Thorp's original novel McClane is a widower, the stewardess is called Kathy, and they talk on the 'phone a few times over the course of the book – the action of which takes place over three days. For the film all of the drama is compressed into just a few hours, with most scenes taking place at night.

As McClane is waiting at baggage reclaim, his estranged wife Holly (Bonnie Bedelia) is preparing to participate in a Christmas Eve party at her place of work – the Nakatomi Corporation building in central Los Angeles. This building was the second 'star' of the film, and was in reality the not-quite-finished 35-storey Fox Plaza office tower in Los Angeles' Century City.

In addition, in view of the destruction that would be inflicted on the building during the film, three floors were recreated on Stage 15 of the 20$^{th}$ Century Fox film lot, and reflected the influence of the Japanese and the American architect Frank Lloyd Wright with interiors full of stone, wood and traditional materials. Surrounding the set was a 260 degree cyclorama (a curved, painted backdrop) of West Los Angeles, which was lit from behind to simulate different times of the day. A staggering 380 feet long, some parts of the backdrop were painted out of focus to simulate what the eye sees. Lighting effects were also incorporated, including animated bulbs to simulate moving traffic. It was so effective that it was re-used in several other productions and still exists in storage today.

As Holly is getting ready to join the party her work colleague Harry Ellis (Hart Bochner) suggests they have dinner together, but Holly declines. She then rings her daughter Lucy (Taylor Fry) at their home in Los Angeles to find out if her husband John has called.

Meanwhile, John McClane is being picked up at LAX airport by a chauffeur called Argyle (De'voreaux White) who is driving a huge, expensive Lincoln Town car limousine with every conceivable extra including cassette player, CD, TV and a car phone. Argyle quizzes McClane about his personal life and discovers he is a New York cop who has come to visit his wife and children, as Holly is now working in LA.

Argyle drives to the Nakatomi building where he drops John off, gives a business card with his carphone number and parks the car in the underground garage, saying he will wait for him there. If he wants to leave the party early, he only has to call. As McClane checks in at the front desk using a touchscreen device (cutting edge technology for

1988), he notices that his wife now goes under the name of Holly Gennero and works on the 30<sup>th</sup> floor. He takes the express elevator up to her location as Argyle parks his limousine. Arriving at the suite of offices, McClane is introduced to Nakatomi executive Joseph Takagi (James Shigeta), who shows him into Holly's office. Harry Ellis is sitting in Holly's seat and leaves as John arrives. Although Ellis claims to have been making a 'phone call it looks as though he has been taking cocaine, partly explaining his hyped-up behaviour later in the movie.

McClane expresses surprise that the Japanese are celebrating Christmas, and Takagi responds with the witticism:

'We're flexible. Pearl Harbor didn't work out, so we got you with tape decks.'

This line of dialogue may have been inspired by the famous Sony advertising slogan 'From these fabulous people who brought you Pearl Harbor', which was dreamed up by marketing expert Jerry Della Femina in the late sixties.

Holly arrives and is clearly pleased to see her husband, who immediately notices that she is wearing an expensive Rolex watch which has been given to her by her employer.

As McClane strips down to his vest to have a wash in Holly's executive bathroom, he mentions that he will be staying at a friend's house over Christmas. Holly pleads with him to stay with her and their children, as she has missed him.

'Guess you didn't miss my name', replies McClane, who points out that she is now known as 'Miss Gennero'.

In the meantime, a Mercedes W124 saloon draws up outside the building and two terrorists, Karl (Alexander Gudonov) and Theo (Clarence Gilyard Jr), jump out and stroll towards the front desk, chatting in a very casual manner. Without warning, they shoot the guard and Karl rolls a disc-shaped stun grenade (a 'hockey puck flashbang') along the floor, shooting a security guard who tries to intervene. As this is happening, a large Ford LN Pacific courier truck arrives in the basement and the remaining ten terrorists – and their leader, Hans Gruber (Alan Rickman) – walk out using a power-operated ramp at the rear of the vehicle.

Theo gets to work on the computer system and lowers steel shutters to seal off the building, while Tony (Andreas Wisniewski) taps into the building's 'phone system using leads with crocodile clips. Up on the $30^{th}$ floor, McClane tries to 'phone Argyle but discovers the lines have gone dead. Unbeknown to him, Karl is cutting through all the phone lines using a chainsaw.

As the terrorists prepare to storm the party, McClane is still in the bathroom where he has followed the advice given by his fellow passenger on the flight to LA. Having taken off his shoes and socks, he makes fists with his toes on the rug and discovers that it does indeed refresh him.

Suddenly the terrorists burst into the room where the party is being held, carrying Heckler and Koch MP5 submachine guns. They fire short bursts into the ceiling to frighten and subdue the guests, but the noise alerts McClane about what is happening. McClane flees the bathroom carrying his handgun, but leaving behind his shoes and socks and only wearing his grey trousers and white vest. He makes his way up the fire escape to the unfinished $32^{nd}$ floor to try and summon help by 'phone. Unfortunately all the lines are dead.

Meanwhile, Hans Gruber is addressing the hostages and claims to be leading a group of anti-capitalist terrorists.

He takes Takagi in the lift to another floor and admires his suit.

'John Philips of London. I have two. Rumour has it that Arafat wears them.' A reference to the then-leader of the Palestinian Liberation Organisation, Yasser Arafat.

Concealed from view in an upper floor, McClane witnesses several terrorists manhandling crates containing anti-tank missiles and wonders what they are planning.

On another floor, Hans admires some architectural models including one planned project in Indonesia and mentions that he himself used to make models when he was young. One of the models on view shows Frank Lloyd Wright's design for the Butterfly Wing Bridge across San Francisco bay, which was never built. It was loaned for use in the production by the Frank Lloyd Wright Foundation. Producer Joel Silver was himself a great fan of this particular American architect.

Hans takes Takagi into an adjacent room and asks him for the codes which will enable him to access $640m worth of bearer bonds which are held in a vault in the building.

'What kind of terrorists are you?' says an astonished Takagi.

'Who says we are terrorists?' replies Gruber. This is a major departure from Thorp's original novel, in which the hostage-takers are anti-capitalist terrorists, not common criminals. However, in the film Gruber's gang maintains the fiction of being freedom fighters almost to the end in order to achieve their goals. John McTiernan agreed with the writers and producers that this change would make the film more enjoyable and interesting.

Located nearby, McClane is observing the scene and crawls on his stomach, pistol in hand, to get a better look.

Although he can see Hans from behind, he doesn't get a clear look at his face.

Gruber repeats his demands for the codes. After screwing a suppressor to end of the barrel of his gun – a Heckler and Koch PZM13 – he points it at Takagi saying he will count to three and then shoot him.

'That's a nice suit. It would be a shame to ruin it.'

Again Takagi refuses to reveal the codes. 'You'll just have to shoot me', he says.

'OK', Gruber responds as he pulls the trigger and kills Takagi. Theo reassures Hans that he can still break into the vault without Takagi's help.

McClane is so shocked by this brutal act of murder that he accidentally moves, making a noise and giving away his presence. Some of the terrorists race into the next room but McClane escapes, hoping that Argyle has heard the shot and is 'phoning the police. Unfortunately the chauffeur is still on the carphone, loud music blaring from his limousine's stereo, and doesn't hear anything.

The most memorable terrorist in the film is Karl, played by Alexander Gudonov. Russian by birth, Gudonov defected to the USA from the Soviet Union in 1979 and brought tremendous physicality to his performance as he had previously trained as a ballet dancer.

In the interim, Theo is struggling to break the codes which will open the vault – the biggest problem being the seventh lock. One of the codewords he is able to guess correctly is *Akagi*, which means 'Red Castle' in Japanese. The *Akagi* was a famous Japanese aircraft carrier which took part in the attack on Pearl Harbor in 1941 and was sunk the following June during the Battle of Midway. As Theo struggles with his problem, McClane is anguished over his perceived failure to prevent Takagi's death and comes up with a new plan – he will trigger the fire alarm, forcing the emergency services to pay a visit and alerting the authorities to what is going on. He sets off the alarm and, within a few minutes, four fire department vehicles race down the road leading to the building. Unfortunately Gruber responds by getting one of his men to 'phone 911, saying it was a false alarm, and the trucks turn back before they arrive at the building.

Suddenly, the terrorist Tony arrives carrying an MP5 submachine gun and a black haversack. He can't see McClane, so he tells him to surrender and insists he won't be harmed. McClane switches on an electric saw, which attracts Tony's attention, and then sticks his pistol in the left side of the terrorist's neck. The two then start fighting and, after a desperate struggle, both of them fall down a metal fire escape and Tony sustains a fatal head injury. McClane searches his clothing and haversack and discovers some useful items including two spare magazines for the MP5 and a hand-held CB radio. He also takes off Tony's trainers but discovers they are too small for his feet. In Roderick Thorp's original novel Leland declines to wear the shoes, not because they are too small but rather because he doesn't like the idea of wearing a dead man's shoes. He puts Tony's corpse in an office chair after scrawling something on his shirt, then climbs on top of the lift car after selecting the button to make it go down to the 30$^{th}$ floor.

As the lift is descending, Gruber is addressing the hostages. Suddenly there is a loud ping as the lift car arrives at the 30$^{th}$ floor. The doors open to reveal Tony sprawled in an office chair. He is wearing a Christmas hat and on his chest, scrawled in red crayon, are the words 'Now I have a machine gun. Ho Ho Ho'.

The terrorists are clearly shaken that their perfect plan is starting to unravel. Some of them take the lift to the top floor, unaware that McClane is riding above the carriage. As the car reaches the top of the building, McClane jumps off and makes his way down the fire escape to a lower level.

Meanwhile Karl (who is Tony's brother) is arguing with Gruber, who says they can't alter their plans because of one person. Ellis is dismissive of McClane's efforts, feeling that he is putting everyone at risk, but Holly sticks up for him by saying that he is only doing his job.

McClane has now made his way to the roof where he attempts to contact the police using his CB radio, but his pleas for help are dismissed by a female police radio operator who thinks he is a crank. McClane becomes more and more angry: 'Do you think I'm ordering a pizza?'

Unfortunately McClane's transmissions are heard by Hans, whose hand-held radio is working on the same frequency. Realising McClane must be on the roof, he dispatches three of his men to deal with him. McClane is forced to terminate his call as the terrorists arrive, and a gun battle ensues.

As McClane fights off the three terrorists, the police radio operator ponders over what to do. Though she still thinks it was a crank call she realises the address given by McClane was the subject of a fire alarm call a few minutes earlier, so she asks the nearest 'Black and White' (police patrol car) to investigate a 'Code 2' at the Nakatomi building.

The call is answered by overweight, middle-aged cop Al Powell (Reginald VelJohnson) who is buying a huge pile of 'Twinkies' in a gas station close to the Nakatomi building.

(A 'Twinkie' is a bar-shaped sponge cake with a cream filling which is full of fat, calories and sugar, and first went on sale in the USA in 1930.) Powell steps outside, looks at the Nakatomi Building just a few hundred yards away and sets off in his car, a 1979 Chevrolet Impala.

As Powell's police car travels to the office block, McClane is involved in a machine gun battle with the terrorists and is forced to seek refuge inside the lift shaft. In order to get there he has to stop the blades of a huge fan using his MP5 and then crawl through between the blades. All the terrorists carry Heckler and Koch MP5s except for Karl, who prefers a futuristic looking Steyr Aug assault rifle.

Gruber is concerned because he knows police are on the way, and he tells Karl to shut McClane in the lift shaft where he can do no harm. Inside the shaft, a bruised and battered McClane realises the only way to escape is to make his way a few yards down the shaft to the air conditioning duct. There is no ladder or handholds, so McClane uses his MP5 as an anchor and hangs from the gun's carrying strap as he descends. Before he can reach the duct the MP5 comes loose and McClane falls, but he manages to grab the lip of the air conditioning duct and pull himself inside it. The fall was an accident during filming, but looked so good it was kept in. For scenes where the camera is looking down the shaft, a simple painted backdrop was used which was placed on top of an airbag to cushion the impact if the stuntman employed accidentally fell.

Outside the shaft, the terrorists realise what McClane has done and riddle the duct with bullets, fortunately missing him. They are unable to complete the task because Gruber is begging them to get downstairs as a police car is approaching the building. Once the terrorists leave, McClane makes his way to the window and is disappointed to see that the cop car has not spotted anything suspicious.

'Who's driving that car? Stevie Wonder?' he quips.

Al Powell goes into the building and chats with Eddie (Dennis Hayden), who is pretending to be the concierge. He doesn't notice anything unusual. Meanwhile, in frustration McClane tries to smash a window with a chair. The noise attracts two terrorists, Heinrich (Garry Roberts) and Marco (Lorenzo Caccialanza), who burst into the room. McClane kills Heinrich and dives for cover under a long conference table as Marco gets on top of the table, puts a fresh magazine into his MP5 and prepares to shoot McClane. But the New York cop is too quick for him and swiftly fires 15 rounds from his handgun through the table, killing the terrorist. This scene allegedly resulted in Bruce Willis sustaining permanent hearing loss. By this stage in the movie McClane's vest, which started off as white, is now olive green.

By this point Al Powell is about to leave the building, having reported in by radio that everything is OK at the Nakatomi Plaza. McClane realises that he has to do something drastic to attract the cop's attention, so he throws Marco's dead body out of the window as he utters the wisecrack 'Welcome to the party, pal'.

Marco's body lands with a crash on the bonnet of Powell's car. The terrorists open fire on the car with an M60 machine gun and drill it full of holes, but Powell gets out of danger by reversing at high speed as he puts out an emergency call for assistance on his radio. Eventually Powell reverses over a parapet and drops to a lower level where he cannot be hit.

Within minutes the police have arrived in force, and this activity has come to the attention of odious TV reporter

Richard Thornburg (William Atherton). Gruber discusses the latest developments with his remaining men. A police response was expected at some stage, so this is not a disaster.

As Gruber is reviewing the situation, McClane calls him on his radio and the criminal leader tries to find out more about the man's identity. The German expresses his distaste for cowboys like John Wayne in American popular culture and McClane responds that he prefers Roy Rogers, uttering a modified version of Rogers' catchphrase: namely 'Yippie Ki Yay, Motherfucker'. These words were subsequently uttered by John McClane in all the *Die Hard* sequels, and became his own catchphrase.

In the meantime Thornburg is requesting a TV outside broadcast truck so he can do an exclusive on the story, while back at the Yakatomi building Gruber realises that Marco is dead and the bag containing the crucial detonators is missing.

McClane exchanges information with Al Powell over the radio, leading Al to suspect he is an ex-cop. Deputy Police Chief Dwayne T. Robinson (Paul Gleason) arrives to take charge, but he is clearly a protocol-obsessed bureaucrat. He is unimpressed by what he has heard about McClane, and doesn't believe Powell's suspicions that he may be a cop.

As a van from the TV station KFLW arrives containing Richard Thornburg and his crew, Holly meets Gruber with some modest demands. One of the hostages is pregnant and is due to give birth in two weeks, so Holly asks if she can be moved to a room with a sofa. Gruber says he will arrange for a sofa to be brought to her. Holly also says that arrangements will have to be made to allow people to visit the bathroom, and Gruber agrees to this as well.

As Holly leaves, Gruber glances at the photos next to her desk. One of them – showing her with John and her kids

– has been placed face down, but Gruber doesn't realise the significance of this. In the basement car park Argyle is watching TV when a news item comes on about the siege, and he finally realises what has been happening.

Meanwhile, a SWAT team from the Los Angeles police department is preparing to assault the building as Powell expresses his concern that the police have underestimated the resourcefulness of the terrorists. As the armed policemen close in on the building, the terrorists close all the steel shutters to make entry harder and track the attackers on CCTV. As Gruber's gang prepare to repel the attackers, Uli (Al Leong) pinches a couple of chocolate bars from a glass cabinet.

The terrorists open fire on the SWAT team and knock out all the spotlights. As things start to go wrong, the SWAT team leader asks for an armoured car to be sent in. The vehicle is a WW2 vintage six-wheeled Ford M8 armoured car, painted black and with its usual gun turret removed. With its all-wheel drive the vehicle climbs up the stone steps in front of the building, but then becomes stuck and is immediately hit by an anti-tank missile fired from the fourth floor of the building. The missile launcher in this sequence, which looks like an elongated version of a WW2 bazooka, was custom-made for the movie and was not a recognisable type. To simulate a moving anti-tank missile, a solid fuel rocket was fired down a wire which was treated with acid to prevent it reflecting light and making it invisible.

One curious plot point is that the terrorists have to move the missile launcher and ammunition in the lift from one of the upper floors of the building to the fourth floor before they can bring it into action, so why didn't they have the weapon ready for use in one of the lower levels to begin with?

And how did this bulky weaponry get into the building in the first place, since it wasn't in the Pacific Courier truck?

McClane is furious when he hears Gruber on the radio ordering a second round to be fired at the armoured vehicle: 'Hans, you motherfucker! You've made your point!' But the German is unrepentant, and another missile strikes the M8 car.

In a fit of pique, McClane retaliates. After prising open the lift doors with an axe he grabs an office chair, sticks a slab of C4 plastic explosive on it, shoves in a detonator, puts a computer monitor on top, and lashes it in place with the power cable. He then flings it down the open lift shaft. It falls to the bottom of the shaft and explodes, killing the terrorists responsible for the missile attack. To create the effect of a huge explosion without damaging the building, a large number of powerful flashbulbs – which burned for a full two seconds – were used.

The explosion is witnessed and filmed by the KFLW TV crew, pleasing Thornburg considerably, while back at the Nakatomi building the sleazy Harry Ellis has an idea to resolve the situation. He realises that Gruber's plan is starting to unravel as a result of McClane's single-handed war against his gang. He knocks on Gruber's door.

'What do you want?' says the German.

'It's not what I want', says Ellis. 'It's what I can give you. Business is business. You use a gun, I use a fountain pen; what's the difference? The guy upstairs is fucking things up. I can give him to you.'

As this is happening, McClane is chatting on the CB radio to Powell who reveals that his wife is having a baby. Suddenly Gruber butts into the conversation. He has now discovered McClane's identity, though he doesn't yet know that Holly is his wife. 'I have someone who wants to talk to you', he says, passing the 'phone to Ellis.

'What did you tell them?' says McClane. He is clearly fearful that Ellis is going to reveal Holly's true identity. Ellis claims that they are old friends and that McClane was a guest at the party. This is clearly part of his strategy to get McClane to do what he wants. He then says that the terrorists plan to kill him if he can't persuade him to hand over the detonators. However, McClane refuses and Gruber shoots Ellis.

Robinson and Powell have heard the whole exchange over the radio and Robinson blames McClane for what has happened. But Powell sticks up for, him claiming he did everything he could. This leads to an argument between the two men.

Gruber then calls Robinson on the radio and reads out a list of demands which include a list of imprisoned terrorists in various locations around the world that must be released. When all the terrorists are freed, the hostages will be taken to the roof where they will be taken by helicopter to Los Angeles International Airport, at which point further instructions will be given. The authorities have just two hours to comply.

Gruber then calls Theo to find out if he is on schedule, and he reports that he has only one lock left to open. He then asks Karl to hunt down McClane and recover the crucial detonators. McClane discusses the latest developments with Powell, and says he is suspicious of Gruber's demands.

The TV networks are now giving extensive coverage to the siege and one of them has an interview with a Dr Hasselldorff, who talks about 'Helsinki Syndrome' in which hostages form a bond with their captives. This is an error on the part of the scriptwriters, as the correct term is 'Stockholm Syndrome' which was first described following an incident in which hostages formed a bond with their captors during a bank siege in Stockholm in 1973.

Meanwhile the FBI arrive in the form of Agent Little Johnson (Grand L. Bush) and Special Agent Big Johnson (Robert Davi), who we are told are not related to one another. The following year Davi played the memorable villain Franz Sanchez in Timothy Dalton's second and final Bond picture *Licence to Kill*. The FBI men announce they are taking charge, much to the chagrin of Dwayne T. Robinson.

As the FBI men are planning their next move, Gruber is checking the area just beneath the roof and momentarily puts down his pistol and torch. As he jumps down he meets McClane, who is armed with his own pistol. Thinking quickly, Gruber puts on an American accent, pretends to be a terrified escaped hostage, and claims that he was trying to get onto the roof. This scene came about after it was realised that it would be a good idea if Gruber and McClane could meet at some point in the film and that this would be possible if Gruber could fake an American accent and wear a suit thus enabling him to pass as a hostage. To make this scene plausible, the earlier one showing McClane witnessing Takagi's execution had to be shot in such a way that it was clear that McClane had not actually seen Gruber's face and so would not recognise him.

McClane offers Gruber a cigarette and he takes one. In the ensuing conversation McClane reveals he is a New York cop and Gruber notices he has bare feet. Gruber claims his name is Bill Clay and McClane gives 'Bill' a pistol. As McClane turns his back on Gruber, the German speaks into his CB radio in his native tongue and points his gun at McClane.

'Put down your gun and give me the detonators.'

McClane refuses to hand them over and Gruber pulls the trigger. Nothing happens, as the gun is empty

'Think I'm fucking stupid, Hans?' blurts out McClane.

Good thinking on the part of McClane. But it is never explained how he twigged that Bill Clay was really Hans Gruber! Suddenly the lift doors open and Karl, Franco and Fritz (Hans Buhringer) arrive. A furious battle ensues with automatic weapons, and Gruber tells his men to shoot at all the glass in the office as he knows McClane's bare feet are his weak point. In fact Bruce Willis's feet were not really naked in most scenes, as he was fitted with fake rubber feet with metal soles – rather like moccasins – to protect him from injury. This was a sensible precaution, as the glass in this scene was real and not the usual plastic safety glass employed in movies. Karl uses another of his 'hockey puck' flashbangs, but Fritz and Franco are killed in the battle while McClane is forced to flee, leaving behind the bag containing the crucial detonators.

As McClane seeks cover, Thornburg's researcher has discovered that McClane is a New York cop and that his wife and children are living in LA. She even discovers their address.

Meanwhile in a bathroom in an upper floor, McClane binds his bloody, wounded feet using makeshift bandages made by ripping up his vest, and then calls Powell on his radio to report that he has killed two more bad guys. Powell reveals that he suffered a work-related trauma some years before when he shot a 13 year old. Since then he has been unable to bring himself to fire a gun.

As the two continue with their conversation, FBI Special Agent Johnson plans to cut power to the building in the belief that this will make things more difficult for the terrorists. Even though many city blocks will be affected, Johnson orders this to be carried out. Instantly the Nakatomi building is plunged into darkness before the battery-operated emergency lighting kicks in. The power cut actually helps Gruber's gang, as it results in the final vault lock opening. The shot of all the lights going out in the building was achieved with a visual effect.

Blissfully unaware that his action is actually aiding the gang, Special Agent Johnson calls in helicopter gunships to strafe the criminals as they are standing on the roof. He calls up Gruber on the radio to tell him that all the terrorists have been released (as Gruber had demanded), and helicopters are on their way. But Hans is planning his own double cross. Once all the hostages are on the roof he is set to blow it up with explosives. By the time the authorities sift through the wreckage and work out what has happened, Hans will be 'lying on a beach earning twenty percent'; his comments reflecting the rather higher interest rates of the late eighties!

Two genuine Bell UH-1 Huey helicopters were used in the production, and all scenes featuring them had to be shot during a two-hour window which had been granted by the authorities. Nine camera crews filmed the action simultaneously, to ensure that the sequence did not have to be repeated.

As McClane continues his radio conversation with Powell, he asks him to tell Holly something. He realises he has been a jerk and should have been more understanding about her job. He wonders, though, what Gruber was doing on the top floor and decides to go upstairs to check out the underside of the roof. There, he is horrified to discover a large quantity of explosives, detonators and timers. As he is trying to call Powell on the radio, Karl sticks the muzzle of a rifle against his head. 'We are both professionals; this is personal', says Karl, who is particularly angry that McClane killed his brother Tony.

Downstairs, Gruber sees a news item on the TV. It is Thornburg interviewing the McClane children. Immediately he makes the connection and flips up the photo beside Holly's desk, realising that Holly is McClane's wife. 'Pleased to make your acquaintance', he says as he holds Holly at gunpoint.

As McClane and Karl continue to fight on the top floor, the two armed Bell UH-1 Huey helicopters fly towards the Nakatomi building. The lead chopper contains both Agent Johnson and Special Agent Johnson who is in an exuberant mood as it reminds him of his days in Vietnam.

Gruber arrives in the vault, holding Holly at gunpoint, as gang members count the liberated bonds. McClane's wife realises the true reason behind the gang's actions.

'You're just a common thief.'

'I'm an exceptional thief!' replies Gruber.

Meanwhile McClane's fight with Karl comes to a climax as he manages to hang the German from the ceiling using a length of chain.

As the two choppers approach the building the hostages are taken onto the roof. McClane arrives and discovers that Holly has been taken to the vault. He realises the hostages are in extreme danger, and forces them to leave the roof by firing his MP5 submachine gun into the air. This does the trick, but Special Agent Johnson thinks he is a terrorist and orders the helicopter crews to open fire on him with machine guns. McClane is now in danger both from 'friendly fire' and the imminent explosion on the roof. Thinking quickly, McClane graps a fire hose, ties it around his waist, and jumps off the top of the building just as the roof explodes in a gigantic fireball. As he swings in front of the windows he pulls out his pistol and fires several times to break the glass, allowing him to enter the building through a broken pane.

As he crashes into an empty office and unties the fire hose, the lead Huey containing both Agents Johnson is consumed by the explosion on the roof and fiery debris rains down the outside of the building. This highly realistic sequence was achieved using a one-sixth scale radio-controlled model chopper built from a kit, which was carefully painted and detailed to match the two real Hueys used in the production and filmed against a detailed miniature of the top floors of the Nakatomi building. Filmed with a high-speed camera to slow down the action, the result was totally convincing. The only thing that went wrong during this model filming was that the small helicopter refused to fall off the top off the building, requiring a nudge from an unseen broomstick held by a special effects technician!

Inside the building, McClane checks his weaponry and discovers he has no bullets left in his MP5 submachine gun and only two rounds in his pistol magazine. He sees some parcel tape on a shelf and has an idea.

In the basement parking garage Argyle sees Theo going into the truck to retrieve a smaller vehicle (a red and white Los Angeles Fire Department Chevrolet van) which is parked inside. As Theo drives the van out the back using small ramps, Argyle smashes his limo into its side, trapping Theo inside and knocking him unconscious. This is a serious continuity error, because at the start of the film when the gang of terrorists exited the rear of the Pacific Courier truck it was clear that the vehicle was now empty. So how did the van get there?

The now bare-chested John arrives at the vault, limping with his injuries as Gruber holds Holly at gunpoint. He orders McClane to drop his MP5. McClane complies and Gruber thinks he is totally disarmed, but fails to realise he has a pistol taped to his back. Once again Gruber makes fun of American cowboy movies 'with John Wayne and Grace Kelly'. McClane corrects him saying that the film he is thinking of (*High Noon*) actually features Gary Cooper.

McClane, Gruber and Eddie start to laugh and – while they are distracted – McClane whips out his pistol and shoots the two criminals. But Gruber is only wounded in the shoulder and, as he falls through a window, he grabs Holly's watch in an attempt to take her with him. After a struggle, McClane manages to remove Holly's watch and Gruber falls backwards to his death. In Roderick Thorp's original novel Joe Leland is trying to save his daughter (called Stephanie), not his wife who had died some years before, and she actually dies as a result of 'Tony' Gruber grabbing her as he falls to his death.

Alan Rickman did the first part of the stunt himself, falling backwards about 70 feet against a green screen and landing on an airbag which was also painted the same colour. The resulting footage was then matted into a shot taken from a camera looking down from the top of the building. The scene was filmed at 300 frames per second to slow down the action. Rickman was made to fall earlier than he expected, so the look of terror on his face was real and – as he recalled many years later – 'No acting was required'.

The shot which follows, filmed from ground level and showing Gruber falling down the side of the building, involved stuntman Kenny Bates being attached to a cable called a descender which allowed him to fall at normal speed before being rapidly decelerated and then brought to a stop before he hit the ground.

As Gruber falls to his death, hundreds of bonds are fluttering around the plaza as a TV van arrives. McClane is reunited with Holly and meets Al Powell for the first time. But all is not well, as the Deputy Chief Police Commissioner Dwayne T. Robinson is angry at McClane for all the death and destruction he has caused. Suddenly the supposedly-dead Karl, who is being brought out of the building, bursts out his body bag – rifle in hand – and takes aim at McClane. He is promptly shot dead by Al Powell. Although a complete musical score for the film was written by Michael Kamen, two pieces of stock music were used in this sequence – namely some music by John Scott from *Man on Fire* (1987) and a short extract from James Horner's score for *Aliens* (1986).

Argyle drives his limo through the metal grille which has sealed off the garage and screeches to a halt. Thornburg attempts to interview Holly and is rewarded for his efforts with a punch from her. The couple get into the limo and drive off as the Christmas song *Let it Snow, Let it Snow, Let it Snow* by Vaughan Monroe plays on the soundtrack.

*Die Hard* opened in the USA on 12 July 1988 and was a huge hit, making $140m at the box office against a budget of $28m which included a $5m fee for its star Bruce Willis. To date four sequels have been made – *Die Hard 2* (1990), *Die Hard with a Vengeance* (1995) which was directed by John McTiernan, *Live Free or Die Hard* (a.k.a. *Die Hard 4.0*) (2007), and *A Good Day to Die Hard* (2013). At the time of writing, a further sequel is planned – *Die Hard: The Beginning* – which features scenes set in the present day with Bruce Willis, and others in 1978 with a younger actor playing John McClane. For me, though, the best *Die Hard* film was the first one, which is perfectly structured and has a power and intensity that none of its sequels have ever achieved.

## *Die Hard* (1988)
## Production Credits

Director: John McTiernan
Screenplay: Jed Stuart and
Steven De Souza
Based on the novel *Nothing
Lasts Forever* by Roderick
Thorpe

**Cast**
John McClane - Bruce Willis
Holly Gennaro McClane -
Bonnie Bedelia
Sgt Al Powell - Reginald Vel
Johnson
Deputy Police Chief Dwayne T
Robinson - Paul Gleason
Richard Thornburg - William
Atherton
Harry Ellis - Hart Bochner
Joseph Takagi - James Shigeta
Hans Gruber - Alan Rickman
Karl - Alexander Gudonov
Franco - Bruno Doyon
Argyle - De'voreaux White
Tony - Andreas Wisniewski
Theo - Clarence Gilyard Jr
Alexander - Joey Plewa
Marco - Lorenzo Caccialanza
Kristoff - Gerard Bonn
Eddie - Dennis Hayden
Uli - Al Leong
Heinrich - Gary Roberts
Fritz - Hans Buhringer
James - Wilhelm von Homburg
FBI Special Agent Big Johnson -
Robert Davi

FBI Agent Little Johnson -
Grand L. Bush
City Engineer - Bill Marcus
Wait (City Worker) - Rick
Ducommun
Captain Mitchell - Matt
Landers
Rivers - Carmine Zozzora
Ginny - Dustyn Taylor
Dr Hasseldorf - George Christy
Young Cop - Anthony Peck
Woman - Cheryl Bates
Man - Richard Parker
Harvey Johnson - David Ursin
Gail Wallens - Mary Ellen
Trainor
Police Supervisor - Diana James
Dispatcher - Shelley Pogoda
Hostages - Selma Archerd, Scot
Bennett, Rebecca Broussard,
Kate Finlayson, Shanna Higgins,
Kym Main, Lucy McClane,
Taylor Fry, John McClane Jr,
Noah Land, Paulina Betty
Carvalho
Convenience Store Clerk - Kip
Waldo
Station Manager - Mark
Goldstein
Thornburg's Assistant - Tracey
Reiner
Guards - Rick Cicetti, Fred
Lerner
Producer - Bill Margolin
Cameramen - Bob Jennings,
Bruce P. Schultz

Soundman - David Katz
Businessman - Robert Lesser
Stewardess - Stella Hall
Girl at Airport - Terry Lynn Doss
Boy at Airport - Jon. E. Greene
Kissing Man - P. Randall Bowers
Girl in Window - Michele Laybourn
Cameraman - Rich Bross
SWAT Member - Conrad Hurtt
Police Officer - Marshall
Dancing Elk Lucas
Dwayne T. Robinson's Driver - Charlie Picerni
Hostage (uncredited) - Gary Pinkston
Gas Station Customer - Stan Rodarte
Police Detective - Mark Winn

## Production Credits
Executive Producer: Charles Gordon
Producers: Lawrence Gordon, Joel Silver
Associate Producer: Lloyd Levin

## Music
Composer: Michael Kamen

## Cinematography
Cinematographer: Jan De Bont

## Film Editing
Film Editors: John F. Link, Frank J. Urioste

Casting: Jackie Burch
Production Design: Jackson De Govia
Art Direction: John R. Jensen
Set Decoration: Phil M. Leonard
Costume Design: Marilyn Vance

## Make-up Department
Hair Stylist: Paul Abascal
Hairstylist (Bruce Willis): Josee Normand
Make-up Artists: Wes Dawn, Jim Kail
Make-up Supervisor: Scott H. Eddo

## Production Management
Unit Production Manager: Beau Marks

## Second Unit Director or Assistant Director
DGA Trainee: Paula Foster
Second Assistant Directors: Michael Alan Kahn, Terry Miller Jr
Second Unit Director: Beau Marks
First Assistant Director: Benjamin Rosenberg

## Art Department
Assistant Property Master: Michael Blaze
Set Dressers: Kirk B. Jones, Donald Kaeding, Steve Nelson, Richard Boris, Mike Bruner,

Efrain Gonzalez, Roland Hill,
Gus Feederie
Construction Foreman: Steve
Callas
Set Designer: E.C. Chen
Assistant Art Directors:
William J. Durrell Jr, Craig
Edgar
Lead Man: Bill Fannon Jr
Construction Coordinator:
Bruce J. Gfeller
Construction Paint Foreman:
Dick Girod
Production Painter: Jaymes
Hinkle
Illustrator: John L. Jensen
Property Master: Tommy
Tomlinson
Construction Foreman: Clete
Cetrone
Scenic Artist: Michael Denering
Set Construction: Stanley E.
Foster
Art Department Coordinator:
Kacy Magedman
Architect (Fox Plaza): Willian
L. Pereira
Plasterer: William M. Shannon
Propmaker Foreman: Robert
Van Dyke
Labourer: Frank White

## Sound Department
Foley Artists: Robin Harlan,
Vanessa Ament
Supervising Dialogue Editor:
George H. Anderson
Assistant Dialogue Editor:
Kevin Barlia

Foley Editor: Rick Mitchell,
Ron Bartlett
Re-recording Mixer: Kevin F.
Cleary, Don Bassman
Assistant Sound Editor: Destiny
Borden
Assistant ADR Editor: Sherrie
Bayer Burke
ADR Mixer: Kevin Carpenter
Machine Operator: Phyllis
Drury
Sound Effects: Richard Shorr,
Stephen H. Flick
Stereo Sound Consultant: David
W Gray
Sound Recordist: Craig Heath
Boom Operator: Dennis Jones
Dialogue Operator: Cindy
Marty
Assistant Sound Editor: Oscar
Mitt
Sound Mixer: Al Overton
Re-recording Mixer: Richard
Overton
Cable Person: Todd Overton
Apprentice ADR Editors: Lisa
M. Risen, Matthew Peerce
Sound Recordist: Robert Renga
ADR Recordist: Dennis Rogers
Dialogue Editor: Jeff Rosen
Supervising ADR Editor: Hank
Salerno
Post-Production Dialogue:
Norman B. Schwartz
Sound Effects Editor: Catherine
Shorr
ADR Editors: James R. Simcik,
Ronald Sinclair, Bill Voigtlander

Sound Effects Editor: David E. Stone
Foley Mixer: Lee Tinkham
Assistant ADR Editor: Rosemarie Wheeler
Sound Effects Recordist: Ezra Dweck
Sound Re-recording Engineer: Bill Henderson
Supervising Sound Editor: Richard Shorr

## Special Effects
Special Effects Foreman: William Aldridge
Special Effects Assistants: Jay Bartus, Hal Bigger, James Camomile, Larry De Unger, Al Di Sarro, Dennis Dion, Richard Zarro, Patrick R Gordon, Jay M. Hirsch, Darrell Pritchett, Joe D. Ramsey, Andrew Sebok, Steve Suits, Rick Thompson, Michael A. Tice, Bruno Van Zeebroeck
Effects Technician (Boss): Daniel Hutten
Special Effects Foreman (Boss): Thaine Ross
Chief Engineer (Boss): Gene Whiteman

## Visual Effects
Model Maker (Boss): Yarek Alfer
Animation Production Assistant (Boss): Maura Alvarez
Visual Effects Art Director (Boss): Brent Boates

Model Electronics (Boss): Richard Chronister
Optical Line-up (Boss): Kevin Clark
Optical Supervisor (Boss): Al Cox
Chief Electronics Engineer (Boss Film): Philip Crescenzo
Visual Effects Producer: Richard Edlund
Stand-by Model Maker (Boss): Alan Faucher
Chief Financial Officer (Boss): Donald R. Fly
Animation Production Assistant (Boss): Meg Freeman
Model Maker (Boss): James G. Anka, Dana Yuricich, Bruce MacCrae, Suzy Schneider, Dennis Schultz, Kent Gebo
Model Painter (Boss): Ron Gress
Model Effects Key Man: Robert L. Johnston
Model Helicopter Consultant (Boss): Larry Jolly
Stage Assistant (Boss): Kelly Kerby
Animation Production Assistant (Boss): Lisa Krepela
Chief Model Maker (Boss): Pat McClung
Visual Effects Editor (Boss): Dennis Michelson
Director of Photography (Boss): William Neill
Camera Operator (Boss): Clinton Palmer

Technical Animation Supervisor (Boss): Samuel E. Recinos
Optical Department Supervisor (Boss): Chris Regan
Model Construction Foreman (Boss): Milius Romyn
Model Effects (Boss): Paul Sabourin
Chief Miniature Moldmaker (Boss): David Schwartz
Optical Camera Operator (Boss): James Sleeper
Model Shop Supervisor (Boss): Mark Stetson
Visual Effects Coordinator: Michael Van Himbergen
Special Project Supervisor (Boss): Garry Waller
Assistant Visual Effects Editor (Boss): Debra Wolff
Optical Line-up (Boss): Peter Yanovitch
Chief Matter Artist (Boss): Matthew Yuricich
First Assistant Camera Operator (Boss): Wayne Baker
Visual Effects Coordinator: Mike Chambers

## Stunts
Stunt Performers: Ken Bates, Janet Brady, Nick Brett, Jophery Brown, Kurt Bryant, Brian Christensen, Gilbert B. Combs, Kerrie Cullen, Kennie Endoso, Andy Epper, Randy Hall, Norman Howell, Kell Johnston, Henry M. King, Julius Le Flore, Fred Lerner, Michael Marasco,

Don McGovern, Don Meier, Alan Oliney, Victor Paul, Charles Picerni Jr, Paul V. Picerni Jr, Steve Picerni, Bernie Pock, Chad Randall, R.A. Rondell, Benjamin Rosenberg, John Sherrod, Russell Solberg, Steve Vandeman, George Wilbur, Glenn Wilder, Dick Ziltor
Stunt Coordinator: Charles Picerni
Stunt Double (Bruce Willis): Keii Johnston
Stunt Double (Hans Buhringer): Henry Kingi
Stunt Double (Alexander Gudonov): Don Charles McGovern
Stunt Driver: Steve Ray

## Camera and Electrical Department
Assistant Camera: Brian Armstrong
Gaffer: Ed Ayer
Electrician: Brink Brydon
Musco Light Operators: Brad Chelesvig, Mike De Meyer, Robert Spurgeon, Ron Kunecke
Best Boys: Blaise Dahiquist, Michael Franz
Dolly Grip: Glen Davis
Key Grip: Bill Decker
Best Boy Grip: John Donnelly
Assistant Camera: John Ellingwood, Michael R. Marquette

Camera Operators: Michael
Ferris, M. Todd Henry
Electrician: Steven C. Hodge
Grip: Brian Holechek, Matthew
Nelson, Jim Rankin
Still Photographer: Robert
Isenberg
Still Photographer (Boss): Virgil
Mirano
Best Boy Grip: Bernie Schwartz
Camera Operator: Michael
Scott
Still Photographer: Peter Sorel
Key Grip (Boss): Patrick Van
Auken
First Assistant Camera (Boss):
Stefanie Wiseman
Electrician: Doug Yonker
Assistant Camera: Les Zell
High Speed Camera Technician:
Scott Dale
Electrician: Moose Enright
Assistant Camera: Ken Fisher,
Nicholas S. MacLean
Grip: Patricia Gregory

## Casting Department
Casting Associate: Ferne Cassel
Extras Casting: Carl Joy

## Costume and Wardrobe Department
Costume Supervisor: Barry
Francis
Costumer : Bruce Willis
Set Costumer: Barbara Siebert
Additional Costumer: Victoria
Snow

Set Costumer (Men): Michael J.
Voght

## Editorial Department
Assistant Editor: Derek Brechin
Negative Cutter: Gary Burritt
Assistant Editors: Bryan Carroll,
Gregory M. Gerlich, Kelly Irvine
Colour Timer: Dale Grahn, Bob
Hagans
Second Assistant Editors: Jeff
Gullo, Edward Malone
Negative Developer (Boss): Paul
Jenson

## Location Management
Location Managers: Joel Marx,
Ken H. Rosen
Assistant Location Manager:
Antoinette Simmrin

## Music Department
Additional Orchestrators: Bruce
Babcock, Chris Boardman
Score Engineer: Walt Borchers
Supervising Music Editor:
Christopher Brooks
Score Engineers: Terry Brown,
Chuck Garsha
Additional Orchestrators: Philip
Giffin, Fiachra Trench
Conductor: Michael Gamen
Music Producer: Stephen
McLaughlin
Score Mixer: Armin Steiner
Composer (Additional Music):
Bruce Babcock
Musician (Oboe): Tom Boyd

Musician (Tuba): Tommy
Johnson
Musician (French Horn): James
Thatcher

## Transportation Department
Transportation Coordinators:
Myra Hill, Dean Mason, Jim
Nordberg
Picture Car Coordinator:
Stanley Webber
Picture Car Mechanic: Tim
Sisson

## Other Crew
Assistant to John McTiernan:
Pamela Alessandrelli
Dubbing Projectionist: Alex
Algarin
Production Assistant: Brook
Altman
Special Weapons Training:
Bobby Bass
Assistant to Joel Silver: Susan
Joy Beallor
Location Liaison: Dan Carroll
Special Ceramic Vessels: Paul
Chaleff
Craft Service: Rick Chavez
Knife Designer: Jack Crain
Trainer for Bruce Willis: Keith
Cubba
Assistant Production
Accountant: Jyllel Syage
Cinetechnician (Boss): Ken
Dudderar
Production Executive: Riley
Kathryn Ellis

Chief Lighting Tech (Boss):
Robert Eyslee
First Aid: Marilynn B. Frank
Police Technical Advisor: Art
Fransen
Production Coordinator:
Elizabeth Galloway
Technical Advisor (Military):
Lt Gary Goldman
Model Furnisher (Butterfly
Bridge): Aaron J. Green
Assistant Production
Accountant: Alison Harstedt
Video Graphics: Richard E.
Hollander
Assistants to Bruce Willis: Clare
Leavenworth, Deborah Johnson
Production Accountant: K.
Lenna Katich
Caterer: Tony Kerum
Assistant to John McTiernan:
Carol Land
Publicity Coordinator: Andrew
Lipschultz
Pilots: Charles A Tamburro,
Michael Tamburro, Tony
Tamburro, Alan Purwin, Peter
McKernan
Second Pilot: Peter McKernan Jr
Video Graphics: Gregory L
McMurry
Production Assistants: Kari Ann
Messina, Lisa Miller, Frank
Reinhard, Phil Robinson
Stage Assistant (Boss): Chrissa
Ownens
Weapons Specialist: Michael
Papac

Stage Assistant (Boss): Jeff Rand

Assistant to Charles Gordon: Annie Saunders
Assistants to Lawrence Gordon: Shari Schneider, Kellett Tighe
Production Associate: Tamara Smith
Maintenance Engineer: Ken Stone
Production Coordinator: Dana Lynne Taylor
Script Supervisor: Marion Tumen
ADR Loopgroup (Voice): Larry Turk

Assistant to Joel Silver: Ladd Vance
Special Ceramic Vessels: Tod M. Volpe
Video and Graphics: John C. Wash
Design Engineer (Boss): Mark West
Assistant to Richard Edlund: Claire Wilson
Production Accountant (Boss): Maryjane Zelicskovics
Digital Distribution: Tyler Atkinson
Production Assistant: M. Rutledge McCall

# A FORCE OF ONE

## The Career of Chuck Norris, One of the Top Action Stars of the Eighties

CARLOS Ray 'Chuck' Norris, who was born in Ryan, Oklahoma on 10 March 1940, was one of the best-known action stars of the eighties. His films lack the subtleties of those made by the likes of Mel Gibson, Clint Eastwood, Bruce Willis, Arnold Schwarzenegger and Sylvester Stallone, but still deliver the goods on a low budget and have their fans. Rather like the *Death Wish* series, Norris's movies are generally hated by the critics but loved by the general public. Some of them have even become cult classics.

As a child, Norris was described as 'non-athletic, shy and scholastically mediocre', and he suffered the stigma of having an alcoholic father – Ray – who worked as an auto mechanic. In 1958, Norris joined the US Air Force as an air policeman and was sent to Osan Air Force base in South Korea. It was there that he first acquired the nickname 'Chuck' and started training in Tang Soo Doo, a form of martial arts. Norris subsequently became proficient in a number of martial arts, including Karate.

After leaving the USAF in 1962, Norris went to work for the Northrop Corporation and opened a chain of Karate schools including one in his then-hometown of Torrance in California. His celebrity clients at his schools included Steve McQueen, Chad McQueen, Bob Barker, Priscilla Presley, Donny Osmond and Marie Osmond.

Norris continued to develop his career as a Karate champion and, in 1990, he became the first Westerner to be given the rank of 8ᵗʰ Degree Black Belt Grand Master. He was subsequently inducted into the Martial Arts History Museum's Hall of Fame, and in 2000 he was presented with the Golden Lifetime Achievement Award by the World Karate Union Hall of Fame.

His acting debut came in the 1968 film *The Wrecking Crew*, one of a series of *Matt Helm* secret agent pictures made by Dean Martin. He subsequently appeared in the Bruce Lee martial arts movie *Way of the Dragon* (1972), one of several made by Lee in Hong Kong in the seventies.

Norris's first proper acting role, though, was in *Breaker, Breaker* (1977), which was followed by *Good Guys Wear Black* (1978), *The Octagon* (1980), *An Eye for an Eye* (1981) and *Lone Wolf McQuade* (1983) – which also starred Barbara Carrera, who appeared as Bond villainess Fatima Blush in *Never Say Never Again* the same year.

Norris had two brothers – Wieland, who was killed in the Vietnam War, and Aaron, who has worked as a stuntman, actor, director and producer and has been involved in some capacity in many of his brother's pictures.

In 1984, Norris starred in *Missing in Action* – the first of eight action pictures he was to make for Cannon Films between 1984 and 1988. The Cannon Group had been set up by two Israeli filmmakers, Menahem Golan and Yoram Globus, who had first come to prominence when they produced *Operation Thunderbolt* (1978), an Israeli film about the Entebbe raid in July 1976 which had also inspired two Hollywood movies – *Victory at Entebbe* (1976) and *Raid on Entebbe* (1977). Curiously, a fourth film about the raid – *Entebbe* – is due to start production in 2017.

In the 1980s the Cannon Group was a potent force in cinema as they made a large number of action films, with many of them starring either Norris or Charles Bronson. They also owned about 1,500 cinemas in Europe.

The first film Norris made for the Cannon Group, *Missing in Action* (1984), was a simple tale about Colonel James Braddock – who had previously fought in the Vietnam War – searching for missing POWs in Vietnam. The storyline was allegedly inspired by James Cameron's initial screenplay of *Rambo: First Blood Part II*, and Cannon reportedly got their film out first in order to lessen the chance of legal action for copyright infringement. The two films are indeed very similar, as they contain some identical plot elements such as American POWs being held in a jungle camp in bamboo cages, a journey downriver in a boat to the location of the camp, a rescue by Huey helicopter, and lots of action scenes in which Vietnamese soldiers are blown to kingdom come. Unlike the *Rambo* picture, the Russians don't make an appearance, but the Vietnamese troops are depicted as incompetent brutal thugs who end up as cannon fodder. The ending is also very similar to the second *Rambo* picture: Braddock lands a Huey in the centre of Saigon and – with several rescued POWs in tow – gatecrashes a press conference which Vietnamese officials are holding to deny the existence of MIAs (Missing In Action), the name given by the American media to POWs who had not been released following the end of the conflict.

The following year a prequel, *Mission in Action 2: The Beginning*, hit the cinemas before *Rambo: First Blood Part II* had even started shooting. In fact, the first two *Missing in Action* films had been shot back-to-back and the prequel was originally intended to be released first, but – as the second film was perceived to be the better of the two – it was premiered first.

*Missing in Action 2* was set some years before the first film in a North Vietnamese prison camp run by the sadistic Colonel Yin (Soon Tech Oh), who is forcing POWs to grow opium for a French drug runner named Francois (Pierre Issot). Braddock eventually agrees to confess to war crimes in exchange for anti-malarial drugs which he needs to treat his fellow POW, Frankie (John Wesley). However, Yin breaks his word and gives Frankie a fatal dose of opium instead. Eventually Braddock manages to kill his captors, destroys the camp, and escapes with the other POWs by helicopter.

A third Braddock film – *Braddock: Missing in Action III* – premiered on 22 January 1988, several months before the third *Rambo* picture (*Rambo III*). It was directed by Chuck Norris's brother, Aaron. This time the plot (which took place in 1988) centred on Braddock's discovery that his Asian wife Lin Tan Cang (Miki Kim) – who he had assumed to be dead – was still alive and living in Vietnam. Furthermore, he has a 12 year old son called Van Tan Cang (Roland Harrah III).

Braddock returns to Vietnam, but his plans go awry when Lin is killed by the sadistic Vietnamese General Quoc (Aki Alcong). The American soldier is captured along with his son, and they are both taken away to be tortured. Eventually Braddock escapes and, after some spectacular battles with the Vietnamese, he escapes to Thailand with his son.

By this time Norris had made what were probably his best two films for Cannon, namely *Invasion USA* (1985) and *The Delta Force* (1986).

*Invasion USA* was one of Norris's most interesting films, and dealt with an incursion by Cuban-led guerrillas into the mainland United States. The film was inevitably compared with John Milius's *Red Dawn* (1984), in which a large force of Soviet paratroops – later backed up by heavy weapons such as tanks – invades the USA.

Despite its title and poster artwork showing Norris standing in front of a smoking White House, *Invasion USA* doesn't feature a full-scale attack on America. Instead, it deals with a large number of terrorists landing on the Florida coast and carrying out attacks on various targets. They are led by Soviet operative Mikhail Rostov (Richard Lynch), who clearly has had some traumatic past dealings with the hero – former CIA agent Matt Hunter (Chuck Norris).

Hunter is approached by the authorities and asked to come out of retirement to deal with the crisis, but he refuses (a familiar action movie cliché). However, when his house in the Everglades is destroyed by the villains (who arrive in four 'Airboats') and his friend John Eagle (Dehl Berti) is killed, he reconsiders his decision.

Later that day, hundreds of armed terrorists land on the Florida beaches in several WW2-vintage landing craft and make their way inland in an assortment of trucks and vans. A housing estate is attacked with anti-tank rockets and left blazing. Then a group of guerrillas disguised as police officers attack a community centre full of Cuban expatriates in Miami, causing them to distrust the police. This leads to race riots and general chaos in the City of Miami.

Next the terrorists attack a shopping mall, and are only thwarted by the intervention of Hunter who drives his pick-up truck through the doors of the complex to surprise the bad guys – an idea later reused in *Lethal Weapon* (1987). Interestingly, the events of *Invasion USA* take place in the pre-Christmas period, as is the case in several Hollywood action blockbusters of the period including *Lethal Weapon* (1987), *Die Hard* (1988), *Cobra* (1986), and *Tripwire* (1989).

The terrorists also try to attack a school bus and a church, but the ex-CIA man again foils their plans by blowing them up with their own bombs. They are literally 'hoisted by their own petard'. The villains have one success, though, as they attack a funfair. Hunter is despondent as he realises there are too many of them to stop, even with the assistance of the National Guard who have now been called out.

Eventually Hunter is apparently arrested and taken to the local command centre in Atlanta, Georgia on the grounds that he is breaking the law by acting like a vigilante. He is apprehended by a police SWAT team, who assault his property while he is watching *Earth vs the Flying Saucers* (1956) on his TV.

As he is taken into custody, he turns to a TV news camera saying that when he meets the terrorist leader, 'it will be time to die'. His nemesis Rostov sees this and goes berserk, smashing up his television set (another idea re-used in *Lethal Weapon*). Rostov has clearly been suffering from PTSD since an incident some years earlier, when Hunter successfully prevented him from carrying out an assassination by rocket launcher after putting a gun to his head and saying the words: 'It's time to die'. Ever since then, Rostov has been plagued by recurrent nightmares in which Hunter utters this disturbing phrase before killing him. As a result, he has become obsessed with killing the ex-CIA man.

He orders all his men to attack the command centre and kill Hunter. But the whole thing is a clever ruse devised by Hunter to get all the guerrillas into one location where they can be surrounded and then killed or captured.

The terrorists subsequently invade the command centre, but find it empty. Suddenly hundreds of National Guard troops surround the building, supported by a large number of M60 Patton tanks with 105mm main guns, M113 Armoured Personnel Carriers, and M151 'Mutt' Jeeps with mounted machine guns. Some of the US troops have M72 LAW rocket launchers and M60 machine guns. Armed Huey helicopters hover overhead. All the troops and equipment in this scene were supplied by the real Atlanta National Guard, greatly adding to its authenticity.

Their combined firepower is awesome. Many of the guerrillas are killed by the intense volley of fire, and the survivors soon surrender. Hunter stalks Rostov through the command centre and finally blows him through a window with an M72 LAW anti-tank rocket (in exactly the same way that Charles Bronson's character Kersey killed gang leader Manny in *Death Wish 3* the same year). *Invasion USA* isn't Shakespeare, and is certainly not an exploration of the human condition, but it is a cracking action yarn filled with gunfights, punch-ups, chases and explosions.

Norris's next film was probably his best, and features the final screen appearance of Lee Marvin. *The Delta Force* (1986) was originally to be a re-telling of the events of the unsuccessful 'Operation Eagle Claw' in April 1980, when the US military attempted to rescue some American hostages who were being held by Iranian militants at the US Embassy in

Tehran. The plan failed after some of the helicopters used in the mission developed engine trouble due to sand ingress, and a crash occurred between a taxiing Lockheed C-130 Hercules and a hovering helicopter.

For the film, the screenplay was originally intended to show what would have happened if the mission had gone to plan. Unfortunately the film's technical advisor, Colonel Charles Beckwith, resigned in protest when he read the script. As a consequence a new screenplay was prepared which was based on the real-life hijacking of TWA Flight 847 in 1985.

In the new version, TWA Flight 847 became Travelways Flight 282 and involved a Boeing 707 which was flying from Cairo to New York via Athens and Rome. On the second leg of the journey the aircraft is hijacked by two terrorists named Abdul Rafai (Robert Forster) and Mustafa (David Menahem) from the fictitious New World Revolutionary Organisation.

The plane is forced to fly to Beirut, where the Jewish hostages are secretly taken off the plane and taken to a militant-controlled area of the city. A dozen extra terrorists then board the plane which departs for Algiers.

All the female hostages and children are released at Algiers as the Delta Force team prepare to storm the plane. At the last moment, the assault is called off when Colonel Nick Alexander (Lee Marvin) realises there are 12 more terrorists aboard the plane than expected.

The terrorists eventually fly back to Beirut, where they transfer the remaining hostages to accommodation in militant-held areas. With the assistance of the Israeli Navy, the Delta Force team land in Beirut – with their vehicles – from a tank landing craft, rescue the hostages, recapture the Boeing, and fly everyone back to Israel.

The film is best remembered for its spectacular stunts and action sequences. Norris's character Major Scott McCoy rides a Suzuki SP600 motorcyle fitted with small but powerful rockets, recalling a similar vehicle ridden by Luciana Paluzzi's character, Fiona Volpe in *Thunderball* (1965).

The entire production was filmed in Israel, and a Lockheed C-130H Hercules registration 89-9196 of the Israeli Air Force was fitted with self-adhesive decals to represent an American Delta Force aircraft.

The film was moderately successful, making nearly $18m at the box office set against a budget of $9m, and led to a sequel – *Delta Force 2: The Colombian Connection* – which was released in 1990, by which time Cannon Films had folded.

Chuck Norris has continued to make films until fairly recently, having appeared in *The Expendables 2* (2012). He also achieved some success in television, having starred in the long-running TV series *Walker: Texas Ranger* between 1993 and 2005.

A staunch supporter of the Republican Party, he is also a devout Christian and has written several books on the subject. He will always be remembered, though, as one of the truly great action stars of the 1980s.

\* \* \*

## Chuck Norris 1980s Filmography

| 1980 | *The Octagon* |
| 1981 | *An Eye for an Eye* |
| 1982 | *Silent Rage* |
| 1982 | *Forced Vengeance* |
| 1983 | *Lone Wolf McQuade* |
| 1984 | *Missing in Action* |
| 1985 | *Missing in Action 2: The Beginning* |
| 1985 | *Code of Silence* |
| 1985 | *Invasion USA* |
| 1986 | *The Delta Force* |
| 1986 | *Firewalker* |
| 1988 | *Braddock: Missing in Action III* |
| 1988 | *Hero and the Terror* |

# I HAVE BEEN EXPECTING YOU, MR BOND!

## How the James Bond Movies Fared During the Action Movie Boom of the Eighties

THE series of James Bond movies made by Eon films since 1962 is recognised as the most successful franchise in film history. To date (2017), 24 have been made (plus two non-Eon Bond movies in 1967 and 1983), and there is every indication that the 007 brand will continue for many years – if not decades – to come. Just like Sherlock Holmes, Bond is one literary character who will continue forever.

By 1980, 11 Bond films had been made (plus the first, disastrous non-Eon films 'spoof' version of *Casino Royale* in 1967), and producer Cubby Broccoli was wondering what direction the series should go in next. After the rather lacklustre *Live and Let Die* (1973) and the even poorer *The Man with the Golden Gun* (1975), the producers went back to an earlier production for inspiration. Ian Fleming's original novel *The Spy Who Loved Me* (1962) was an oddity. Unlike all the other books of the series, it was told from the perspective of the young female heroine, Vivienne Michel, who encounters two American gangsters called Sluggsy and

Horror at the 'Dreamy Pines Motor Court'. She is saved from being raped and murdered by the intervention of James Bond – who only appears two thirds of the way through the rather short book – and subsequently gives her the greatest sexual experience of her life. Even Ian Fleming realised it was not suitable material for a 007 film, so he left instructions with his lawyers that only the title could be used in any movie.

Accordingly, a new story was devised by screenwriters Richard Maibaum and Christopher Wood in which an Ernst Stavro Blofeld-like character, Carl Stromberg (Kurt Jurgens), captures US, Soviet and British atomic submarines using a modified super-tanker, the *Liparus* (which has opening bows and inbuilt submarine pens), and then attempts to bring about a nuclear Armageddon with their Polaris missiles.

Essentially, *The Spy Who Loved Me* was a remake of *You Only Live Twice* (1967), in which SPECTRE attempts to bring about a nuclear holocaust by capturing US and Soviet spacecraft. There are a huge number of similarities between the two films, even down to the fact that they were both directed by Lewis Gilbert and feature colossal sets designed by Ken Adam and stunt work by Bob Simmons. Both the 'crater' set in *You Only Live Twice* and the supertanker/submarine pen built for *The Spy Who Loved Me* must rank as some of the most impressive set designs in cinema history.

*The Spy Who Loved Me* was a great success – both critically and commercially – when it was released in the summer of 1977. It was originally intended that the next film in the series would be *For Your Eyes Only* (and this claim appears in the end titles of *The Spy Who Loved Me*), but the success of *Star Wars* and the imminent launch of the first US Space Shuttle made the producers change their minds, resulting in the next film being *Moonraker*.

*Moonraker* had a similar style to *The Spy Who Loved Me* – it employed many of the same production crew including director Lewis Gilbert, stunt arranger Bob Simmons and set designer Ken Adam, and also saw the return of the character 'Jaws' played by Richard Kiel. Additionally, it had some of the best model work of the series, supervised by Derek Meddings who was regarded as one of the world's greatest experts in miniature filming, having honed his craft on various Gerry Anderson TV shows such as *Thunderbirds* and *UFO*.

*Moonraker* was a great success, but received mixed reviews from critics when it was released in the summer of 1979. There was a consensus that – although the stunts, special effects, music and production design were excellent – the emphasis had now shifted to outright comedy, epitomised by the scene in the pre-credits sequence in which 'Jaws' finds his parachute won't deploy and starts flapping his arms in the hope that he will fly. The various scenes in which 'Jaws' enjoys romantic moments with his true love and then switches sides to work for the good guys are also embarrassingly awful, as are his few lines of dialogue. In *The Spy Who Loved Me* it was implied that he could not speak (Christopher Wood's novelization of the movie makes this clear), and he had no dialogue – something that made him more sinister. (Interestingly, the same thing happened in Universal's *Frankenstein* series of films. In the original *Frankenstein*, 1931, the monster doesn't speak, but in the follow-up *The Bride of Frankenstein*, 1935, he has a few lines of dialogue – something which actor Boris Karloff felt was a mistake, as it made the character less unsettling.)

Thus when pre-production started on *For Your Eyes Only*, there was a feeling that the new film should have a more serious feel to it, similar in style to *From Russia with Love* (1963). The pre-credits sequence doesn't really fit the tone of the rest of the movie. After visiting his wife Tracey's grave – a reference to the tragic end of *On Her Majesty's Secret Service* (1969) – Bond is picked up by a Bell Jet Ranger helicopter marked in Universal Exports livery. A few minutes into the flight, the pilot is electrocuted and the chopper comes under the control of a bald man with a cervical collar who is in a wheelchair. He flies the rotary-wing aircraft using TV monitors and a radio-control unit. This hairless villain is only seen from behind and is never named, but is clearly none other than Bond's old nemesis Ernst Stavro Blofeld. At the time, Eon was unable to use the character of Blofeld or the SPECTRE organisation due to an ongoing legal dispute with *Thunderball's* executive producer Kevin McClory, so this appearance was as far as Eon's lawyers felt they could go.

The part of 'Blofeld' was played by John Hollis but voiced by Robert Rietti, who had over-dubbed many characters' voices in various Bond films including Draco in *On Her Majesty's Secret Service*. 'Blofeld' mentions that it had been ten years since he and Bond last met, but that would have been during the events of *Diamonds are Forever* (1971) when Blofeld – then played by Charles Gray – had a full head of hair and was clearly not disabled (though he was last seen in a mini-submarine which was being bashed against the side of a drilling rig), whereas his appearance as a bald man in a wheelchair, wearing a cervical collar, is more consistent with the end of *On Her Majesty's Secret Service* in which Blofeld is alive, though clearly suffering from a neck injury.

'Blofeld' takes control of the helicopter and puts it through a series of aerobatic manoeuvres, with the intention of scaring Bond before killing him. The excitement of this sequence is increased by the use of some Junker-87 'Stuka' dive bomber sound effects previously used in *Battle of Britain* (1969). Bond cannot take over the controls because the Jet Ranger has been specially fitted with a glass bulkhead which prevents access to the cockpit from the passenger cabin. But the intrepid secret agent opens the door, puts his feet on the skids and makes his way forward along the side of the fuselage, eventually entering the cockpit. There, he pushes the dead pilot out the door, rips out the wires of the radio control receiver and takes control of the helicopter. Quickly, he scoops up the wheelchair-bound villain on one of the helicopter's skids. As Bond prepares to drop him down a factory chimney the criminal pleads for his life, even offering to buy Bond 'a delicatessen in stainless steel' if he will spare him. This must be one of the ridiculous lines in movie history, and would have been more suited to *Moonraker!*

The opening graveyard sequence was designed to introduce the public to a new actor as Bond. After his first three 007 pictures, Roger Moore was negotiating to play Bond on a picture-by-picture basis and, in the late summer of 1980, there was speculation that another actor might be picked for the role. Michael Billington – who had been considered for the role of Bond on several occasions, and had appeared in the TV series *UFO* and *The Onedin Line* as well as having a small role in *The Spy Who Loved Me* – was all set to take over as Bond, and was even flown to the Greek islands as well as having costume fittings, but at the last moment a deal was struck with Roger Moore who went on to play Bond in *For Your Eyes Only* plus two further films in the series.

The rest of the film was fairly serious and did indeed have some similarities with *From Russia with Love*. The earlier Bond movie had a 'McGuffin' in the form of a Lektor, a decoding device similar to a wartime German 'Enigma' machine. This time, Bond was on the trail of an Automatic Targeting Attack Communicator (ATAC).

One scene which indicated the seriousness of the new approach was the sequence where Bond kicks a Mercedes car containing the villain Locque off a cliff, resulting in his death. Roger Moore was reluctant to do this, saying it was 'Bond-like, but not Roger Moore Bond-like', and had to be persuaded to comply with director John Glen's wishes.

The film ends with a comic sequence involving British Prime Minister Margaret Thatcher (Janet Brown) talking to Bond on the 'phone while her husband Denis (John Wells) lurks in the background. The sequence is funny, though rather cringe-inducing, and not in keeping with the tone of the rest of the film.

*For Your Eyes Only* was a commercial success, but received some bad reviews. Many fans didn't like Bill Conti's musical score, which was very different from John Barry's many contributions to the series.

The next film in the series, *Octopussy* (1983), dealt with the Cold War but retained a few comic elements which had become a trademark of the Roger Moore years. Again, it was originally intended that a new actor should take over as Bond and American James Brolin – who was Barbra Streisand's husband, and had appeared in *Capricorn One* (1979) – had no less than three screen tests for the role.

Eventually, Cubby Broccoli decided to continue with Roger Moore and one reason for his decision was that he felt that it would be the wrong time to introduce a new Bond, as Sean Connery was making a return as Bond in *Never Say Never Again* which was due to be released the same year.

The best bit of *Octopussy* was the pre-credits sequence. Sent to an undisclosed Latin American country (possibly Argentina or Cuba) to obtain details of a new type of radar fitted in the nose cones of fighter aircraft, Bond is forced to make his escape in a miniature jet plane. The aircraft – a homebuilt Bede BD-5J 'Acrostar' – really existed, and was originally scheduled to feature in *Moonraker*.

Making his escape from the airfield in the Acrostar, Bond is engaged by a surface-to-air missile battery. Production paperwork indicated that this was supposed to be a British Aerospace Rapier system, as used in the 1982 Falklands War. However, a real Rapier launcher has four missiles (later versions had eight), whereas the mock-up version seen on screen only has two. Bond successfully evades the missile, but it does a U-turn and comes back at him (a piece of 'Hollywood Science', as no missile can do this). Eventually Bond flies the Acrojet through the open doors of a hangar, and out a gap between the rapidly closing doors at the far end. The missile tries to follow him, hits an aircraft, and the hangar explodes in a massive conflagration. This sequence was filmed at RAF Northolt and the jaw-dropping scene of the Acrojet flying through the hangar was achieved by mounting the aircraft on a pole attached to a cut-down Jaguar car. The pole and Jaguar were hidden by various objects and people inside the hangar, while the climactic explosion was effected using a miniature.

The rest of the movie deals with Bond's attempts to investigate the theft of a Fabergé Egg in India, which puts him on the trail of a renegade Soviet General Orlov (Steven Berkoff). Orlov plans to explode a nuclear weapon at a US airbase in West Germany, which he hopes will result in nuclear disarmament in the West and a strengthening of Russia's position (it should be noted that Frederick Forsyth's

1984 novel *The Fourth Protocol* and the subsequent 1986 film, which starred Pierce Brosnan, had a similar plot).

The film premiered on 6 June 1983, and although it did well at the box office – making $187.5m against a budget of $27.5m – it received varied reviews, with *Entertainment Weekly* declaring it the third worst Bond film ever made.

A few months later, a second James Bond film made its debut – *Never Say Never Again*, produced by Kevin McClory and Jack Schwartzman, and featuring none other than 52 year old Sean Connery in his seventh and final appearance as 007. The origins of this film go back to a famous 1963 court case in which Kevin McClory and Jack Whittingham sued Ian Fleming for using material from a 1959 first draft screenplay, *Longitude 78 West* (written by Fleming, McClory, Whittingham and Ivor Bryce), without permission in his 1961 novel *Thunderball*.

The pursuers won their case, and one outcome was that Kevin McClory was made executive producer of the 1965 Eon film *Thunderball* and was also given the right to make another version of the same film after a period of ten years had elapsed. From 1975 onwards McClory attempted to achieve this goal, involving Sean Connery and novelist Len Deighton in an abortive project entitled *Warhead 1975* which involved robot sharks infiltrating the New York sewer system! Connery even made a trip to New York to scout possible locations, which included the Statue of Liberty.

All of McClory's attempts to make the film were thwarted by Eon Productions' lawyers but, in 1982, Hollywood lawyer and producer Jack Schwartzman became involved and a screenplay was devised which met the requirements of the earlier legal settlement. Eon Films' famous opening gunbarrel sequence couldn't be used and neither could Monty Norman's James Bond theme. John Barry was reportedly approached about doing the music but declined because of his loyalty to Cubby Broccoli, and composer Michel Legrand was used instead.

Breaking with tradition, *Never Say Never Again* has no pre-credits sequence and opens with a title scene in which Bond approaches a guerrilla camp in the jungle in order to rescue a female hostage. After fighting various soldiers he frees the girl only to be stabbed by her – she has been turned.

Later, back in London at MI6 headquarters, M (Edward Fox) reviews video footage of the episode, which is revealed to be a training exercise. In this incarnation, M is a health nut and sends Bond to Shrublands Health Farm to lose weight, get fit, and de-tox as he feels that he has lost his edge.

From that point on, the plot is similar to *Thunderball* with a few changes. In the 1965 film Bond only had brief encounters with Count Lippe, but in the new version the equivalent character (now called just 'Lippe', and played by wrestler Pat Roach who had two stunt roles in *Raiders of the Lost Ark* in 1981) fights with Bond in a lengthy sequence in which the pair end up demolishing much of Shrublands.

The equivalent character to Fiona Volpe (Luciana Paluzzi) in the original film was Fatima Blush, memorably played by Barbara Carrera. Blush had appeared in early drafts of the *Thunderball* scripts, and the legal agreement which allowed McClory to make his film stipulated that he could use any material that was in early drafts of the screenplay and the novel, provided it had not appeared in the 1965 film. This is the reason that the sequences involving a US Navy submarine (which appear in the novel but not in the 1965 film) play a prominent role in the 1983 remake. Incidentally, the scenes showing the submarine underwater were lifted from *Ice Station Zebra* (1968).

This time around, Largo was played by Klaus Maria Brandauer who gave a brilliant performance suggesting an incipient psychosis, rather like John Simm's Master in *Doctor Who* (2007). Rather oddly, Blofeld was played by Max Von Sydow, who with his white beard resembled Santa Claus. He looked nothing like the previous cinematic incarnations of Blofeld, the best-known of which would be Donald Pleasance's portrayal in *You Only Live Twice* (1967). With his bald head and large vertical scar passing through one eye, he was memorably described by John Brosnan (author of *James Bond in the Cinema*) as resembling 'an egg that had cracked on the boil'. Interestingly, none of the screen Blofelds have been anything like the description given by Ian Fleming in his various Bond novels. It is hard to pass judgement on Von Sydow's overall performance, though, because most of it ended up on the cutting room floor, as did the majority of the scenes featuring Miss Moneypenny (Pamela Salem).

The plot of *Thunderball* involved SPECTRE hijacking an RAF Avro Vulcan bomber armed with nuclear weapons and landing it in the shallow waters of the Bahamas. In the new version, the aircraft was a Rockwell B-1 bomber of the US Air Force. Shots of the missiles being loaded onto the aircraft were achieved using a Concorde airliner which had a similar delta wing, while all other sequences involving the B-1 and the nuclear-tipped Tomahawk cruise missiles used traditional miniature work shot against a blue screen.

The film ends with Bond defeating Largo and recovering the nuclear warheads. The final scene (shot in the garden of Kevin McClory's home in the Bahamas) shows Bond and Domino (Kim Basinger) splashing about in a swimming pool. They are interrupted by a British diplomat, Nigel Small-Fawcett (Rowan Atkinson), who is mistaken for an intruder and thrown in the pool by Bond.

Small-Fawcett has a message from 'M.' He wants him to agree to be reactivated and return to MI6, but Bond declares 'never', turning to the camera and winking, thus breaking the 'fourth wall' in the process. He is really telling the audience that his involvement with Bond is now over.

*Never Say Never Again* was released in December 1983. Although most critics said it was worth watching just for the pleasure of seeing Sean Connery play James Bond one last time, there was a general consensus that it was really not that different from the current Roger Moore movies. Sean Connery had previously expressed his dislike for the apparent silliness and lack of seriousness of the Moore films, but *Never Say Never Again* had its comic moments as well – particularly all the scenes featuring Rowan Atkinson, which many felt should be consigned to the cutting room floor. Much later, Atkinson played a Bond-like character in a series of humorous TV adverts for Barclaycard, which led to the two *Johnny English* films.

*Never Say Never Again* also made less money than *Octopussy*, though John Brosnan – writing in *It's Only a Movie* (his regular column in *Starburst* magazine) – said that his award for the best James Bond movie of 1983 went to *Never Say Never Again*, while his nomination for the worst James Bond movie of 1983 would go to you-know-what!

Up until his death, Cubby Broccoli always refused to comment on *Never Say Never Again* or even confirm that he had seen it, but in the documentary *Everything or Nothing* (2012) about the history of the Bond films, his daughter (and heir) Barbara commented that the relative failure of *Never*

*Say Never Again* was down to the producers focusing on just one aspect of the Bond films' success, namely Sean Connery in the lead role.

In 1985, Roger Moore made his final appearance as Bond at the age of 58 in *A View to a Kill*. By this point the screenwriters had run out of book titles to use, and were resorting to the names of some of Ian Fleming's Bond short stories stuck onto an all-new screenplay.

This time the story plumbed new depths of silliness, with villain Max Zorin (Christopher Walken) planning to destroy Silicon Valley. The film also featured one of the worst pre-credits sequences in Bond history, with a potentially tense skiing sequence being ruined by the insertion of the Beach Boys song *California Girls* into the soundtrack, which a moment earlier had included a homage to the theme from *On Her Majesty's Secret Service*. The rest of John Barry's score wasn't up to his usual high standards, although the title song (performed by Duran Duran) was very impressive.

The film was poorly received, but at this point in the mid-eighties when it seemed the series had reached a new low – on a par with *The Man with the Golden Gun* (1974) – there was exciting news. With the retirement of Roger Moore, a younger actor was to take over the role.

As has always been the case, several actors were considered for the part – including Kiwi actor Sam Neill – but in 1986 it was announced that Irish actor Pierce Brosnan, 33, was to play the part of Bond in *The Living Daylights*. Brosnan's most recent role was in the American TV series *Remington Steele* (1982-87), which had just been cancelled. However, a clause in Brosnan's contract meant that the actor was legally obliged to do another series of the detective drama if the producers changed their mind. Unfortunately for

Brosnan, the producers did just that as all the publicity about him taking over as Bond revived interest in the programme and – at the last moment – he was required to do a further batch of episodes, meaning that he had to turn down Bond.

Now that Brosnan was out of the picture, Eon Productions offered the role to Timothy Dalton, a 40 year old Welsh actor who had been considered for the part of Bond as long ago as 1969, when he was just 23. It is fascinating to speculate what *On Her Majesty's Secret Service* might have been like with Dalton playing the lead role, particularly as he would have excelled at some of the highly emotional scenes.

A highly-experienced Shakespearean performer, Dalton remains probably the best actor ever to have played James Bond. In preparation for the role, Dalton read all of Ian Fleming's Bond books and totally immersed himself in the character. One thing Dalton realised was that the Bond of the books was nothing like the cinematic Bond, who indulged in jokes and wisecracks.

Fleming's Bond was a deeply flawed character who smoked and drank a lot, was frequently tense, anxious, traumatised and depressed, and even suffered a nervous breakdown following the death of his wife. He rarely made wisecracks, and had quite a serious approach to life.

Opening in the summer of 1987, *The Living Daylights* was enthusiastically received by Bond fans and critics alike, who applauded Dalton's highly realistic and naturalistic performance. In his regular column in *Starburst*, John Brosnan praised the film, saying that seeing Bond portrayed by 'an actor' had a kind of 'shock effect' at first, as he was so used to Roger Moore just playing himself. The official James Bond Fan Club also welcomed the film, which they saw as a return to the grittier style of the early Connery movies.

Whereas *A View to a Kill* had one of the worst pre-credits sequences in the history of the Bond movies, *The Living Daylights* had one of the best, involving a rogue agent (Carl Rigg) infiltrating a training exercise on the Rock of Gibraltar in which MI6 agents are being hunted by SAS troops.

The film opens with an RAF Lockheed C-130 Hercules flying over the Rock of Gibraltar. 'M' (Robert Brown) has a desk on board the aircraft. He addresses his officers, who are standing with their backs to the camera (so that the face of the new Bond cannot be seen). Eventually the Double O agents parachute out of the plane and sky-dive towards the ground, only opening their parachutes at low level – what the military call a Low Altitude Low Opening (LALO) drop. This sequence is enhanced by some magnificent aerial photography, on a par with the paratroop sequences in *A Bridge Too Far* (1977) and *The Wild Geese* (1978), and John Barry's excellent score is one of the best of the series.

After the MI6 men have landed, they are hunted down by SAS troops armed with paint guns. But then a rogue agent (Carl Riggs) kills one of the troops and makes agent 004 fall to his death. It is at this point that we get our first glimpse of the new Bond. Dalton looks magnificient, clad entirely in black, his face creased with tension as he turns round on the rock face to investigate the noise. Bond hears an engine start up and chases the rogue agent, who is trying to escape in a British Army Land Rover filled with boxes of ammunition. Jumping onto the canvas roof, Bond has difficulty holding on as the vehicle careers downhill along narrow winding roads. Eventually he uses his combat knife to cut through the roof of the truck and enters the driver's compartment of the vehicle. After a brief fight, the Land Rover goes over the edge of the road and falls hundreds of feet to the sea (a scene filmed at Beachy Head in England), but Bond escapes just before the Land Rover explodes by deploying his reserve parachute. He lands on the deck of a yacht where he shares a drink with a pretty girl.

The title sequence then follows with the song *The Living Daylights* by Norwegian pop group A-Ha. This was the result of a collaboration between the band and composer John Barry, who apparently found the experience a stressful one and cited it as one of the reasons he never worked for the series again.

The rest of the movie features a very complicated plot typical of 80s Bonds. 007 is sent to Bratislava, Czechoslovakia to assist the defection of KGB officer General Georgi Koskov (Jeroen Krabbe). Once in the UK, Koskov reveals that the KGB's old policy of 'Smiert Spionam' (Death to Spies) has been reactivated by his superior, General Leonid Pushkin (John Rhys-Davies). Bond is sceptical of this claim, but is sent to Tangier to assassinate the General. By this time Koskov has apparently been abducted from an MI6 safe house and returned to the USSR.

Once in Tangier, Bond fakes Pushkin's assassination, but Bond and Koskov's girlfriend Kara (Maryam d'Abo) are drugged and taken to Afghanistan. Eventually they escape and learn that Koskov is involved in a drugs deal with the Mujahadeen, enabling him to buy Western arms for the Soviets from his friend – arms dealer Brad Whitaker (Joe Don Baker).

The film is full of spectacular action sequences, including one of the best fight scenes in the series between killer Necros (Andreas Wisniewski) and an MI6 operative at the safe house, greatly enhanced by John Barry's score. There were also scenes of combat with Soviet forces in Afghanistan, similar to those in *Rambo III* which would be released the following year.

The movie also features the return of the James Bond Aston Martin, in this case a V8 Vantage model which looks similar to the DBS used by George Lazenby in *On Her Majesty's Secret Service*. This time the car didn't have an ejector seat, but did feature a number of spectacular gadgets including forward firing missiles, sideways firing lasers emitting from the wheelhubs, outriggers, and a jet engine for extra speed. Two different Aston Martins were used in the production – an Aston Martin V8 Volante convertible for scenes set in the UK, and a hardtop V8 saloon for those taking place in Czechoslovakia. A sequence apparently showing the convertible being 'winterised' was shot to give the impression they were the same car. The film was a great success, making $191.2 million against a budget of $40m and was generally well-received by critics.

The final James Bond film of the eighties was *Licence to Kill*, which was released in the summer of 1989. Originally it was to be called *Licence Revoked*, but early market research in the USA revealed that most Americans didn't understand that title as they thought it referred specifically to a driver's licence. For the first time the title didn't come from an Ian Fleming novel or short story, though the plot incorporated elements of *Live and Let Die* and some Bond short stories.

The film opens with Bond helping his old CIA chum Felix Leiter (David Hedison) to apprehend a drug lord called Franz Sanchez (Robert Davi), with the assistance of some DEA colleagues. 61 year old Hedison had previously appeared as Leiter in *Live and Let Die* in 1973, and this was the first time in the Bond films that the character had been played more than once by the same actor. The pre-credits sequence concludes with Bond and Leiter parachuting out of a helicopter in order to attend the CIA man's wedding to Della (Priscilla Barnes).

The title sequence then follows. The music for the film was written by Michael Kamen (who also scored *Die Hard* and *Lethal Weapon*), as John Barry was unavailable (and reportedly uninterested in returning to the series). Unfortunately his title song *Licence to Kill* comes across as a pastiche of previous Bond scores. Indeed, some elements were blatantly lifted from *Goldfinger*, requiring royalties to be paid to the composers of that track.

After the title sequence, the story resumes with the aftermath of Leiter's wedding. Unfortunately the couple's happiness doesn't last long, as Sanchez soon escapes from custody and wreaks revenge on the couple. Della is apparently raped (off-screen) and then murdered, while Leiter is lowered into a tank containing a shark, resulting in him losing a leg (an idea lifted from the original novel of *Live and Let Die*).

The rest of the film is concerned with Bond's efforts to obtain revenge on Sanchez. In the process, he has to go against M's orders and has his licence to kill revoked. In order to achieve his goal, Bond has to travel to Sanchez's base in the Republic of Isthmus. (This was a fictional state, possibly based on Panama. If Steven de Souza had been involved in this production, the action would have probably taken place in 'Val Verde'. See the chapter on *Commando*.)

Bond pretends to be a hitman for hire in order to get close to Sanchez, and eventually foils his plan to distribute cocaine which involves dissolving it in petrol and transporting it in large Kenworth tankers.

The plot also involves Stinger missiles, a reference to current events in Afghanistan. From 1986 onwards the CIA supplied the Afghan Mujahadeen with these weapons, which were the first truly effective shoulder-launched surface-to-air missiles, and turned the tide of the war as they enabled the Afghans to down large numbers of Soviet Mil-24 'Hind' gunships.

There is a scene towards the end of the movie where one of Sanchez's henchman attempts to destroy a Kenworth tanker driven by Bond with one of the Stingers. He aims at the radiator of the approaching tanker but Bond sees the missile coming, tilts the tanker to one side using a ramp, and the missile passes harmlessly underneath the vehicle. It's an exciting scene, but another example of 'Hollywood Science' as the Stinger – being a heat-seeking missile – would have simply homed in on the hot radiator and engine block of the truck, regardless of any manouevres Bond made.

John Gardner – who wrote the novelization of the film – was aware of this glaring scientific error and tried to offer an explanation in the book version, suggesting that these were special versions of the Stinger missile which didn't actually have a guidance system and simply travelled in a straight line!

*Licence to Kill* was the first Bond film which was made entirely outside the UK (*Moonraker* was mostly made abroad with studio work in Paris, although the space sequences were shot at the 007 Stage at Pinewood Studios), with location work in Mexico and Florida.

Its London premiere was on 13 June 1989, and it was moderately successful making £156 million against a budget of $32 million. However, it received considerable criticism for its seriousness and levels of violence. In addition, it was perceived as being not like a typical Bond film and more like an episode of the TV series *Miami Vice*. In his regular 'It's Only a Movie' column in *Starburst*, John Brosnan said that *Licence to Kill* simply couldn't compete with the new breed of Hollywood action movies such as *Die Hard* and *Lethal Weapon*.

On the other hand, author Raymond Benson (who has written nine James Bond novels in recent times) has defended the film, saying that it is more like an Ian Fleming story than any of the films made since the sixties.

In summary, the Bond films of the eighties reflected what was happening on the international stage, particularly the changing nature of the Soviet threat. In 1980 the Cold War was at its peak and the possibility of a nuclear war seemed very real. By 1990 the USSR was a busted flush. The war in Afghanistan had been lost, and the Berlin Wall had collapsed.

While the Bond films incorporated these developments in its plots, they refrained from copying current Hollywood action movies and retained a style of their own. After *Licence to Kill* Bond did not return for six years until the arrival of *GoldenEye*, played by the actor who was due to take over the role in 1986: Pierce Brosnan. But that is another story.

\* \* \*

Further Reading

*The James Bond Movies of the 1980s*
By Thomas A. Christie
Crescent Moon Publishing, 2013
ISBN-10: 1861714858
ISBN-13: 978-1861714855

# WISHING FOR DEATH

## Charles Bronson in the 1980s

CHARLES Bronson (born Charles Dennis Buchinsky) was an American actor of Lithuanian descent who had a long, successful career in film and television which lasted from 1951 until 1999. He died in 2003.

Best known for his craggy, lined face and powerful build, Bronson was born in 1921 in the coal mining town of Ehrenfield, Pennsylvania. After leaving school, Bronson became a coal miner and continued in this occupation until he enlisted in the United States Army Air Force in 1943, eventually becoming a tail-gunner in Boeing B-29 Superfortress bombers of the 61$^{st}$ Bombardment Squadron, based on the Pacific island of Guam. Bronson flew 25 combat missions with the unit, and received the Purple Heart for wounds received in battle.

After World War II, Bronson worked in many odd jobs until joining a theatrical group in Philadelphia, Pennsylvania. In 1950 he married his first wife, Harriett Tendler, and moved to Hollywood where he enrolled in acting classes.

His first role was as an uncredited sailor in *You're in the Navy Now* (1951). Further roles in films and TV series followed in the 1950s, including an appearance as Vincent Price's mute assistant Ygor in *House of Wax* (1953) which holds the distinction of being the only 3D movie to be made by a one-eyed director (Andre De Toth)!

It was in 1960, though, that Bronson's career really took off. Following a small role in 1959's *Never So Few*, its director John Sturges cast him in as Bernardo O'Reilly in *The Magnificent Seven* (1960), followed two years later by one of his most famous parts – Fl. Lt Danny Velinski, 'The Tunnel King' – in *The Great Escape* (1963). Although Velinski was supposedly an expert at tunnelling, he also had a tendency to claustrophobia and Bronson was able to portray this affliction with great accuracy as he himself suffered from this disorder following his years as a coal miner!

Further roles followed in the 1960s, including memorable performances in two war films – *The Battle of the Bulge* (1965) and *The Dirty Dozen* (1967) – and several Westerns. By the 1970s Bronson was one of the top action stars in the world, and in 1975 his career reached its peak when he was ranked as the world's 4th top box-office draw, coming in behind Robert Redford, Barbra Streisand and Al Pacino.

By 1980 Charles Bronson was 58, and already considered far too old for most action roles. This was the reason director John Carpenter declined to use in him in *Escape from New York* (1981), casting Kurt Russell instead. But despite his advancing years, Bronson made some of his most interesting films in the 1980s, with most being action movies. Many of these were produced by Cannon Films, seven of which were directed by J. Lee Thompson with whom Bronson reportedly had a very good working relationship. Two were helmed by Peter Hunt – best-known for directing *On Her Majesty's Secret Service* (1969) – and a further pair by Michael Winner, who had previously directed Bronson in *The Mechanic* (1972), *The Stone Killer* (1973), and *Death Wish* (1974).

J. Lee Thompson is best-known for directing two classic war movies – *Ice Cold in Alex* (1958) and *The Guns of Navarone* (1961), in which he replaced the original director, Alexander MacKendrick, at short notice – plus the original version of *Cape Fear* (1962). He was particularly good with action sequences and had a reputation for working with great speed and efficiency, something that endeared him to Bronson.

Thompson had previously directed Bronson in *St Ives* in 1976, and *The White Buffalo* the following year. The next time they worked together was on the 1980 picture *Caboblanco*, but it was their third collaboration *10 to Midnight* (1983) which, I believe, deserves greater recognition.

In this film, Bronson plays veteran detective Leo Kessler who is teamed up with a much younger partner – Paul McCann (Andrew Stevens) – to hunt down sexual psychopath Warren Stacey (Gene Davis). Fans of war fiction will recognise that 'Leo Kessler' is also the *nom de plume* of writer Charles Whiting, who wrote a number of novels about German armoured forces under that particular pen-name.

Stacey has his own *modus operandi* which involves him stripping naked before each knife murder (and wearing latex gloves) in order to avoid getting blood on his clothing. In fact, Stacey and his victims only appear completely naked in the cinema and VHS/DVD versions of the movie. A 'TV version' of each murder scene was also shot in which both Stacey and his victims retain their underwear.

The film is like a cross between *Dirty Harry* and *Psycho*, as it features elements from both movies – a maverick cop who is prepared to bend the rules to get the bad guy behind bars, and a sexual psychopath who uses a knife as a substitute for his penis. The villain – an office equipment repairman – is also physically very attractive, though lacking in social skills. It is his rejection by various females which makes him kill. He also drives a VW Beetle. These two points suggest the character may have been inspired by the real life serial killer Ted Bundy who was handsome, could be urbane and charming when interviewed, and drove a Beetle.

After Stacey's first murder of a fellow office worker Betty (who had rejected his advances), he is interviewed by Kessler and McCann. The veteran detective is convinced that he has found his man, but can't prove it because Stacey has concocted a perfect alibi and has ensured there are no bloodstains on his clothes. Eventually Kessler tampers with the evidence and puts a spot of blood on the clothes Stacey was wearing on the night of Betty's murder. However, Stacey's criminal defence lawyer smells a rat and puts pressure on McCann to investigate further. Eventually Kessler is forced to confess that he faked the evidence and Stacey is released.

After being freed, Stacey decides to target Kessler's daughter – Laurie (Lisa Eilbacher) – who is a nurse at the local General Hospital. After killing three of her nurse colleagues, he chases Laurie into the street where he is confronted by her father, gun in hand. Stacey taunts him, saying that he will claim to be insane and will therefore be released from prison eventually and that the world will hear from him again.

Kessler merely says 'no, we won't', and shoots him in the forehead just before the police arrive – an ending which is similar to that in *Dirty Harry*.

Another high point of J. Lee Thompson's collaboration with Bronson was the 1986 thriller *Murphy's Law*, in which he plays maverick detective Jack Murphy who has been framed for the murder of his ex – wife Jan (Angel Tomkins). The real killer – rather unusually for this period – is a woman, ex-convict Joan Freeman (Carrie Snodgress), who is angry at Murphy for putting her in jail some years before. In order to clear his name, Murphy has to flee jail while still handcuffed to foul-mouthed petty criminal Arabella McGee.

These plot points – a man framed for murder he didn't commit and handcuffed to a woman – are reminiscent of the first (1935) and second (1959) cinema adaptations of *The Thirty Nine Steps*.

The two – who are like chalk and cheese – have to work together to resolve the case. As you can see, the plot contains many action movie clichés and tropes, but the film is a joy to watch. Generally reviled by the critics, it can now be considered a cult classic.

One of the most controversial films that Charles Bronson ever made was *Death Wish* (1974). Loosely based on a 1972 novel by Brian Garfield, it told the story of a New York architect – Paul Kersey (played by Bronson) – whose life is ripped apart when his family is attacked by muggers who break into his apartment while he is out. His wife is killed, and his daughter is raped and left in a catatonic state following the attack. When the police are unable to find the attackers, let alone prosecute them, Kersey takes matters into his own hands. Using a nickel-plated .32 Colt Police Positive revolver gifted by a friend, Kersey starts his own private war against New York muggers.

Eventually Kersey kills a total of eight muggers over a few nights, but by this time a NYPD detective – Frank Ochoa (Vincent Gardenia) – has tracked him down and is prepared to make an arrest. However, the Police Department is now faced with a dilemma – media reports of the activities of the 'vigilante killer' has led to a huge drop in the number of muggings, and there is strong popular support for his actions. Eventually Ochoa makes a deal with Kersey: if he will move to another city he will not be prosecuted, and details of the case will never be made public.

The film ends with Kersey arriving in Chicago by train, where he encounters a group of hoodlums. They make obscene gestures at him but Kersey merely points his right hand like a gun and smiles. It is implied that his vigilante activities will continue.

*Death Wish* was a surprise hit, making $22 million at the box office against a budget of just $3 million. It was popular with the general public because it hit a raw nerve; at that time there was a feeling in the USA (and elsewhere) that not enough was being done to prevent violent crime, and that the justice system was failing to punish offenders properly. In New York, cinema audiences reportedly cheered every time Kersey shot a mugger.

One of the critics of the film was the author of the original novel, Brian Garfield, who was appalled that the film apparently endorsed vigilantism when his novel had done the opposite. He was so concerned that he wrote a follow-up, *Death Sentence*, which was published in 1975.

Director Michael Winner took a more sanguine view. In his autobiography, he recalls how the original novel 'had only sold about three copies, one of which was bought by the author's mother'. He also mentioned in the same tome how producer Dino De Laurentiis hated the title *Death Wish* and wanted the film to be called *The Sidewalk Vigilante* (!). De Laurentiis' view was that a film title should never have the word 'death' in it. In this belief he was totally wrong – think how many film titles have featured this word: *Death Becomes*

*Her, Deathwatch, Death on the Nile* etc., plus of course two classic *Doctor Who* TV stories – *The Seeds of Death* (1969) and *The Ambassadors of Death* (1970).

In 1982 a sequel was released, simply called *Death Wish II* – again directed by Michael Winner. Eight years on from the original film, Paul Kersey is living and working in Los Angeles and is dating an L.A. radio reporter named Geri Nichols (Jill Ireland). As is widely known, Jill Ireland was Bronson's second wife between 1968 and 1990, when she tragically died of breast cancer. *Death Wish II* is one of 14 films the couple made together.

After picking up Kersey's still-traumatised daughter Carol (Robin Sherwood) from the mental hospital, the three of them visit a fairground in Los Angeles. While waiting in line for ice cream, they are jostled by five gang members who steal Kersey's wallet. The architect chases after one of them but, after catching him, discovers that he does not have the wallet but exerts revenge by beating him with a baseball bat. Unfortunately the gang now have Kersey's ID, including his address, so they later turn up at his house where they rape the maid – Rosario (Silvana Gallardo) – and kidnap Carol. When Kersey returns home he is knocked unconscious. The gang flee the scene, taking Carol hostage. Later she is raped by one of the gang and is so upset by this trauma that she tries to escape, jumps out of a window, and ends up impaled on some railings.

When the police arrive, Lt Mankewiez (Ben Frank) asks for help with identifying the muggers, but Kersey claims he can't remember anything. After Carol's funeral, he decides to embark on a fresh war against muggers, rapists and criminals in general. Using a cheap hotel as a base, wearing a woollen cap and armed with a 0.380 calibre Beretta 84 handgun, he resolves to hunt down and kill every member of the gang who attacked his daughter and housekeeper. This is where *Death Wish II* actually improves on the original. In the first film, Kersey kills several muggers but isn't able to shoot the actual attackers who harmed his family because he doesn't know their identities or even their appearance. This time he knows what all the gang members look like and so he is able to specifically target them, making his revenge seem even more understandable and justified than in the first film.

Over the next few nights Kersey kills the gang members until just one of them, Nirvana (Thomas F. Duffy), is left. Unfortunately he is Tasered, captured by police and taken to a secure mental institution before Kersey can kill him. But Kersey is not going to give up that easily. Using a photocopier and some Tippex he prepares a fake doctor's ID badge using a real one as a master. Obtaining access to the Mental Institution with his fake ID, he prepares to shoot Nirvana. But the tall, powerfully-built thug throws a table at him and the two engage in a life-and-death struggle in which Nirvana stabs Kersey with a scalpel several times. It is probably the best-staged fight scene in the whole *Death Wish* series, and is worthy of a Bond film. Eventually Kersey manages to electrocute Nirvana after he gets his hand stuck in an ECT machine. The huge thug falls dead. At this point a hospital orderly arrives, but he knows Kersey's back story. As his family had themselves suffered a similar tragedy, he lets him go.

Meanwhile Geri has discovered previous drafts of Kersey's fake ID in his wastebasket and, hearing news of Nirvana's death on the radio, realises the truth. She places her engagement ring on a newspaper and leaves.

A few months later, Kersey is invited to a party and is asked if he can attend. 'What else would I be doing?' he says. The film ends with a shot of a shadowy figure walking in the night, implying that his vigilante activities are continuing.

Although hated by critics, the film was popular with audiences, though the British Board of Film Censors made some cuts to the rape sequences. Even today, TV versions and DVD and Blu-Ray releases have Carol's rape scene (which is quite explicit) omitted and merely implied.

In 1985, a third *Death Wish* film premiered. Rather unusually, *Death Wish III* – which was also directed by Michael Winner – was partly filmed in London. Although some footage was shot in New York, Lambeth on the South Bank of the Thames stood in for the poorer parts of New York while St Thomas's Hospital represented a police station.

The film opens with Kersey returning to New York for the first time since he was banned at the end of the first film. He has come to visit his old friend and Korean War buddy Charley (Francis Drake). Unfortunately, Charley is attacked by a gang and collapses dead in Kersey's arms, resulting in him being arrested for the murder. While in jail he is recognised by Inspector Richard Shriker (Ed Lauter) as the New York vigilante from 1974.

Kersey is thrown in a holding cell where he meets Manny Fraker (Gavin O'Herlihy), the leader of the gang who killed Charley. The two fight, and when Kersey is released he is threatened by Manny.

Shriker then offers Kersey a deal – he can kill as many criminals as he wants, as long as he informs him about anything he should know about. Kersey then moves into a dingy apartment in the area. The block is largely populated by elderly people terrified of the gang. They include Bennett Cross (Martin Balsam), a WW2 veteran.

Kersey starts his own private war against the gang. He buys a used car as bait and, when two gang members try to break into it, he shoots them. This scene appears in Brian Garfield's original novel, but was not featured in the first *Death Wish* movie. Unfortunately, one of his neighbours – Maria (Marina Sirtis, best known for playing Deanna Troi in *Star Trek: The Next Generation*) – is raped by the gang and dies from her injuries. There is further tragedy when Public Defender Kathryn Davis (Deborah Raffin), who had been starting a relationship with Kersey, is killed when her car is shunted into oncoming traffic by Manny.

Hersey launches an all-out assault on the gang, helped by Maria's widower Rodriguez (Joseph Gonzalez). Bennett even gives Kersey a Browning 0.30 in calibre machine gun he had brought back from the Korean War, and he subsequently stands in the street firing the gun from the hip, Rambo-style.

Eventually Shriker helps Kersey to kill as many gang members as possible. Kersey returns to Bennett's flat to collect more ammunition but Manny arrives, only to be shot by Kersey. But Manny has not been killed, as he was wearing a bulletproof vest. He prepares to shoot the two men but, as Striker distracts him, Kersey picks up an M72 LAW anti-tank rocket launcher and uses it to blow him through the wall. The gang are so stunned by the loss of their leader and their losses that they retreat.

As with all films in the series, *Death Wish III* was not popular with the critics but it made enough at the box office ($16 million against a budget of $10 million) to warrant further sequels.

The next in the series – *Death Wish 4: The Crackdown* – was released in 1987, and was directed by none other than J. Lee Thompson. This time the storyline was completely different and featured Kersey attempting to wipe out a drug gang. In this story, Kersey had a girlfriend – Karen (Kay Lenz) – who dies in the final act.

The last of the *Death Wish* pictures, *Death Wish V: The Face of Death*, was the poorest of the series and the only one not to make a profit. This time Kersey has another girlfriend – Olivia Regent (Lesley-Anne Down) – who ends up dead, providing Kersey with the motivation to go after some gangsters. Unlike the other *Death Wish* films, which were mainly made on location, this one was filmed entirely in a studio. The film received generally negative reviews and it was generally agreed that at age 73 Bronson was too old for this kind of picture. Bronson only made three further films – *Family of Cops* (1995), *Family of Cops 2* (1997) and *Family of Cops 3* (1997) – before dying in 2003.

That would seem to be the end of the *Death Wish* series, but in 2006 Sylvester Stallone announced that he was to star in a rebooted version of the original film. This was subsequently cancelled, but in 2016 it was revealed that Bruce Willis was to play Paul Kersey in a remake which this time would draw more heavily on material in the original book and would be 'anti-vigilante' rather than 'pro-vigilante'. Whether you like or hate the *Death Wish* films, there is no doubt that they played a significant role in the history of the movies, particularly during the eighties.

\* \* \*

# Charles Bronson 1980s Filmography

| 1980 | *Cabo Blanco* |
| 1980 | *Borderline* |
| 1981 | *Death Hunt* |
| 1982 | *Death Wish II* |
| 1983 | *10 to Midnight* |
| 1984 | *The Evil That Men Do* |
| 1985 | *Death Wish III* |
| 1986 | *Murphy's Law* |
| 1987 | *Death Wish 4: The Crackdown* |
| 1987 | *Assassination* |
| 1988 | *Avenging Angels* |
| 1989 | *Kinjite: Forbidden Subjects* |

# MAKING MY DAY

## *Dirty Harry* in the 1980s

Born in 1931, Clint Eastwood remains a potent force in American cinema. Though he has now retired from acting, he is still active as a director at the age of 85 which must be something of a record, as even Alfred Hitchcock made his last film when he was 75.

Eastwood's first film role was as a lab technician in *Revenge of The Creature* (1955), a sequel to *Creature from the Black Lagoon* (1954). Minor roles in many 1950s features followed, but his breakthrough role came in 1959 when he was cast as Rowdy Yates in the long-running TV Western series *Rawhide* (1959-65). Eastwood appeared in 271 episodes of the series, and this led directly to one of his most famous roles – 'The Man With No Name' – in the spaghetti Western *A Fistful of Dollars* (1964), directed by Sergio Leone. Eastwood appeared in two further sequels – *For a Few Dollars More* (1965) and *The Good, The Bad and The Ugly* (1966). This title was so effective that it was used by *Car* magazine for its monthly review of all available new cars during the 1970s.

Following the success of these three films – which were all made in Spain on a low budget – Eastwood's career soared, with appearances in a number of top-notch Hollywood films such as *Coogan's Bluff* (1968) and *Paint Your Wagon* (1969). During this period, Eastwood also made two excellent war movies – *Where Eagles Dare* (1968) and *Kelly's Heroes* (1970) – which were both directed by Brian G. Hutton. *Kelly's Heroes* was the last film that Eastwood made in which he was part of an ensemble cast. From that point on, most of his films featured him in the lead role. Later he set up his own production company, Malpaso Films, to ensure he had greater creative control, and he started to direct many of his movies, starting with *Play Misty for Me* in 1971.

That same year, Eastwood made a film that is regarded as a milestone in the history of action movies. The screenplay of what was eventually called *Dirty Harry* had gone through a number of drafts and had its origins in a script called *Dead Right*, which was written by Harry Julian Fink and Rita M. Fink, about a New York City police inspector named Harry Callahan who is determined to stop a serial killer called Travis. The screenplay went through a number of drafts, and at one point the action was moved to Seattle.

The actor originally earmarked for the role of Inspector Harry Callahan was Frank Sinatra, who at the time was 55 and not too old to play the character, who was envisaged as a man in his fifties. As you will have discovered when reading the chapter in this book on *Die Hard* (1988), Sinatra was also considered for the lead role in that movie, so if things had turned out differently the veteran actor and singer might have played two of the greatest action movie roles of the 20th Century!

Other actors who were considered for the part included Steve McQueen, Burt Lancaster, and Paul Newman. McQueen passed on the role on the grounds that the part was too similar to that of the titular character he had played in *Bullitt* (1968). He also declined to star in *The French Connection* (1971) for the same reason. Newman in turn demurred, as he felt the character was too right-wing. Eventually the role was given to 41 year old Eastwood and – in view of the younger age of the actor now playing Callahan – additional action scenes were scripted.

The story now took place in San Francisco, where serial killer Scorpio (Andrew Robinson) has threatened to kill a number of people with his sniper rifle unless his demands are met. Eventually he kidnaps a young girl and demands that $200,000 be paid for her return. Callahan agrees to act as the delivery man for the ransom money, but takes precautions to ensure a successful outcome including wearing a radio bug, taping a knife to his ankle, and having his partner Chico (Reni Santoni) tail him.

After taking the money from Callahan and assaulting him, Scorpio announces that he is going to kill him and also let his kidnap victim die. Callahan is only saved from death by the prompt arrival of Chico, who has been monitoring the conversation on radio. The wounded Callahan stabs Scorpio in the leg, and the injured criminal flees the scene without the cash.

Eventually the two policemen track down Scorpio to his lair in nearby Kezar Stadium, where Callahan tortures Scorpio into revealing his kidnap victim's location. The girl is found, but she is already dead.

Later the District Attorney (Josef Sommer) informs Callahan that they cannot prosecute Scorpio as the search of his living quarters (which was carried out without a search warrant) was invalid and it was also illegal to torture him and to not have read him his rights.

Scorpio is freed, and eventually hijacks a school bus full of kids. Instead of delivering further ransom money, Callahan intercepts the vehicle and chases Scorpio into a quarry. The film ends with Callahan shooting Scorpio dead and then throwing his police badge into the water, implying that he has effectively resigned from the police force.

The film was a great success, receiving much praise for its action, realism and grittiness, and two years later a sequel – *Magnum Force* – followed. Unfortunately this proved to be the poorest of the *Dirty Harry* films, and much of the criticism centred on the character of Harry Callahan himself.

The plot of the second film centred on a group of four motorcycle cops within the San Francisco police force who have taken the law into their own hands and were hunting down and executing known criminals. Eventually Callahan kills all the vigilantes and their leader Lt Neil Briggs (Hal Holbrook), but many fans of the original film pointed out that logically Callahan should have supported the vigilantes and his sudden conversion to liberal causes was inconsistent with his character as portrayed in the first film. He also has a sort-of-relationship with a woman in the film, something that was at odds with his image as a loner. John Milius, who drafted the original screenplay, blamed the weaknesses of the film on Michael Cimino who had made many changes including the addition of a girlfriend.

A third *Dirty Harry* film, *The Enforcer*, premiered in 1977. This time the maverick Inspector was teamed up with a female partner, Inspector Kate Moore played by Tyne Daly, who later became well-known for playing Detective Mary Beth Lacey in the long-running TV series *Cagney and Lacey*.

The bulk of the plot deals with a terrorist group, the People's Revolutionary Strike Force (PRSF) – led by Bobby Maxwell (De Veren Bookwalter) – who are intent on acquiring a cache of high-tech weapons in order to further their goals. The PRSF was based on the real-life Symbionese

Liberation Army, who kidnapped heiress Patty Hearst and forced her to participate in crimes including bank robberies.

Eventually the PRSF use a stolen gas company van and uniforms in a raid on a military warehouse, where they acquire a large stock of weapons including M16 automatic rifles, M72 LAW anti-tank rockets, and Tasers. Armed with their new weapons, the gang kidnap the Mayor of San Francisco (John Crawford) and hold him hostage in the disused and derelict island prison at Alcatraz in San Francisco bay. Callahan and Moore sail out to the island, but Moore is killed by Maxwell after rescuing the Mayor. As the gang leader climbs to the top of a watch tower, Callahan kills him with an M72 rocket. He then returns to his partner's corpse as reinforcements arrive.

At that point it seemed we had heard the last of Dirty Harry but, in 1983, taking advantage of the boom in action movies in the eighties and a desire on the part of the general public and fans to see more, Callahan returned in what many fans consider to be the best of the series: *Sudden Impact*. This time the film was directed by Eastwood himself, and featured his then-current partner Sondra Locke with whom he had made a few films starting with *The Gauntlet* in 1976.

The plot was different from previous *Dirty Harry* movies, as it centred around artist Jennifer Spencer (Sondra Locke) who had been brutally gang-raped a decade earlier. Her sister had also been sexually attacked in the same incident, and had been left in a catatonic state.

Ten years on, Spencer sees one of her attackers – Michael Maurer (George Wilburn) – and pretends to be interested in him. She gets into his car with him, goes to a remote location, and then shoots him in the head with a .38 Colt Detective Special revolver after putting a bullet through his genitals. She then decides to hunt down all the remaining members of the gang who attacked her and kill them in a similar fashion, one at a time.

This part of the plot therefore bears a certain similarity to the first two *Death Wish* movies. It is also very like the very disturbing film *I Spit on Your Grave* (1982) in which a female writer (coincidentally also called Jennifer), after being gang-raped and left for dead, decides to castrate and kill all her attackers. That film, by the way, holds the unenviable distinction of having the longest rape scene in cinema history.

*Sudden Impact* started off as a straightforward 'revenge for a rape' story written for Sondra Locke by Charles B. Pierce and Earl E. Smith, but was converted into a *Dirty Harry* story by Joseph Stinson who added additional plot threads.

One of these elements involved a group of young thugs who are released by a judge on the grounds that Callahan had carried out a search and seizure which was unreasonable (harking back to the scene with the District Attorney in *Dirty Harry*).

Another plot thread involves the crime lord Threlkis (Michael V. Gazzo). Callahan causes him to have a fatal heart attack at his granddaughter's wedding after he threatens him with prosecution in a murder case, implying that he has compromising evidence that he does not really have.

Four of Threlkis's hitmen subsequently come after Callahan. The Inspector kills three of them, but a fourth escapes. In a separate incident, he also comes under attack from the gang of young thugs who had been released by a judge earlier in the movie. They try to attack Callahan in his car using Molotov cocktails, but the Inspector simply picks up an unexploded petrol bomb and throws it back at them, causing them to drive over the edge of a wharf and into the sea, thus resulting in their deaths.

Because of these incidents Callahan is ordered to take a break, and he moves to the seaside town of San Paulo where – coincidentally – Jennifer Spencer has now relocated, as it is the home of the people who had attacked her under the boardwalk ten years earlier. Callahan subsequently meets her while jogging with his dog, Meathead.

Meanwhile, Jennifer kills a second rapist – Kruger (Jack Thibeau) – at the beach. Callahan discovers that the victims and local woman Ray Parkins (Audrie J. Neenan) – who had set up Jennifer and her sister to be gang-raped a decade earlier – are friends of local Police Chief Lester Jannings's son, Alby (Matthew Child). Callahan and Spencer meet a second time at a local outdoor café, where the Inspector reveals that he is investigating the death of George Willburn – a revelation which upsets Spencer.

Spencer subsequently kills another of the rapists, Tyrone (Wendell Wellman), plus Parkins. She is unable to kill Mick (Paul Drake), as he is arrested by Callahan and thrown in jail. Unfortunately Mick is subsequently bailed from jail by Kruger's two brothers-in-law, Eddie (Russ McCubbin) and Carl (Robert Sutton).

Mick and his two henchmen beat up Callahan and throw him into the ocean. Meanwhile, Spencer arrives at Alby's home with the intention of killing him but refrains from doing so when she discovers he is brain-damaged and catatonic. His father, Chief Jannings (Pat Hingle), arrives and holds her at gunpoint, explaining that his son could not live with the guilt of what he had done and had tried to kill himself in a car crash. He then admits he had covered up the crimes but will now ensure that the other remaining rapist, Mick, will be punished.

At that point Mick bursts in with his two henchmen and shoots Chief Jannings using Spencer's .38 revolver, ensuring the crime will be blamed on her. He then takes Spencer to the boardwalk and announces his intention of repeating the rape. But this time Spencer breaks free and announces that if he wants to sexually assault her this time 'he will have to rape her dead body'. Spencer runs away, hotly pursued by Mick and his two associates.

Meanwhile Callahan has swum ashore, having survived the assault. He returns to the motel to find his friend Horace dead and his dog wounded. Furious at this appalling crime, he retrieves his new weapon (a .44 Automag) and returns to the boardwalk, where he eventually kills Eddie, Carl and Mick. Spencer is sure that Callahan is going to turn her in, but when police reinforcements arrive the Inspector hands over the .38 revolver – which now has Mick's prints on it – saying that he is sure ballistics will show it was used in all the murders.

*Sudden Impact* was not well-received by critics, but it was hugely popular – making nearly $68 million at the box office against a budget of $22 million. Eastwood's catch phrase in the movie – 'Go ahead; make my day' – also entered popular folklore, and it was even used by US President Ronald Reagan. Like 'Play it again, Sam' and 'Beam me up, Scotty', the line is often misquoted as 'Go ahead, punk – make my day'.

The success of *Sudden Impact* led to a fifth (and final) *Dirty Harry* film – *The Dead Pool* – which premiered in 1988. This time, Eastwood's co-stars were Liam Neeson, Jim Carrey, and Patricia Clarkson. Carrey made his film debut in this production, and has since carved out a career as a comic actor. It was also an also an early role for Irish actor Liam Neeson, who in recent years has been associated with the three *Taken* films which can be regarded as having their roots in action films of the eighties.

The film opens with Callahan finally having achieved fame as a crime-fighter, having put local crime boss Lou Janero (Anthony Charnota) in prison which results in a cover feature in *San Francisco Magazine*. Even though he is behind bars, Janero attempts to take revenge on Callahan by having four of his men attack him while he is in his car. Callahan shoots three of the attackers and knocks the fourth down with his car.

Soon afterwards, Callahan is assigned a new partner – Asian-American, martial arts-skilled officer Al Quan (Evan C. Kim). Their first case together involves the case of rock singer Johnny Squires (Jim Carrey), who is murdered in his trailer outside a refrigerated meat store during the filming of a pop video directed by Peter Swan (Liam Neeson).

Soon after this, Swan's executive producer Dean Madison is killed during an armed robbery on a Chinese restaurant. The crime is witnessed by Callahan and Quan, who try and stop it. This leads to the obligatory sequence found near the beginning of all the *Dirty Harry* movies, in which the Inspector foils a crime single-handed with his .44 Magnum while uttering his current catchphrase, which on this occasion is 'You're shit out of luck'.

One of the criminals escapes the volley of fire from Callahan's powerful weapon, only to be tackled by Quan who swiftly incapacitates the robber with his martial arts skills, thus earning the Inspector's respect. The two then rummage through Madison's clothes and discover a piece of paper with a list of names on it, including those of Callahan and Johnny Squares.

It transpires that both Swan and Madison were engaged in a 'Dead Pool' game, in which they tried to predict the forthcoming deaths of celebrities and then wrote them on a list. In the meantime, another person – film critic Molly Fisher (Ronnie Claire Edwards), who was on the list – is killed in her apartment by an intruder claiming to be Swan.

As investigations continue, Callahan is ordered to co-operate with local news reporter Samantha Walker (Patricia Clarkson), who is threatening to sue the Police Department over an earlier incident in which her film camera was destroyed by Callahan. The reporter agrees to drop the lawsuit if she can do an exclusive profile of Callahan. The two subsequently go on a couple of dinner dates, with the second being rudely interrupted by Janero's men who try to murder the policeman. Callahan subsequently puts an end to these attacks by visiting San Quentin prison and telling Janero that another prisoner, the powerfully-built Butcher Hicks (Diego Chairs), will attack him if anything happens to him.

Soon afterwards Callahan and Quan manage to save a disturbed man, Gus Wheeler (Louis Giambalvo), who has confessed to the murders and is threatening to set himself on fire.

Later, Callahan and Quan interview Swan and learn that he has in the past been harassed by a deranged fan called Harlan Rook (David Hunt), who had accused him of stealing his ideas. Callahan realises this may be who is behind the recent murders.

Rook then kills his next victim – talk show host Nolan Kennard (Bill Wattenburg) – using an ingenious device: a radio controlled toy car filled with plastic explosives. Callahan finds a toy wheel at the scene of the crime, but still isn't sure how it was done. Later, as he and Quan are driving through the streets of San Francisco they spot a model car following them, operated from a radio-control unit in Rook's car.

A car chase through the streets of San Francisco then follows, obviously inspired by the stunts in *Bullitt*. Eventually Callahan and Quan are trapped in an alleyway, but Callahan escapes by allowing the model car to drive under the chassis of his vehicle and then, at the last moment, reversing at full throttle. The bomb explodes, but the engine block of Callahan's car absorbs the blast and the two policemen only receive minor injuries.

Later, Rook (pretending to be Swan) invites Clarkson to Swan's film studio for an interview. But the police are closing in. They raid the deranged's fan's apartment, finding torn posters of Swan's films and copious quantities of explosives. Callahan races to the film studio, but is relieved of his .44 Magnum revolver. The Inspector escapes, and Rook shoots at him but soon runs out of bullets (as a .44 Magnum only holds six rounds). Callahan eventually shoots him with the harpoon gun (seen earlier in the film) just before the police arrive.

*The Dead Pool* premiered on 13 July 1988 and was only moderately successful, making just $48 million at the box office against a budget of $31 million. Although it was well-received by fans and the general public alike, it remains the least profitable of all the *Dirty Harry* films.

My own rating of the various *Dirty Harry* films in order of best to worst would be as follows:

1. *Dirty Harry*
2. *Sudden Impact*

3. *The Dead Pool*
4. *The Enforcer*
5. *Magnum Force*

The five *Dirty Harry* films have also contributed to popular culture, and have influenced many action films and TV series. John McClane in *Die Hard* is probably more like Harry Callahan than the Joe Leland character in *Nothing Lasts Forever*, the book on which the 1988 film was based. The *Lethal Weapon* series of films can also be seen to be updated, higher-octane versions of *Dirty Harry*.

The films are also notable for their many catch phrases which have passed into common parlance.

'Are you feeling lucky?'; 'A man's got to know his limitations'; 'Opinions are like assholes: everyone's got one'; 'Go ahead: make my day'; 'You're shit out of luck'. All phrases which have been used by politicians and speech writers at some point.

Following *The Dead Pool* there were rumours that a sixth *Dirty Harry* film might be made, and one possible plotline involved Harry travelling to London where he would battle with English gangsters. In the event this never happened, but with Hollywood's current penchant for remakes and reboots it is entirely possible that a new version of the original film may be made and Harry Callahan may once again make our day!

# ILLUSTRATIONS

Action Stars of the 1980s

Harrison Ford (1942-)
Image Credit: Chandran Rutnam/Asian Film Location
Services (Pvt) Ltd.
(Creative Commons by ShareAlike 3.0 Unported)

**Arnold Schwarzenegger (1947-)**
Image Credit: Michael Arthur Worden Evans
(Public Domain Image)

**Sylvester Stallone (1946-)**
Image Credit: Alan Light
(Creative Commons by Attribution 2.0 Generic)

**Sigourney Weaver (1949-)**
Image Credit: David Shankbone
(Creative Commons by ShareAlike 3.0 Unported)

**Mel Gibson (1956-)**
Image Credit: Alan Light
(Creative Commons by Attribution 2.0 Generic)

**Danny Glover (1946-)**
Image Credit: Gage Skidmore
(Creative Commons by Attribution 2.0 Generic)

**Bruce Willis (1955-)**
Image Credit: Associated Press
(Public Domain Image)

**Chuck Norris (1940-)**
Image Credit: Yoni S. Hamenahem
(Creative Commons by ShareAlike 3.0 Unported)

**Roger Moore (1927-)**
Image Credit: Allan Warren
(Creative Commons by ShareAlike 3.0 Unported)

Timothy Dalton (1946-)
Image Credit: Bart Molendijk
(Creative Commons by ShareAlike 3.0 Netherlands)

Charles Bronson (1921-2003)
Image Credit: Georges Biard
(Creative Commons by ShareAlike 3.0 Unported)

**Clint Eastwood (1930-)**
Image Credit: NASA Dryden Flight Research Center
Photo Collection
(Public Domain Image)

# INDEX

# D

# G

# H

# M

# R

# W

# Y

# Z

# About the Author

Dr Colin M. Barron was born in Greenock, Scotland in 1956, and was educated at Greenock Academy (1961-74) and Glasgow University (1974-79) where he graduated in Medicine (M.B. Ch.B.) in 1979. He worked for the next five years in hospital medicine, eventually becoming a Registrar in Ophthalmology at Gartnavel General Hospital and Glasgow Eye Infirmary.

In December 1984 he left the National Health Service to set up Ashlea Nursing Home in Callander, which he established with his first wife Sandra and ran until 1999. He was the chairman of the Scottish branch of the British Federation of Care Home Proprietors (BFCHP) from 1985 to 1991, and then a founding member and chairman of the Scottish Association of Care Home Owners (SACHO) from 1991 to 1999.

Colin has a special interest in writing – his first non-fiction book *Running Your Own Private Residential and Nursing Home* was published by Jessica Kingsley Publishers in 1990. He has also written around 150 articles for various publications including *This Caring Business, The Glasgow Herald, Caring Times, Care Weekly, The British Medical Journal, The Hypnotherapist, The Thought Field* and many others. He was a regular columnist for *This Caring Business* between 1991 and 1999.

Colin has always had a special interest in hypnosis and alternative medicine. In 1999 he completed a one-year Diploma course in hypnotherapy and neuro-linguistic programming with the British Society of Clinical and Medical Ericksonian Hypnosis (BSCMEH), an organisation created by Stephen Brooks who was the first person in the UK to teach Ericksonian Hypnosis. He has also trained with the British Society of Medical and Dental Hypnosis (BSMDH) and with Valerie Austin, who is a top Harley Street hypnotherapist. Colin is also a licensed NLP practitioner. In 1992 he was made a Fellow of the Royal Society of Health (FRSH). He is a former member of various societies including the British Society of Medical and Dental Hypnosis - Scotland (BSMDH), the British Thought Field Therapy Association (BTFTA), the Association for Thought Field Therapy (ATFT), the British Complementary Medicine Association (BCMA), and the Hypnotherapy Association.

Colin has been using TFT since early in 2000, and in November 2001 he became the first British person to qualify as a Voice Technology TFT practitioner. He used to work from home in Dunblane and at the Glasgow Nuffield Hospital.

Colin has also had 40 years of experience in public speaking, and did some training with the John May School of Public Speaking in London in January 1990.

In May 2011 his wife Vivien, then 55, collapsed at home due to a massive stroke. Colin then became his wife's carer but continued to see a few hypnotherapy and TFT clients. In late July 2015 Colin suffered a very severe heart attack and was rushed to hospital. Investigation showed that he had suffered a rare and very serious complication of myocardial infarction known as a ventricular septal defect (VSD) - effectively a large hole between the two main pumping chambers of the heart.

Colin had open heart surgery to repair the defect in August 2015, but this first operation was unsuccessful and a second procedure had to be carried out three months later. On 30th November he was finally discharged home after spending four months in hospital.

As a result of his wife's care needs and his own health problems Colin closed down his hypnotherapy and TFT business in April 2016 to concentrate on writing books and looking after his wife.

Colin's books for Extremis Publishing include *The Craft of Public Speaking* (2016) and *Planes on Film: Ten Favourite Aviation Films* (2016).

His interests include walking, cycling, military history, aviation, plastic modelling, and reading.

For more details about Colin and his work, please visit his website at: **www.colinbarron.co.uk**

Author Images are Copyright ©2017, Raymond McFadyen.

# The Craft of Public Speaking

By Colin M. Barron

Public speaking is one of the most important skills in personal and professional life. Yet too often this key ability is neglected, leading to presentations which are dull, uninspired and poorly delivered.

*The Craft of Public Speaking* examines some of the crucial aptitudes which are fundamental to delivering an effective presentation for listeners. These include preparation, structure and rehearsal, in addition to some of the more overlooked aspects of oration such as the use of visual aids, adding humour, and dressing for success. As well as discussing how to deliver effective live addresses in public settings, the book also covers interview techniques for TV and radio along with how to organise seminars and conferences.

Dr Colin M. Barron has delivered hundreds of lectures and presentations to audiences during a long career, giving speeches on a wide variety of different subjects over many years. In *The Craft of Public Speaking,* he shares the essential knowledge that you will need to become a truly successful public speaker.

# Planes on Film
## Ten Favourite Aviation Films

### By Colin M. Barron

One of the most durable genres in cinema, the aviation film has captivated audiences for decades with tales of heroism, bravery and overcoming seemingly insurmountable odds. Some of these movies have become national icons, achieving critical and commercial success when first released in cinemas and still attracting new audiences today.

In *Planes on Film: Ten Favourite Aviation Films*, Colin M. Barron reveals many little-known facts about the making of several aviation epics. Every movie is discussed in comprehensive detail, including a thorough analysis of the action and a complete listing of all the aircraft involved. With information about where the various planes were obtained from and their current location, the book also explores the subject of aviation films which were proposed but ultimately never saw the light of day.

With illustrations and meticulous factual commentary, *Planes on Film* is a book which will appeal to aviation enthusiasts, military historians and anyone who has an interest in cinema. Written by an author with a lifelong passion for aircraft and their depiction on the silver screen, *Planes on Film* presents a lively and thought-provoking discourse on a carefully-chosen selection of movies which have been drawn from right across the history of this fascinating cinematic genre.

# The Spectrum of Adventure

## A Brief History of Interactive Fiction on the Sinclair ZX Spectrum

### By Thomas A. Christie

The Sinclair ZX Spectrum was one of the most popular home computers in British history, selling over five million units in its 1980s heyday. Amongst the thousands of games released for the Spectrum during its lifetime, the text adventure game was to emerge as one of the most significant genres on the system.

*The Spectrum of Adventure* chronicles the evolution of the text adventure on the ZX Spectrum, exploring the work of landmark software houses such as Melbourne House Software, Level 9 Computing, Delta 4 Software, the CRL Group, Magnetic Scrolls, and many others besides.

Covering one hundred individual games in all, this book celebrates the Spectrum's thriving interactive fiction scene of the eighties, chronicling the achievements of major publishers as well as independent developers from the machine's launch in 1982 until the end of the decade in 1989.

# A Righteously Awesome Eighties Christmas
## Festive Cinema of the 1980s

### By Thomas A. Christie

The cinema of the festive season has blazed a trail through the world of film-making for more than a century, ranging from silent movies to the latest CGI features. From the author of *The Christmas Movie Book*, this new text explores the different narrative themes which emerged in the genre over the course of the 1980s, considering the developments which have helped to make the Christmas films of that decade amongst the most fascinating and engaging motion pictures in the history of festive movie production.

Released against the backdrop of a turbulent and rapidly-changing world, the Christmas films of the 1980s celebrated traditions and challenged assumptions in equal measure. With warm nostalgia colliding with aggressive modernity as never before, the eighties saw the movies of the holiday season being deconstructed and reconfigured to remain relevant in an age of cynicism and innovation.

Whether exploring comedy, drama, horror or fantasy, Christmas cinema has an unparalleled capacity to attract and inspire audiences. With a discussion ranging from the best-known titles to some of the most obscure, *A Righteously Awesome Eighties Christmas* examines the ways in which the Christmas motion pictures of the 1980s fit into the wider context of this captivating and ever-evolving genre.

For details of new and forthcoming books
from Extremis Publishing,
please visit our official website at:

# www.extremispublishing.com

or follow us on social media at:

www.facebook.com/extremispublishing

www.linkedin.com/company/extremis-publishing-ltd-/